Habitations of Modernity

HABITATIONS OF MODERNITY

ESSAYS IN THE WAKE OF SUBALTERN STUDIES

Dipesh Chakrabarty

With a foreword by
Homi K. Bhabha

THE UNIVERSITY OF CHICAGO PRESS · CHICAGO AND LONDON

Dipesh Chakrabarty is professor of history and of South Asian languages and civilizations at the University of Chicago. He is the author of *Provincializing Europe: Postcolonial Thought and Historical Difference* and *Rethinking Working-Class History: Bengal 1890–1940*.

The University of Chicago Press, Chicago 60637
The University of Chicago Press, Ltd., London
© 2002 by The University of Chicago
All rights reserved. Published 2002
Printed in the United States of America

11 10 09 08 07 06 05 04 03 02   1 2 3 4 5

ISBN: 0-226-10038-3 (cloth)
ISBN: 0-226-10039-1 (paper)

Library of Congress Cataloging-in-Publication Data

Chakrabarty, Dipesh.
 Habitations of modernity : essays in the wake of subaltern studies /
Dipesh Chakrabarty ; with a foreword by Homi K. Bhabha.
     p.   cm.
 Includes bibliographical references and index.
 ISBN 0-226-10038-3 (cloth : alk. paper) — ISBN 0-226-10039-1 (paper : alk. paper)
     1. India—Historiography.   2. India—Politics and government.   3. Social
justice—India.   I. Title.
 DS435 .C46   2002
 954'.007'2—dc21

                                                            2002019210

To
ASHIS NANDY

and
KRISHNA RAJ

in appreciation

CONTENTS

PART THREE: THE ETHICAL AND THE IN-HUMAN

FOREWORD

The essence of language is friendship and hospitality.
—Emmanuel Levinas

To be asked to write a foreword purely out of friendship is to be granted a rare and generous freedom. While the professional critic may squint at the work's brilliance, and the acolyte is often overcome by its aura, the friend approaches the work unburdened by the need to praise or blame. The spirit of friendship lives in the shadows cast by raised banners and gleaming standards, and in the midst of the cut and thrust of argumentation, friendship seeks out the unconditional voice of conversation. For conversation, as you might hear it among the Chatterjees and the Banterjees at a Calcutta *adda,* chooses to follow the improvisational over the instrumental. Wandering away from the "gravitational pull of any explicit purpose," the conversation transforms what is contingent, turning what comes up in the course of conversation into the sufficient grounds of a common, collaborative dialogue of interests and affiliations.

All that I know about the utter seriousness of idle conversation, I learned from Dipesh Chakrabarty during our early morning telephone calls in Chicago. While those around us of firmer resolve and fleeter foot pulled on their Adidases and headed for the lake, we would retire to the telephone, teacups in hand, to resume our little *adda à deux.* While they jogged, our tongues wagged. Suddenly the midwestern morning would be painted in the distant colors of other days, dawning belatedly in Calcutta and Bombay, or turning to dusk in Canberra and London. We spoke each day, looking out onto the same bleached sky, Dipesh *there* and I *here,* the distance between us measured by a telephone wire along which we threaded the narratives of our lives and days. What we shared in those meetings of everyday voices was a desire to be at home in the place and time in which we found ourselves. And that desire was no less true for being unrealizable. The uncanny homing instinct that we shared did not come from a belief, or a sense of relief, in the sufficiency of our present situations. Far from it. We were anchored in the wayward memories of our making, and what drew us together in the midst of our journeys was our desire to shadow each other, to be each other's stranger and friend, to share our different darknesses and doubts. No one has understood better than Joseph Conrad what compels the joyous and difficult conversations of those who wander "over the face of the earth, the illustrious and the obscure, earning beyond the seas our fame, our money or only a crust of bread." For it is they—or indeed *we*—who are bound to each other, in history and story, "in the name of that doubt which is the inseparable part of our knowledge" (*Lord Jim,* chap. 21).

What is the task of the foreword written out of friendship, and cast in the conversational mode?

The friend turns to the finished text in a spirit of dialogue that is contingent, interruptive, insurgent. His purpose is to protect the author from the embrace of the sententious. For there is always an urgent, if invisible, line to be drawn between the author's sovereignty and the writer's survival. This is the jagged lifeline of the text that will be revived, long after the work is published, each time it is read and reread. The author performs his histrionic gestures of sincerity and authenticity in order to conquer the world with the facility of the phrasemaker or the compass of the mapmaker. The writer, on the other hand, risks his very integrity and singularity in order to touch a world that he can no more conquer than he can master language. In disclosing what human history renders disjunct or diverse, the writer reveals a worldly knowledge that draws humanity together in a *practice of doubt,* a kind of knowledge that arises not because modern man knows too much for truth to be resolved, but because "human kind cannot bear very much reality." The conversational friend plays on such doubts and distinctions between sovereignty and survival. And in so doing, he draws forth the unquiet spirit of writing that haunts the author's histrionic gesture. The task of the foreword is to ask, What, my friend, have you risked in this work? Are you willing to drive us beyond the limit of our understanding and the directive line of your reasoning? Are you declaiming these truths from the repose of your disciplinary divan, making disciples of us all? Or will you set us free to wander in those places that you leave open to the future—

those gaps where emotions and insights have yet to find adequate forms of speech? Tell us why suddenly your voice fails, and your passion takes shape, in the inchoate, the interruptive, the contingent? And why is it that in that very fading of your voice we see you practice the art of a darker doubt in which your words bind us to a common history and a shared conversation?

My friendship with Dipesh has provoked these questions "in the name of that doubt which is the inseparable part of our knowledge," and reading *Habitations of Modernity* now helps me understand them. The historian's practice of doubt, Dipesh suggests, must not be read merely as a hermeneutic of suspicion, peeling away the protocols of disciplinary power to reveal the presence of the obscure, subaltern subject. This line of argument often leads to the injunction "Only Historicize" and seeks to emancipate those who have been "hidden from history." But these outlaws, these peoples without a history, are frequently delivered to history by being marched through the defiles of a secular modernity. When they arrive at the signposts of progress, they are shorn of their stories and traditions; they are no longer hidden from history, but they have turned into spectral figures, transparent testimonies to the worldly triumph of a secular capitalist modernity. When modern world history contemplates its achievements and transformations in this light, it fails to represent the passions and perversities of those modernities that have a pre- or post-colonial genealogy. In the company of Ranajit Guha and Ashis Nandy, Dipesh argues that the modern social sciences may develop philanthropic pedagogies that seek to spread "scientific rationality, democratic politics, and modern aesthetics" (p. 39) across the world, but in so doing, they endow themselves with a surveillant vision and a disciplinary prescience, failing to understand that "there are parts of society that remain opaque to the theoretical gaze of the modern analyst. . . . [I]t seems . . . that cultural practices have a dark side. We cannot see into them, not everywhere" (p. 45).

When the glass of theory turns dark, must we abandon ourselves to experience and pragmatism? Do we espouse a practice of doubt only when our speculative systems are defeated? Enter that historical and theoretical darkness, Dipesh argues, free oneself and others from the benighted conditions of oppression, but also register a deep doubt about the enlightened career of the "self-inventing hero of modern life" (p. 46). The dynamic of darkness and doubt leads Dipesh to probe what progressive historians have too easily dismissed as the "problem of the undesirable past" as it encroaches on contemporary politics. There is no question that these dark sides of history—sati, child marriage, communal violence, infanticide, poverty—must be transformed into a growing democratic dialogue between empowered groups and freer individuals. But the dream of a total root-and-branch social transformation—be it liberal, socialist, anarchist, or marxist—even when it is dreamed on behalf of the rights of the subaltern or the oppressed, is part of a political imaginary that can only think in terms of "the whole called *the state*" (p. 35). In resisting the sublatory narratives of state-centered transcendent histories and polities, Dipesh dares us to imagine a modal and moral form of political agency founded on the subaltern's "fragmentary and episodic" experience of history and citizenship:

> Can we *imagine* another moment of subaltern history, one in which we stay—permanently, not simply as a matter of political tactic—with that which is fragmentary and episodic? . . . If the statist idea of the political defined the mainstream of political thought, then here may be an alternative conceptual pole to it: an idea of the political that did not require us to imagine totalities. . . . What kind of (modern) social justice would one envisage as one embraced the fragment? . . .
>
> . . . This is an *ideal* figure. No actual member of the subaltern classes would resemble what I imagine here. The question is, Are there moments in the life practices of the subaltern classes that would allow us to construct such an agent? The Buddhist imagination once saw the possibility of the joyful, renunciate *bhikshu* (monk) in the miserable and deprived image of the *bhikshuk* (beggar). We have not yet learned to see the spectral doubles that may inhabit our Marxism-inspired images of the subaltern. (pp. 34, 36)

In these concluding figures of spectral doubles we see, once again, the struggle between the author's sovereign sententiousness and the writer's subaltern, survivalist ethic played out in the act of identifying the subaltern spirit of the Buddhist imagination. Dipesh's call for a political imaginary of the future—"Can we *imagine* . . . [T]here may be . . ."—at once casts doubt on the present state of theory and politics, while sowing seeds to be harvested in the history of another time. In our contemporary moment we suddenly see the passing of a proleptic future, a wayward passage of time—future's present—that only the conversation of friends can bring to life. As the subaltern agent doubles as monk and beggar, we are warned that this may be only an idealized figure, history's wager with fiction, as no actual member of the subaltern classes may resemble the image. Indeed, we have yet to learn to *see*. . . . And yet, we do see. In this counterfactual dialogue of spectral doubling, where the Buddha and Gramsci greet each other in a virtual embrace, a kind of actuality is revealed. For the spectral signifies an inviolable, ethical proximity—

"a mode of relating . . . in which (historical and contingent) difference is neither reified nor erased but negotiated" (p. 140)—that Dipesh has brought to life in his remarkable haunting of history's many human and in-human habitations.

Homi K. Bhabha

ACKNOWLEDGMENTS

The essays included here were written over the past ten years or so. The intellectual and personal debts that I incurred in those years are acknowledged in more detail in my *Provincializing Europe*. In order to avoid repetition, let me just say that discussions with members of the editorial collective of *Subaltern Studies* and the experience of reading their work have been absolutely essential to this enterprise. Friends such as Shahid Amin, David Arnold, David Bennett, Gautam Bhadra, Alice Bullard, Philip Darby, Greg Dening, Simon During, Michael Dutton, Leela Gandhi, Keya Ganguly, David Hardiman, Christopher Healy, Robin Jeffrey, Sudipta Kaviraj, David Lloyd, Shail Mayaram, Jon Mee, Donna Merwick, Meaghan Morris, Stephen Muecke, Aamir Mufti, the late D. R. Nagaraj, Gyan Pandey, Rajyashree Pandey, M. S. S. Pandian, Sanjay Seth, Ajay Skaria, Susie Tharu, and Patrick Wolfe have been patient listeners and have given affection, encouragement, and criticism in equal parts. They deserve very special thanks.

Two institutions have supported my work in the past ten years: the University of Melbourne and the University of Chicago. I am grateful to my colleagues at and the students, staff, and administrators of these universities for all the help and stimulation that they have afforded me. The Australian National University (ANU) has, on several occasions, hosted me as a visiting fellow in various departments: the Department of Asian and Pacific History in the Research School of Pacific Studies, the Department of History in the School of Social Sciences, the Humanities Research Centre (HRC), and the Centre for Cross-Cultural Research.

Iain McCalman, the director of the HRC, and Benjamin Penny of ANU deserve a special expression of grateful and warm thanks for the untiring support that they have given my work.

Intellectual collaboration over the years with Leila Abu-Lughod, Sara Castro-Klaren, Fernando Coronil, Walter Mignolo, Timothy Mitchell, and Stephen Vlastos, among others, has given me a sharper sense than I would have had otherwise of the diversity that global modernity contains. I also warmly acknowledge the excellent assistance and good counsel that I received from Richard Delacy in preparing this book for publication.

The friendship of Arjun Appadurai, Homi Bhabha, Carol Breckenridge, C. M. Naim, Sheldon Pollock, and Clinton Seely at the University of Chicago has been a privilege that I have had the good fortune to enjoy since joining that institution. My rich interactions with these colleagues—especially my daily early-morning phone conversations with Bhabha, conversations that seem to course their way through the mundane, the spiritual, and the philosophical with equal ease—and their warm affection have been among the assets of my life. To Bhabha I am also grateful for agreeing to write a foreword to this book. My existence in Chicago has also been enriched by the recent presence of Kunal and Shubhra Chakrabarti from Delhi and Beppe Karlsson from Uppsala, all three visitors to the university in the academic year 2000–2001.

Over the years, Partha Chatterjee, Barun De, Ranajit Guha, Anthony Low, Asok Sen, and Gayatri Spivak have taught me a great deal through their writings, criticisms, and conversations. I continue to learn from their work.

The warm and generous friendship of my editor, Alan Thomas, has eased the path of this book through the procedures of the press. My thanks to him and to the readers he chose for the critical and helpful comments that guided the work of revision. I also thank him for suggesting the book's title.

And, last but not least, it is a pleasure to acknowledge the support that I have received from my parents, from my sister and her family, from Kaveri, and from Arko. It will remain a lasting regret that my father, who lived and emotionally supported me through the years during which I worked on these essays and on *Provincializing Europe*, did not live to see the resulting books in print.

Earlier versions of the essays collected here were published in the following journals and anthologies and are reprinted here with permission: Chapter 1 in *A Companion to Postcolonial Studies*, ed. Henry Schwartz and Sangeeta Ray (Oxford: Blackwell, 2000), and in *Nepantla: Views from South* 1, no. 1 (2000): 9–32. Chapter 2 in *Economic and Political*

Weekly, 8 April 1995, 751–59. Chapter 3 in *Emergences,* nos. 7–8 (1995–96): 168–77 (www.tandf.co.uk). Chapter 4 in *Journal of Human Values* 5, no. 1 (1999): 3–13 (Copyright © Management Centre for Human Values, Indian Institute of Management, Calcutta, 1999. All rights reserved. Reproduced with the permission of the copyright-holder and the publishers, Sage Publications India Pvt Ltd., New Delhi, India). Chapter 5 in *South Asia* 14, no. 1 (June 1991): 15–32, and in *Economic and Political Weekly,* 7–14 March 1992, 541–47. Chapter 6 in *Communal/Plural,* 1, no. 1 (1993) (www.tandf.co.uk). Chapter 7 in *Dangerous Liaisons,* ed. Donna Merwick (Melbourne: Department of History, University of Melbourne, 1994). Chapter 8 in a special issue of *South Asia* 18 (1995): 109–30, and in *Economic and Political Weekly,* 10 August 1996, 21–43.

I dedicate the book to Ashis Nandy and Krishna Raj. Nandy strikes me as one of the most democratic of Indians whom I have personally met. His faith in Indian democracy is profound and moving. Krishna Raj I have never met personally. Yet I have admired from a distance the breadth of vision and the spirit of tolerance for rival views with which he edits the distinguished Indian journal *Economic and Political Weekly.* I offer this book to them as a token of my appreciation of their contributions to Indian democracy.

INTRODUCTION

Modernity is easy to inhabit but difficult to define. If *modernity* is to be a definable, delimited concept, we must identify some people or practices or concepts as *nonmodern*. In the nineteenth century and the early twentieth, the task seemed clear to political philosophers such as J. S. Mill and L. T. Hobhouse. Following the tenets of the European Enlightenment, many Western intellectuals thought of modernity as the rule of institutions that delivered us from the thrall of all that was unreasonable and irrational. Those who fell outside its ambit could be described as *premodern*. Western powers in their imperial mode saw modernity as coeval with the idea of progress. Nationalists saw in it the promise of development.

Many Indian writers continued, as we shall see, to think along these lines well into the 1970s. But today—after anticolonial, feminist, environmentalist, and other new social movements have radicalized our sense of democracy—these older definitions produce a moral dilemma. Can the designation of something or some group as *non-* or *premodern* ever be anything but a gesture of the powerful? For a country such as India, the question takes very specific forms.

India is, constitutionally, a democracy. It holds elections that are, on the whole, regular, fair, and free. It has an active and free press. Every adult Indian, theoretically speaking, enjoys political rights guaranteed by the country's constitution. Even the nonliterate members of the peasantry and the urban working classes enjoy these entitlements. Public life in India is necessarily influenced by the active political presence of these classes. They bring into the sphere of the political their own ideas of well-being, justice, gods, spirits, religion, magic, and so on. This is not a case of the so-called intrusion of the traditional into the realm of the modern. The subaltern classes are as caught up in modern institutions as the middle and upper classes are. And this is what produces some of the most challenging questions of Indian modernity.

How do we, for instance, characterize the intellectual worlds of the peasant and the subaltern classes who are our contemporaries yet whose life practices constantly challenge our "modern" distinctions between the secular and the sacred, between the feudal and the capitalist, between the nonrational and the rational? The old imperial option of looking down on them through some version of the idea of *backwardness* has lost its appeal. Increasingly, we want the process of democratization to be itself democratic. The farther afield the process of democratization ranges, and the more radical that process becomes, the more we are challenged to rethink our stance as self-conscious political subjects of modernity.

So how would one write of forms of modernity that have deviated from all canonical understandings of the term? There have been several scholarly responses to this question. Most revolve around contesting the idea that modernity has any necessary, ideal-typical form. Some scholars prefer the label *alternative or plural modernities,* while others write about *modernity at large.*[1] These are useful, critical ideas, but they still leave us with the problem that we must first distinguish what modernity is before we can go on to determine what it is not. And the concept *modernity* loses value as a concept if everything in the world is by definition modern (alternatively or not). Some, of course, question the value of the very idea of modernity, but the word is all around us, and it may already be too late to legislate its uses.[2]

It is, of course, entirely possible that the word *modernity* has outlived its utility as a rigorous concept and is mostly of rhetorical value in today's debates. Yet it is a word that we cannot do without in the everyday context of discussions of democracy and development. It comes into use in the same way as words like *medieval* or *feudal* circulate in ordinary speech as expressions of moral value. *Premodern, backward, medieval*—these historicist tropes survive in our rhetoric even when we no longer unquestioningly believe in the universality or applicability of these ideas. But the rhetoric itself may be taken as a sign that, in spite of our contemporary intellectual incredulity toward them, historicist or stagist ideas of history and modernity are never far from our thoughts. We must, therefore, engage and reengage our ideas about modernity in a spirit of constant vigilance.

This is where this book may have a claim on the attention of the non-specialist reader. The primary questions that motivate it are not peculiar to India. At the heart of them all are certain problems now shared among postcolonial historians all over the world. How do we think about the global legacy of the European Enlightenment in lands far away from Europe in geography or history? How do we envision or document ways of being modern that will speak to that which is shared across the world as well as to that which belongs to human cultural diversity? How do we resist the tendency in our thinking to justify the violence that accompanies imperial or triumphalist moments of modernity? How do we also construct critiques of popular violence that have, from time to time, torn apart—and/or given birth to—communities and nations of modern times?

My work has been associated for about two decades now with the Oxford University Press series *Subaltern Studies,* launched in 1982 under the intellectual leadership of Ranajit Guha. In the discussions that followed the publication of these volumes, modernity, the nation-state, and the idea of history itself emerged as important and controversial topics. The rise of an aggressive, cultural nationalism in India in the 1980s— a Hindu Right that deliberately targeted Muslim and Christian minorities for discriminatory treatment—understandably colored much of what was said in these debates. Feeling besieged, Indian scholars on the Left often pinned their hopes for the future to a purist allegiance to the tenets of Marxism and liberalism. They argued that the "linguistic" and "poststructuralist" turn in the writings of *Subaltern Studies* historians—along with the "critiques of modernity" developed by writers such as Ashis Nandy—played straight into the hands of Hindu cultural nationalists. The critics of modernity, if they can be so called, argued, on the other hand, that the ailments of India belonged to the pathologies of modernity itself. The debate, thus, became completely polarized, both sides elaborating mutually exclusive positions encouraged by the contingencies of political and social conflicts in India and feeding on similar ideologically driven controversies in the universities of the West.[3] But the polarization exaggerated the differences between the two sides.

My purpose in this book is to suggest ways of going beyond the sterile opposition of entrenched black-and-white distinctions that has been produced by these controversies. We are all, one way or another, products of world capitalism and the institutions, practices, and ideas that have accompanied it. What is at issue in these essays is the very nature of modernity in colonial and postcolonial India. India, one may reasonably argue, became decidedly capitalist through the period of British rule and after, but this has not meant the hegemony of bourgeois or liberal practices in Indian social life. It is now accepted almost universally that the electoral and populist aspects of Indian democracy have encouraged people to challenge older hierarchies of power and status. But that does not mean that social relations and the relations of production in the country have become bourgeois or liberal in any recognizable way. Today's India is more democratic if one considers the impact of universal adult franchise on Indian public life generally. More and more conflicts in contemporary India get caught up in political processes than ever before. A small, local conflict can burgeon into a massive drama drawing into its dynamics political parties, institutions, and personalities. Yet greater democracy does not mean that the rules of public debate in India or the cultural codes for the expression of authority and power in everyday life are necessarily liberal or even nonviolent. Yes, Indian public life is more democratic than before—and, in that sense, modern—but it is not thereby necessarily rendered more civil. Verbal, physical, and symbolic violence underwriting relations of domination and subordination are to be seen in every department of life: from relations of production to relationships in the family.

The fundamental problem of how one might characterize Indian modernity has remained at the center of scholarly disputations on the subject. The labeling exercise on the part of the Left and the liberal intelligentsia has, on the whole, been an attempt to qualify categories characteristic of European metahistories by attaching to them negative particles or prefixes. *Not bourgeois, not capitalist, not liberal,* and so on— these have been our predominant ways of summing up Indian modernity. "Incomplete modernity" or an "incomplete bourgeois revolution," as some of the essays collected here will show, was the catchphrase of Indian intellectuals on the Left in the 1970s and 1980s. Ranajit Guha's label—*dominance without [bourgeois] hegemony*—was perhaps the most successful attempt of all to find a positive way of describing the situation, but, even there, the negative function of the word *without* can hardly be missed.

The negative labeling of positive phenomena is, ultimately, unsatisfactory. But it cannot be ascribed to any failure of intelligence or erudition. The problem, it has seemed to me for some time, lies in the very categories of social science and political philosophy with which we think. Unlike in the case of the categories of the mathematical sciences or other disciplines that allow a formal presentation of problems, it is difficult for social-science categories to attain a universality that is completely free of historical and contingent differences between societies. While such categories are eminently translatable across societies and should, indeed, be so translated in the interest of social justice, they are also dogged by problems that arise from such acts of translation. This happens because societies are not tabulae rasae. They come with their own plural histories that have already been imbibed by their members through certain shared dispositions, skills, competencies, and sentiments. Our use of negative labels may be read as an index of the problems of translation that we, academic intellectuals, encounter in describing Indian social acts through the filter of European-derived social sciences and political philosophies.

These questions are taken up in the essays that follow. There is, as such, no one single argument to which the essays sum, but they contain intersecting themes. I have found it convenient to collect the essays in three parts in order to highlight some of the themes addressed in them.

The first part, "Questions of History," is organized around historiographic debates. I begin with a "small history" of *Subaltern Studies*. It explains how *Subaltern Studies* came to speak to certain problems of political modernity and democracy in India and attempts to give a thumbnail sketch of the history of the series. The next two essays broaden the scope of the discussion by raising questions about the role of the past in constructions of modernity in colonial countries. Sumit Sarkar's criticisms of *Subaltern Studies* and Ashis Nandy's critiques of the discipline of history, respectively, provide my starting points in these chapters.

The second part, "Practices of Modernity," contains essays that focus on specific cultural and institutional sites of modern India. I have included here a speculative reading of *khadi,* the Gandhian dress of the male politician in India; an essay on the politics of civic consciousness (or the lack thereof) visible in Indian public spaces; and a piece examining the governmental roots of modern ethnicity.

The third part, "The Ethical and the In-Human," contains three essays working their way toward an appreciation of some of the ethical dilemmas and ambiguities that arise when we write—as, indeed, we must—on behalf of projects for greater social justice. The first of these essays investigates the relation between law and narrative in the structuring of modern political desires. The final two essays relate to the memories and politics of the popular violence that rocked British India when it was divided in 1947 to create the modern nation-states of India and Pakistan. Both these essays relate primarily to contemporary discussions in India of the significance of the Partition. I must acknowledge here a criticism that is often made of this discussion by Pakistani intellectuals: that Indian scholars tend to see the Partition predominantly as a tragedy, missing the fact that it gave birth to the new nation of Pakistan. I do not think that I escape this criticism.

Some of the essays included here bear the birthmarks of the debates within which they were born. I worked on these essays during the same years I was working on my *Provincializing Europe.*[4] There is, naturally, some overlap between the intellectual concerns of the two books. This is particularly true of chapter 7 and parts of chapter 1 in this book. But I have let the shared similarities stand because I felt that I pursued a direction of analysis here that was significantly different from the goals that I had set myself in writing *Provincializing Europe.*

What all these essays are searching for is a better understanding of the complexities of modernity in India and for principles of humaneness that may elude our political theories. They seek to write about modernity self-reflexively. The turn toward the ethical at the end of the book is also a plea to keep in view—even as we write politically and in search of a more just world—the dilemmas of what Hannah Arendt once sagaciously called "the human condition."[5] Far too hastily, it has often seemed to me, we now equate being human with being political. I recognize the equation as one belonging to the mood of contemporary democracies. I inevitably share in that mood but recognize that it sometimes makes us cut intellectual corners. The essays here struggle with that tendency—from which I claim no immunity—by pointing toward problems of analysis that admit no easy solutions. It would be foolish to claim either success or finality for the intellectual positions that I adopt in these essays. I bring them together in the knowledge that the debates in which they participate are still with us, in one form or another. I obviously make an assumption here: that self-reflexivity about the political and the modern is itself something political. The more we become aware that some of the intellectual and moral quandaries thrown up by the exigencies of democracy and development may not admit of any a priori solutions, the less capable we are of justifying—in an a priori manner—the violent and undemocratic steps that the process of becoming modern appears also to entail.

PART ONE

QUESTIONS OF HISTORY

ONE A Small History of *Subaltern Studies*

In a wide-ranging critique of postcolonial studies, Arif Dirlik suggests that, while the historiographic innovations of *Subaltern Studies* are welcome, they are mere applications of methods pioneered by British Marxist historians, albeit modified by "Third World sensibilities." Dirlik writes: "Most of the generalizations that appear in the discourse of postcolonial intellectuals from India may appear novel in the historiography of India but are not discoveries from broader perspectives. . . . [T]he historical writings of *Subaltern Studies* historians . . . represent the application in Indian historiography of trends in historical writings that were quite widespread by the 1970s under the impact of social historians such as E. P. Thompson, Eric Hobsbawm, and a host of others."[1]

Without wishing either to inflate the claims of *Subaltern Studies* scholars or to deny what they may, indeed, have learned from the British Marxist historians, I would like to demonstrate that Dirlik's reading of *Subaltern Studies* seriously misjudges that which makes the series a postcolonial project. To that end, I provide here a "small" history of the series. I call this history *small*, not simply because of its brevity, but also because,

3

following Benjamin's "small history" of photography, the narrative here has a very particular end in focus.[2] I argue—against critics who have advised otherwise—why subaltern studies could never be a mere reproduction in India of the English tradition of writing "history from below."

SUBALTERN STUDIES AND DEBATES IN MODERN INDIAN HISTORY

The academic subject called *modern Indian history* is a relatively recent development, a result of research and discussion in various universities mainly in India, the United Kingdom, the United States, and Australia after the end of British imperial rule in August 1947. In its early phase, this area of scholarship bore all the signs of an ongoing struggle between tendencies affiliated with imperialist biases in Indian history and a nationalist desire on the part of historians in India to decolonize the past. Marxism was understandably mobilized in aid of the nationalist project of intellectual decolonization.[3] Bipan Chandra's *The Rise and Growth of Economic Nationalism in India,* Anil Seal's *The Emergence of Indian Nationalism,* A. R. Desai's *Social Background of Indian Nationalism,* D. A. Low's collection *Soundings in Modern South Asian History,* the many seminal articles published by Bernard Cohn (now collected in *An Anthropologist among the Historians*), debates around Morris David Morris's assessment of the results of British rule in India, and the work of other scholars in the 1960s raised new and controversial questions regarding the nature and results of colonial rule in India.[4] Did the imperialist British deserve credit after all for making India a developing, modern, and united country? Were the Hindu-Muslim conflicts that resulted in the formation of the two states of Pakistan and India consequences of the divide-and-rule policies of the British, or were they reflections of divisions internal to South Asian society?

Official documents of the British government of India—and traditions of imperial history writing—always portrayed colonial rule as being beneficial to India and its people. They applauded the British for bringing to the subcontinent political unity, modern education institutions, modern industries, a sense of nationalism, the rule of law, and so on. Indian historians in the 1960s—many of whom had English degrees and most of whom belonged to a generation that grew up in the final years of British rule—challenged that view. They argued instead that colonialism had had deleterious effects on economic and cultural developments. Modernity and the nationalist desire for political unity, they claimed, were not so much British gifts to India as fruits of struggles undertaken by the Indians themselves.

Nationalism and colonialism thus emerged, not surprisingly, as the two major areas of research and debate defining the field of modern Indian history in the 1960s and 1970s. At one extreme of this debate was the Cambridge historian Anil Seal, whose 1968 *Emergence of Indian Nationalism* described *nationalism* as the work of a tiny elite reared in the education institutions that the British set up in India. This elite, as Seal put it, both "competed and collaborated" with the British in their search for power and privilege.[5]

A few years later, this idea was pushed to an extreme in the collection *Locality, Province, and Nation,* to which Seal, his colleague John Gallagher, and a posse of their doctoral students contributed.[6] Their writings discounted the role of ideas and idealism in history and foregrounded an extremely narrow view of what constituted political and economic "interest" for historical actors. They argued that it was the penetration of the colonial state into the local structures of power in India—a move prompted by the financial self-interest of the raj rather than by any altruistic motives—that eventually, and by degrees, drew Indian elites into the colonial governmental process. According to this argument, the involvement of Indians in colonial institutions set off a scramble among the indigenous elites, who combined—opportunistically and around factions formed along "vertical" lines of patronage[7]—to jockey for power and privilege within the limited opportunities for self-rule provided by the British. Such, the Cambridge historians claimed, was the real dynamic of that which outside observers or naive historians may have mistaken for an idealistic struggle for freedom. Nationalism and colonialism both came out in this history as interdependent phenomena. The history of Indian nationalism, said Seal, "was the rivalry between Indian and Indian, its relationship with imperialism that of the mutual clinging of two unsteady men of straw."[8]

At the other extreme of this debate was the Indian historian Bipan Chandra, in the 1970s a professor at the prestigious Jawaharlal Nehru University in Delhi. Chandra and his colleagues saw Indian history of the colonial period as an epic battle between the forces of nationalism and those of colonialism. Drawing on both Marx's writings and Latin American theories of dependency and underdevelopment, Chandra argued that colonialism was a regressive force that distorted all developments in India's society and polity. The social, political, and economic ills of post-Independence India—including those of mass poverty and religious and caste conflict—could be blamed on the political economy of colonialism. However, he saw nationalism in a different, contrasting light—as a regenerative force, as the antithesis of colonialism, something that united and produced an "Indian people" by mobilizing them for struggle against the British. Nationalist leaders such as Gandhi and Nehru were the authors of such an anti-imperial movement for unity. Chandra claimed that the conflict of interest and ideology between the colonizers and the Indian people was the most important conflict of British India. All others—whether of class or of caste—were secondary to this principal contradiction and were to be treated as such in histories of nationalism.[9]

Yet, as research progressed in the 1970s, there emerged a series of increasingly serious difficulties with both these narratives. It was clear that the Cambridge version of nationalist politics without ideas or idealism would never ring true to scholars in the subcontinent who had themselves experienced the desire for freedom from colonial rule.[10] On the other hand, the nationalist historian's story of there having been a "moral war" between colonialism and nationalism wore increasingly thin as research by younger scholars in India and elsewhere brought new material to light. New information on the mobilization of the poor (peasants, tribals, and workers) by elite nationalist leaders in the course of the Gandhian mass movements in the 1920s and 1930s, for example, suggested a strongly reactionary side to the principal nationalist party, the Indian National Congress. Gyanendra Pandey at Oxford, David Hardiman and David Arnold at Sussex (all of them later to become members of the *Subaltern Studies* collective), Majid Siddiqi and Kapil Kumar in Delhi, Histesranjan Sanyal in Calcutta, Brian Stoddart, Stephen Henningham, and Max Harcourt in Australia, and others elsewhere documented the way in which nationalist leaders would suppress with a heavy hand peasants' or workers' tendency to exceed the self-imposed limits of the nationalist political agenda by protesting the oppression meted out to them, not only by the British, but by the indigenous ruling groups as well.[11]

From the point of view of a younger generation of historians, whom Ranajit Guha, following Salman Rushdie, has called *midnight's children*, neither the Cambridge thesis propounding a skeptical view of Indian nationalism nor the nationalist-Marxist thesis glossing over—or assimilating to a nationalist historiographic agenda—real conflicts of ideas and interests between the elite nationalists and their socially subordinate followers was an adequate response to the problems of postcolonial history writing in India.[12] The persistence of religious and caste conflict in post-Independence India; the war between India and China in 1962, which made official nationalism sound hollow and eventually gave rise to a fascination with Maoism among many urban, educated young people in India; the outbreak of a violent Maoist political movement in India (known as the Naxalite movement), which drew many urban youths into the countryside in the late 1960s and early 1970s—all these and many other factors combined to alienate younger historians from the shibboleths of nationalist historiography. This alienation was further strengthened by the rise in popularity of peasant studies among Anglo-American academics in the 1970s. All this historiographic discontent, however, was still floundering in the old liberal and positivist paradigms inherited from English traditions of history writing even as it was searching for a path toward decolonizing the field of Indian history.

SUBALTERN STUDIES AS PARADIGM SHIFT, 1982 – 87

Subaltern Studies intervened in this situation in 1982. Intellectually, it began on the very terrain that it was to contest: historiography that had its roots in the colonial education system. It started as a critique of two contending schools of history: the Cambridge school and that of the nationalist historians. Both these approaches, declared Guha in a statement that inaugurated the series *Subaltern Studies,* were elitist. They wrote up the history of nationalism as the story of an achievement by the elite classes, whether Indian or British. For all their merits, they could not explain "the contributions made by people *on their own,* that is, *independent of the elite* to the making and development of this nationalism."[13] It will be clear from this statement of Guha's that *Subaltern Studies* was part of an attempt to align historical reasoning with larger movements for democracy in India. It looked for an antielitist approach to history writing, and, in this, it had much in common with the "history-from-below" approaches pioneered in English historiography by Christopher Hill, E. P. Thompson, E. J. Hobsbawm, and others. Both *Subaltern Studies* and the history-from-below school were Marxist in inspiration; both owed a certain intellectual debt to the Italian Communist Antonio Gramsci in trying to move away from deterministic, Stalinist readings of Marx.[14] The declared aim of *Subaltern Studies* was to produce historical analyses in which the subaltern groups were viewed as the subjects of history. As Guha put it once in the course of introducing a volume of *Subaltern Studies:* "We are indeed opposed to much of the prevailing academic practice in historiography . . . for its failure to acknowledge the subaltern as the maker of his own destiny. This critique lies at the very heart of our project."[15]

But, at the same time, Guha's theorization of the project signaled certain key differences that would increasingly distinguish the project of

Subaltern Studies from that of English Marxist historiography. With hindsight, it can be said that there were three broad areas in which *Subaltern Studies* differed from the history-from-below approach of Hobsbawm or Thompson (allowing for differences between these two eminent historians of England and Europe). *Subaltern historiography* necessarily entailed a relative separation of the history of power from any universalist histories of capital, a critique of the nation form, and an interrogation of the relation between power and knowledge (hence of the archive itself and of history as a form of knowledge). In these differences, I would argue, lay the beginnings of a new way of theorizing the intellectual agenda for postcolonial histories.

The critical theoretical break came with the way in which Guha sought to redefine the category *the political* with reference to colonial India. He argued that both the Cambridge and the nationalist historians conflated the political domain with the formal side of governmental and institutional processes. As he put it: "In all writings of this kind [i.e., elitist historiography] the parameters of Indian politics are assumed to be or enunciated as those of the institutions introduced by the British for the government of the country. . . . [Elitist historians] can do no more than equate politics with the aggregation of activities and ideas of those who were directly involved in operating these institutions, that is, the colonial rulers and their élèves—the dominant groups in native society."[16]

Using *people* and *subaltern classes* synonymously, and defining both as the "demographic difference between the total Indian population" and the dominant indigenous and foreign elite, Guha claimed that there was, in colonial India, an "autonomous" domain of the "politics of the people" that was organized differently than the domain of the politics of the elite. Elite politics involved "vertical mobilization" and "a greater reliance on Indian adaptations of British parliamentary institutions" and "tended to be relatively more legalistic and constitutional in orientation." In the domain of "subaltern politics," on the other hand, mobilization for political intervention depended on horizontal affiliations such as "the traditional organization of kinship and territoriality" or on "class consciousness," "depending on the level of the consciousness of the people involved." Subaltern politics tended to be more violent than elite politics. Central to subaltern mobilizations was "a notion of resistance to elite domination." "The experience of exploitation and labour endowed this politics with many idioms, norms and values which put it in a category apart from elite politics," wrote Guha. Peasant uprisings in colonial India, he argued, reflected this separate and autonomous grammar of mobilization "in its most comprehensive form." Even in the case of resistance and protest by urban workers, the "figure of mobilization" was one that was "derived directly from peasant insurgency."[17]

Guha's separation of elite and subaltern domains within the political had some radical implications for social theory and historiography. The standard tendency in global Marxist historiography until the 1970s was to look on peasant revolts organized along the axes of kinship, religion, caste, etc. as movements exhibiting a "backward" consciousness, the kind that, in his work on social banditry and "primitive rebellion," Hobsbawm had called *prepolitical*. This was seen as a consciousness that had not quite come to terms with the institutional logic of modernity or capitalism. As Hobsbawm put it with reference to his own material: "They are pre-political people who have not yet found, or only begun to find, specific language in which to express their aspirations about the world."[18] By explicitly rejecting the characterization of peasant consciousness as prepolitical, and by avoiding evolutionary models of consciousness, Guha was prepared to suggest that the nature of collective action against exploitation in colonial India was such that it effectively led to a new constellation of the *political*. To ignore the problems that peasants' participation in the modern political sphere could cause for a Eurocentric Marxism would lead, according to Guha, only to elitist histories. For one would, then, not know how to analyze the consciousness of the peasant—the discourses of kinship, caste, religion, and ethnicity through which they expressed themselves in protest—except as a backward consciousness trying to grapple with a changing world whose logic it could never fully comprehend.

Guha insisted that, instead of being an anachronism in a modernizing colonial world, the peasant was a real contemporary of colonialism and a fundamental part of the modernity to which colonial rule gave rise in India. The peasant's was not a backward consciousness—a mentality left over from the past—baffled by modern political and economic institutions yet resistant to them. Guha suggested that the (insurgent) peasant in colonial India did in fact read his contemporary world correctly. Examining, for instance, over a hundred known cases of peasant rebellions in British India between 1783 and 1900, Guha showed that these always involved the deployment by the peasants of codes of dress, speech, and behavior that tended to invert the codes through which their social superiors dominated them in everyday life.[19] Inversion of the symbols of authority was almost inevitably the first act of rebellion by insurgent peasants.

Elitist histories of peasant uprisings missed the signification of this gesture by seeing it as prepolitical. Anil Seal, for example, dismissed all nineteenth-century peasant revolts in colonial India as having no "specific political content," being "uprisings of the traditional kind, the reaching for sticks and stones as the only way of protesting against distress."[20] Marxists, on the other hand, explained these gestures as either expressing a false consciousness or performing a "safety-valve" function in the overall social system.[21] What both these explanatory strategies missed, Guha contended, was the fact that, at the beginning of every peasant uprising, there was inevitably a struggle on the part of rebels to destroy all symbols of the social prestige and power of the ruling classes: "It was this fight for prestige which was at the heart of insurgency. Inversion was its principal modality. It was a *political* struggle in which the rebel appropriated and/or destroyed the insignia of his enemy's power and hoped thus to abolish the marks of his own subalternity."[22]

I have emphasized the word *political* in this quotation in order to point up a creative tension between the Marxist lineage of *Subaltern Studies* and the more challenging questions that the series raised from the very beginning about the nature of power in non-Western colonial modernities. Guha's point was that the arrangements of power in which peasants and other subaltern classes found themselves in colonial India contained two very different logics of hierarchy and oppression. One was the logic of the quasi-liberal legal and institutional framework introduced by the British. Imbricated with this was another set of relationships in which hierarchy was based on the direct and explicit domination and subordination of the less powerful through both ideological-symbolic means and physical force. The semiotics of domination and subordination were what the subaltern classes sought to destroy every time they rose up in rebellion. The semiotics could not be separated in the Indian case from what in English we inaccurately refer to as either *the religious* or *the supernatural*.

The tension between a familiar narrative of capital and a more radical understanding of it can be seen in Guha's *Elementary Aspects* itself. There are times when Guha tends to read *domination and subordination* in terms of an opposition between feudal and capitalist modes of production. There is a respectable tendency in Marxist or liberal scholarship to read certain kinds of undemocratic relationships—personalized systems of authority and practices of deification, for instance—as survivals of a precapitalist era, as not quite modern. They are seen as indicative of the problems of the transition to capitalism, the assumption being that a full-blown capitalism would or should be logically incompatible with feudal-type relationships.

These statements repeat a familiar structure that is often given to the European story of the transition to capitalism. First, the peasants' land is expropriated. Then the peasants join the ranks of the urban and industrial workers, whereupon they negotiate the disciplining process of the factory. Next, they engage in machine breaking and other forms of Luddite protest until trade unions arrive on the scene and certain formal freedoms—indicative of a growing democratic consciousness—are put in place. In this fundamentally Eurocentric and stagist view of history, however modulated by theories of "uneven development," the peasant is a figure of the past and must mutate into the industrial worker in order to emerge, eventually, as the citizen-subject of modern democracies. Where this mutation does not quite occur yet the peasant still becomes an actor in the modern political sphere, as in anticolonial nationalisms, the peasant remains, as we have seen, the bearer of what Hobsbawm calls a *prepolitical consciousness.*

Guha's *Elementary Aspects* does sometimes speak within this tradition of analysis. Direct domination, Guha tells us, is a feature of lingering feudalism:

> Taking the subcontinent as a whole capitalist development in agriculture remained merely incipient . . . until 1900. Rents constituted the most substantial part of income yielded by property in land. . . . The element that was constant in this [landlord-peasant] relationship in all its variety was the extraction of the peasant's surplus by means determined rather less by the free play of the forces of a market economy than by the extra-economic force of the landlord's standing in local society and in the colonial polity. In other words, it was a relationship of domination and subordination—a political relationship of the feudal type, or as it has been appropriately described, a semi-feudal relationship which derived its material sustenance from pre-capitalist conditions of production and its legitimacy from a traditional culture still paramount in the superstructure.[23]

This particular Marxist narrative, however, underrepresents the force and larger significance of Guha's critique of the category *prepolitical.* For, if one were to accept the Marxism of this quotation, one could, indeed, come back at Guha and argue that the sphere of the political hardly ever abstracted itself from other spheres—those of religion, kinship, culture—in feudal relationships of domination and subordination and that, in that sense, feudal relationships of power could not properly be called *political.* The lingering existence of feudal-type relationships in the Indian scene could then be read—as Guha indeed does at the beginning of the quotation just offered—as a mark of the incompleteness of the transition to capitalism. By this logic, the so-called semifeudal relationships and the peasant's mentality could, indeed, be seen as leftovers from an earlier period, still active, no doubt, but under world-historical notice of extinction. All India needed was to institute more capitalist institutions, and the process of the conversion of the peasant into the citizen—the properly political figure of personhood—would begin. This, indeed, was Hobsbawm's logic. That is why his prepolitical characters—even when they are "broken into" capitalism, and even when Hobsbawm acknowledges that the "acquisition of political consciousness" by these "primitive rebels" is what makes "our century the most revolutionary in history"—always remain in the position of being classic "outsiders" to the logic of capitalism: "It comes to them from outside, insidiously by the operation of economic forces which they do not understand and over which they have no control."[24]

In rejecting the category *prepolitical,* however, Guha insists on the specific history of modern democracy in India and on differences in the histories of power in colonial India and in Europe. This gesture is radical in that it fundamentally pluralizes the history of power in global modernity and separates it from any universal history of capital. "Hobsbawm's material," Guha writes, "is of course derived almost entirely from the European experience, and his generalizations are perhaps in accord with it. . . . Whatever its validity for other countries the notion of pre-political peasant insurgency helps little in understanding the experience of colonial India."[25] If we see the colonial formation in India as a case of modernity in which the domain of the political, as Guha argues in introducing *Subaltern Studies,* is irreducibly split into two distinct logics that get braided together all the time—the logic of formal-legal and secular frameworks of governance and that of relationships of direct domination and subordination that derive their legitimacy from a different set of institutions and practices, including those of dharma (*dharma* is often translated as "religion")—then Guha's writings help open up a very interesting problem in the global history of modernity and citizenship.

Ultimately, this is the problem of how to think about the history of power in an age when capital and the governing institutions of modernity increasingly develop a global reach. Marx's discussion of capitalist discipline assumed that the rule of capital entailed the transition to capitalist power relationships: the overseer's penalty book replacing the slave driver's lash. Foucault's work shows that, if we want to understand the key institutions of modernity that originated in the West, the juridical model of sovereignty celebrated in modern European political thought must be supplemented by the notions of discipline, bio-power, and governmentality. Guha claims that, in the colonial modernity of India, this supplementation must include an extra pair of terms: *domination* and *subordination.* Not because India is anything like a semimodern or semi-capitalist or semifeudal country. And not because capital in India rules merely by "formal subsumption."

Guha goes beyond the argument that reduces questions of democracy and power in the subcontinent to propositions about an incomplete transition to capitalism. He does not deny the connections of colonial India to the global forces of capitalism. His point, however, is that the global history of capitalism need not reproduce everywhere the same history of power. In the calculus of modernity, power is not a dependent variable and capital an independent one. Capital and power can be treated as analytically separable categories. Traditional European-Marxist political thought that fuses the two is therefore always relevant but inadequate for theorizing power in colonial-modern histories. The history of colonial modernity in India created a domain of the political that was heteroglossic in its idioms and irreducibly plural in its structure, interlocking within itself strands of different types of relationships that did not make up a logical whole. One such strand critical to the functioning of authority in Indian institutions was that of direct domination and subordination of the subaltern by the elite. As Guha put it in his first contribution to *Subaltern Studies,* this strand of domination and subordination ubiquitous in power relationships in India "was traditional only insofar as its roots could be traced back to pre-colonial times, but it was by no means archaic in the sense of being outmoded."[26]

The social domination and subordination of the subaltern by the elite was, thus, an everyday feature of Indian capitalism itself. This was a capitalism of colonial origins. Reading critically some key texts of Marx, Guha argued that modern colonialism was quintessentially the historical condition in which an expansive and increasingly global capital came to dominate non-Western societies without effecting or requiring any thoroughgoing democratic transformation in social relationships of power and authority. The colonial state—the ultimate expression of the domain of the political in colonial India—was both a result and a condition of possibility of such domination. As Guha put it: "Colonialism could continue as a relation of power in the subcontinent only on the condition that the colonizing bourgeoisie should fail to live up to its own universalizing project. The nature of the state it had created by the sword made this historically necessary." The result was a society that no doubt changed under the impact of colonial capitalism but one in which "vast areas in the life and consciousness of the people" escaped any kind of "[bourgeois] hegemony."[27] The "Indian culture of the colonial era," Guha argued elsewhere, defied understanding "either as a replication of the liberal-bourgeois culture of nineteenth-century Britain or as the mere survival of an antecedent pre-capitalist culture."[28] This was capitalism, but a capitalism without capitalist hierarchies, a capitalist dominance without a hegemonic capitalist culture—or, in Guha's famous terms, *dominance without hegemony.*

SUBALTERN STUDIES AND THE REORIENTATION OF HISTORY

Guha's two formulations—that both nationalism and colonialism were involved in instituting in India a rule of capital in which bourgeois ideologies exercised dominance without hegemony and that the resulting forms of power in India could not be termed *prepolitical*—had several implications for historiography. Some of these were worked out in Guha's own writings and some in those of his colleagues. It is important, however, that we clarify these implications, for they are what made *Subaltern Studies* an experiment in postcolonial historiography.

First of all, Guha's critique of the category *prepolitical* challenged historicism by rejecting all stagist theories of history. If, as has been discussed, the term *prepolitical* took its validity from categorizing certain kinds of power relationships as *premodern, feudal,* etc., Guha's discussion of power in colonial India resists such a clear distinction between the modern and the premodern. Relationships in India that looked feudal when seen through a stagist view of history were contemporaneous with all that looked modern to the same point of view. From Guha's perspective, however, the former could not be looked on through geologic or evolutionist metaphors of "survival" or "remnant" without such historicism becoming elitist in its interpretation of the past.

Subaltern Studies, then, was, in principle, opposed to nationalist histories that portrayed nationalist leaders as ushering India and its people out of some kind of precapitalist stage into a world-historical phase of "bourgeois modernity," properly fitted out with the artifacts of democracy: the rights of citizenship, a market economy, freedom of the press, and the rule of law. There is no doubt that the Indian political elite internalized and used this language of political modernity, but this democratic tendency existed alongside and interlarded with undemocratic relationships of domination and subordination. This coexistence of two domains of politics, said Guha, "was the index of an important historical truth, that is, the *failure of the bourgeoisie to speak for the nation.*"[29] There was, in fact, no unitary nation to speak for. Rather, the more important question was how and through what practices an official nationalism emerged that claimed to represent such a unitary nation. A critical stance toward official or statist nationalism and its attendant historiography marked

Subaltern Studies from the beginning. Postcolonial history was, thus, also a postnationalist form of historiography.[30]

Guha's quest for a history in which the subaltern was the maker of his own destiny brought into focus the question of the relation between texts and power. Historical archives are usually collections of documents, texts of various kinds. Historians of peasants and other subaltern social groups have long emphasized the fact that peasants do not leave behind their own documents. Historians concerned with recuperating the peasant experience in history have often turned for help to the resources of other disciplines: anthropology, demography, sociology, archaeology, human geography, etc. In his well-known study of nineteenth-century rural France, *Peasants into Frenchmen*, Eugen Weber provides a succinct formulation of this approach: "The illiterate are not in fact inarticulate; they can and do express themselves in several ways. Sociologists, ethnologists, geographers, and most recently demographic historians have shown us new and different means of interpreting evidence."[31] In the 1960s and 1970s, E. P. Thompson, Keith Thomas, and others turned to anthropology in search of the experiences of the subaltern classes.[32]

Guha's approach is interestingly different from that of these historians. He begins his *Elementary Aspects* by recognizing the same problem as do Weber, Thomas, Thompson, and others: that peasants do not speak directly in archival documents, which are usually produced by the ruling classes.[33] Like these historians, Guha too uses a diversity of disciplines in tracking the logic of peasant consciousness at the moment of rebellion. But he thinks of the category *consciousness* differently. In insisting on the autonomy of the consciousness of the insurgent peasant, he does not aim to produce generalizations that sum up what every empirical peasant participating in rebellions in colonial India must have thought, felt, or experienced.

Guha's critique of the term *prepolitical* legitimately barred this path of thinking, which, however well intentioned, ends up making peasants into relatively exotic objects of anthropology. Guha thought of consciousness—and therefore of peasant subjecthood—as something immanent in the very practices of peasant insurgency. *Elementary Aspects* is a study of the *practices* of insurgent peasants in colonial India, not of a reified category called *consciousness*. The aim of the book was to bring out the collective imagination inherent in the practices of peasant rebellion. Guha makes no claim that the insurgent consciousness that he discusses is indeed conscious, that it existed inside the heads of peasants. He does not equate consciousness with the subject's view of himself. Rather, he examines rebel practices to decipher the particular relationships—between elites and subalterns and among subalterns themselves

—that are acted out in them and then attempts to derive from these re-lationships the elementary structure, as it were, of the consciousness or imagination inherent in those relationships.

In keeping with the structuralist tradition with which he affiliates his book by the very use of the word *elementary* in its title, Guha describes his hermeneutical strategy through the metaphor of reading. The avail-able archives on peasant insurgencies are produced by the counterin-surgency measures of the ruling classes and their armies and police forces. Guha, therefore, emphasizes the need for the historian to de-velop a conscious strategy for reading the archives. The aim of this strat-egy is, not simply to discern and sift the biases of the elites, but to analyze the very textual properties of these documents in order to get at the his-tory of power that produced them. Without such a scanning device, Guha argued, historians tend to reproduce the same logic of representa-tion as that used by the elite classes in dominating the subaltern.[34] The interventionist metaphor of reading resonates as the opposite of E. P. Thompson's use—in the course of his polemic with Althusser—of the passive metaphor of listening in describing the hermeneutical activity of the historian.[35] This emphasis on reading also left *Subaltern Studies* his-toriography open to the influences of literary and narrative theory.[36]

In thus critiquing historicism and Eurocentrism and using that cri-tique to interrogate the idea of the nation, in emphasizing the textual properties of archival documents, in considering representation as an as-pect of power relationships between the elite and the subaltern, Guha and his colleagues moved away from the guiding assumptions of the history-from-below approach of English Marxist historiography. With Guha's work, Indian history took, as it were, the proverbial linguistic turn. From its very beginning, *Subaltern Studies* positioned itself on the unorthodox territory of the Left. What it inherited from Marxism was already in conversation with other and more recent currents of Euro-pean thought, particularly structuralism. And there was a discernible sympathy with early Foucault in the way in which Guha's writings posed the knowledge-power question by asking, What are the archives, and how are they produced?

SUBALTERN STUDIES SINCE 1988: MULTIPLE CIRCUITS

Ranajit Guha retired from the editorial team of *Subaltern Studies* in 1988.[37] In the same year, an anthology entitled *Selected Subaltern Stud-ies* published from New York launched the global career of the proj-ect. Edward Said wrote a foreword to the volume describing Guha's statement regarding the aims of *Subaltern Studies* as "intellectually insurrectionary."[38] Gayatri Spivak's "Deconstructing Historiography," which had first appeared in *Subaltern Studies VI* (1986), served as the introduction to this collection.[39] This essay and a review essay by Rosalind O'Hanlon first published in the journal *Modern Asian Studies* in 1988 offered two important criticisms of *Subaltern Studies* that had a serious effect on the later intellectual trajectory of the project.[40] Both Spivak and O'Hanlon pointed to the absence of gender questions in *Subaltern Studies*. Both also made a more fundamental criticism of the theoretical orientation of the project, pointing out that, in effect, *Subaltern Studies* historiography operated with an idea of the subject—in Guha's words, "to acknowledge the subaltern as the maker of his own destiny"—that had not wrestled at all with contemporary critiques of the very idea of the subject itself. Spivak's famous "Can the Subaltern Speak?"—a critical and challenging reading of a conversation between Foucault and Deleuze—forcefully posed these and related questions by raising deconstructive and philosophical objections to any straightforward program of "letting the subaltern speak."[41]

Subaltern Studies scholars have since tried to take these criticisms into account in their work. The charge that they do not tackle gender issues or engage feminist scholarship has been met to some degree by Ranajit Guha, Partha Chatterjee, and Susie Tharu, among others.[42] Partha Chatterjee's 1986 *Nationalist Thought and the Colonial World* creatively applied Saidian and postcolonial perspectives to the study of non-Western nationalisms, using India as an example.[43] With this work, which extended Guha's criticisms of nationalist historiography into a full-blown, brilliant critique of nationalist thought, and Gyanendra Pandey's book on the history of the Partition of India in 1947, the postcolonial critique may truly be said to have become a postnationalist critique as well.[44]

The influence of deconstructionist and postmodern thought in *Subaltern Studies* may be traced in the way in which the work of Gyanendra Pandey, Partha Chatterjee, and Shahid Amin has in the 1990s come to privilege the idea of the fragment over that of the whole or totality. Pandey's *The Construction of Communalism in Colonial North India* (1990) and his 1992 essay "In Defense of the Fragment," Chatterjee's 1994 *The Nation and Its Fragments*, and Amin's experimental and widely acclaimed 1995 *Event, Memory, Metaphor* all question, on both archival and epistemological grounds, even the very possibility of constructing a totalizing national history in narrating the politics of subaltern lives.[45] This move has also understandably given rise to a series of writings from *Subaltern Studies* scholars in which history itself as a European form of knowledge has come under critical investigation. Gyan Prakash, Ranajit Guha, Partha Chatterjee, Shahid Amin, Ajay Skaria, Shail Mayaram, and others have made significant contributions to the analysis of colonial dis-course.[46] With this growing engagement with the works of Homi Bha-bha,[47] Gayatri Spivak, and Edward Said, *Subaltern Studies* has emerged as a project in conversation with postcolonial studies.

Where does *Subaltern Studies*—both the series and the project—stand today? At the crossing of many different pathways, it seems. The original project has been developed and furthered in the work of indi-vidual members of the collective. David Arnold's study of British colo-nialism in India in terms of histories of contested bodily practices, *Colo-nizing the Body,* David Hardiman's studies of the political and economic culture of subaltern lives caught in emergent forms of capitalism in the Indian state of Gujarat, *The Coming of the Devi* and *Feeding the Baniya,* and Gautam Bhadra's study of a number of texts having to do with peasant society in eighteenth- and nineteenth-century Bengal, *Iman o nishan,* are examples of projects in which the possibilities of the original theoretical historiographic project are worked out and illustrated through concrete, historical examples.[48]

At the same time, it must be acknowledged that *Subaltern Studies* has exceeded the original historiographic agenda that it set for itself in the early 1980s. The series now has, as I said at the outset, both global and regional locations in the circuits of scholarship that it traverses. This ex-pansion beyond the realms of Indian history has earned for the series both praise and criticism. Much of the controversy follows, roughly, the contours of the global and ongoing debate between Marxists and post-modernists.

Like Marxists elsewhere, Indian Marxists charge that the postmod-ernist valorization of the fragment in subaltern historiography hurts the cause of the unity of the oppressed and helps Hindu extremists. Many of the Marxist opponents of *Subaltern Studies* believe that such unity is aided by a social analysis that helps bring the different publics of the op-pressed together by finding global and totalizing causes behind their op-pression.

Defenders of *Subaltern Studies* point out, in reply, that the public sphere—in India and elsewhere—has fragmented under the pressure of democracy and that it cannot be united artificially by a Marxism that in-sists on reducing the many diverse experiences of oppression and mar-ginalization to the single axis of class or even to the triple axes of class, gender, and ethnicity. Achieving a critical perspective on European forms of knowledge, they would add, is part of the interrogation of their colonial inheritance that postcolonial intellectuals must carry out. Their critique of nationalism, they would insist, has nothing in common with the nationalist chauvinism of the Hindu parties.

It is not my purpose here to evaluate this debate, which I treat in more detail in chapter 2. The point of this exercise has been to rebut the charge that *Subaltern Studies* lost its way by falling into the bad company of postcolonial theory. Through a discussion of what Guha wrote in the 1980s, I have sought to demonstrate some necessary connections between the original aims of the *Subaltern Studies* project and current discussions of postcoloniality. *Subaltern Studies* was not a case of the application to Indian material of methods of historical research already worked out in the metropolitan Marxist tradition of history from below. It was in part a product of this lineage, but the nature of political modernity in colonial India made this project of history writing nothing short of an engaged critique of the academic discipline of history itself.[49]

What distinguished the story of political modernity in India from the usual and comparable narratives of the West was the fact that modern politics in India was not founded on an assumed death of the peasant. The peasant did not have to undergo a historical mutation into the industrial worker in order to become the citizen-subject of the nation. The peasant who participated in forms of mass-nationalist struggles against the British was not a prepolitical subject. The formal granting of the rights of citizenship to the Indian peasant after the achievement of independence from the British simply recognized his already-political nature. But this fact also meant that the imagination that could properly be called *political* in the Indian context did not conform to the ideas of thinkers in the West, who theorized the political as a story of human sovereignty in a disenchanted world. If the peasant was not prepolitical and was not to be treated simply as an object of anthropology, then the very history of the politicization of the masses in India showed that the political included actions that challenged the theorist's usual and inherited separation between politics and religion. It can be seen in retrospect that *Subaltern Studies* was a democratic project meant to produce a genealogy of the peasant as citizen in contemporary political modernity.[50]

TWO Subaltern Histories and Post-Enlightenment Rationalism

Yes, I know all that. I should be modern.
Marry again. See strippers at the Tease.
Touch Africa. Go to the Movies.

Impale a six-inch spider
under a lens. Join the Test-
ban, or become The Outsider.

Or pay to shake my fist
(or whatever-you-call-it) at a psychoanalyst.
And when I burn

I should smile, dry-eyed,
and nurse martinis like the Marginal Man.
But sorry, I cannot unlearn

conventions of despair.
They have their pride.
I must seek and will find

my particular hell only in my Hindu mind:
must translate and turn
till I blister and roast.
                    A. K. Ramanujan, "Conventions of Despair"

In the 1990s, *Subaltern Studies* came in for a substantial amount of hostile criticism, particularly in India, on the grounds that the Marxist critique that informed the earlier volumes in the series had been replaced by a critique of the rationalism that marked the European Enlightenment. In an essay on the "fascist" nature of the Hindu Right, the eminent Indian historian Sumit Sarkar spelled out why a critique of Enlightenment rationalism is dangerous in India today. His propositions can be arranged as follows: (1) "Fascist ideology in Europe . . . owed something to a general turn-of-the-century move away from what were felt to be the sterile rigidities of Enlightenment rationalism." (2) "Not dissimilar ideas have become current intellectual coin in the West, and by extension, they have started to influence Indian academic life." (3) It has "already become evident" that these "current academic fashions" (Sarkar mentions "postmodernism") "can reduce the resistance of intellectuals to the ideas of Hindutva [Hinduness]." Sarkar is critical of the kind of social analysis that came out of, for instance, the "History of Consciousness" program at the University of California, Santa Cruz: "The 'critique of colonial discourse' . . . has stimulated forms of indigenism not easy to distinguish from the standard Sangh parivar [a collection of organizations belonging to the Hindu Right] argument . . . that Hindutva is superior to Islam and Christianity (and by extension to the creations of the modern West like science, democracy or Marxism) because of its allegedly unique roots." He warns that "an uncritical cult of the 'popular' or 'subaltern,' particularly when combined with the rejection of Enlightenment rationalism . . . can lead even radical historians down strange paths" that, for him, bear "ominous" resemblance to Mussolini's condemnation of the "teleological" idea of progress and to Hitler's exaltation of the German *volk* over hairsplitting intelligence.[1]

Gautum Bhadra and I, identified as two "members of the *Subaltern Studies* editorial team," are Sarkar's examples of historians who have been led down "strange paths" by their "uncritical adulation of the subaltern" and their "rejection of Enlightenment rationalism."[2] Similar points have been made against other *Subaltern Studies* scholars in recent times.[3] The accusations are not unique to the Indian situation. Readers may be reminded of Christopher Norris's *The Truth of Postmodernism,* which argued that postmodernist critiques of universalism and Enlightenment rationalism preached, in effect, a form of cultural relativism that was at least politically irresponsible, if not downright dangerous.[4] Maintaining a critical position with respect to the legacies of the European Enlightenment does not, however, entail a wholesale rejection of the tradition of rational argumentation or of rationalism itself. Responding to Sarkar's charges allows me to demonstrate why a critical take on the legacies of the Enlightenment may, in fact, be part of the contemporary struggle to democratize historiography.

HYPERRATIONALISM AND THE COLONIAL MODERN

At stake in this Indian debate is an important question about how and in what terms one may, in writing subaltern histories, see the subaltern classes as political actors. Theoretical conceptions of the political are always secular. But political action by peasants during and after the nationalist movement often involved the agency of gods and spirits. Is this necessarily an undesirable form of political imagination? Should the peasant be educated out of this tendency? The constitution makers of India accepted the need for a separation of religious and political institutions. By talking about Hinduness and the Hindu heritage, the new Hindu Right appears to mix politics with religion. But what is religion? The idea of a personal religion—the freedom to pursue religion as part of one's rights of citizenship—is guaranteed by the Indian constitution. But what of religious practices that do not base themselves on the idea of a personal or spiritual preference or quest? Most Hindu religious festivals and rituals having to do with different deities are of that nature. What happens when these particular gods come into the sphere of the modern political?

There has been since colonial times an intellectual tradition in India that has often equated idolatry with the practices of the superstitious. Intellectuals of the Left belong, on the whole, to that tradition. Basing political action on sentiments having to do with the birthplace of the mythical god-king Ram and inciting anti-Muslim and anti-Christian feelings in the name of Hinduness—as the Hindu Right has done—have been, for them, examples of the irrational in political life. They have sought to secure Indian secularism in the cultivation of a rational outlook. Subaltern histories that appeared to emphasize and endorse political imaginations in which gods have agency have, therefore, incurred the wrath of the Indian old Left.

Yet, however unhappy the category may be, religion is a major and enduring fact of Indian political life. Political sentiments in the subcontinent are replete with elements that could be regarded as religious, at least in origin. But Indian historians—the best of whom today are of a Marxist or Left-liberal persuasion—have never been able to develop any framework capable of comprehending the phenomenon. Sarkar's own handling of it in the past reflects this shared failure. His *The Swadeshi Movement in Bengal,* a study of the nationalist movement that broke out in Bengal around the year 1905 against the British decision to partition Bengal, is undoubtedly one of the most important monographs of modern Indian history.[5] Yet there is a remarkable failure of the intellect in this book every time it is a question of interpreting or explaining the role that religion played in this political movement.

The Swadeshi movement was, as Sarkar himself so carefully documents, absolutely full of Hindu religious sentiments and imagination. It was this movement that, more than any other phase in modern Bengali history, helped bring to life and immortalize, for both Muslims and Hindus, the image of Bengal as a mother goddess demanding love and sacrifice from her children. But Sarkar's understanding of this religious imagination remains wholly instrumentalist. He is willing to grant that a modern political movement may have to use religion as a means to a political end (and particularly so in a peasant society), but he can only disapprove of moments when, for the historical actors involved, religion looked like becoming an end in itself. He writes:

> What seems indisputable is that the other-worldly pull of religion tended to assert itself particularly at moments of strain and frustration. *Religion cultivated at first as a means to the end of mass contact and stimulation of morale, could all too easily become an end in itself.* The process of inversion is reflected clearly in Aurobindo's [a nationalist leader] famous Uttarpara speech . . . "I spoke once before with this force in me and I said then that this movement is not a political movement and that nationalism is not politics but a religion, a creed, a faith. I say it again today, but I put it in another way. I say no longer that nationalism is a creed, a religion, a faith; I say that it is the Sanatan Dharma which for us is nationalism." (emphasis added)[6]

The pull of Hindu gods and goddesses is hardly of a kind that one could call *otherworldly*. But, even setting that point to one side, it is clear that, while religion as a means is acceptable to Sarkar, religion as an end in itself is not. For him, the political as a domain necessarily remains separate from the religious. He never considers the possibility that a religious sensibility might also use a political structure and a political vocabulary as means to achieve an end or in the interest of an imagined life form in which the political could not be told apart from the religious. For that is indeed the burden of Aurobindo's speech, from which Sarkar seems to have his ear turned away.

Why does this happen? Why does one of our most capable and knowledgeable historians fail to give us any insight into moments in the history of our political and public life when the European distinction between the sacred and the secular appears to collapse? The answer is not far to seek. It is because Sarkar looks on history as the story of a perpetual struggle between the forces of reason and humanism, on the one side, and those of emotion and faith, on the other, and we are left in no doubt as to which side Sarkar himself is on. Of the Swadeshi movement, he writes in a manner that also discloses to us his view of this ideological battleground on which he positions himself: "[An] . . . important . . . theme [of the Swadeshi movement] is the ideological conflict between modernism and traditionalism—between an attitude which broadly speaking demands social reforms, tries to evaluate things and ideas by the criteria of reason and present-day utility, and bases itself on a humanism seeking to transcend limits of caste and religion; and a logically opposite trend which defends and justifies existing social mores in the name of immemorial tradition and the glorious past, and which tends to substitute emotion and faith for reason."[7]

This strong split between emotion and reason, I suggest, is part of the story of colonialism in India. Scientific rationalism, or the spirit of scientific inquiry, was introduced into colonial India from the very beginning as an antidote to (Indian) religion, particularly Hinduism, which was seen—both by missionaries and by administrators, and in spite of the Orientalists—as a bundle of superstition and magic. Hinduism, wrote the Scottish missionary Alexander Duff in 1839, is "a stupendous system of error."[8] Indeed, early missionary-founded schools in Bengal were more liberal and secular in their curricula than were their counterparts in England. Missionaries did not perceive much contradiction between rationalism and the precepts of Christianity and assumed that an awakening to reason, rather than the more provocative strategy of direct conversion, would itself lead to the undermining of the superstitions that made up Hinduism. As Michael Laird writes of the period: "Apart from a genuine desire to advance learning for its own sake, the missionaries also believed that western science would undermine belief in the Hindu scriptures; the new geography, for example, could hardly be reconciled with the *Puranas*. . . . [They] thus acted as instigators of an intellectual awakening, or even revolution, . . . [and their] schools were obvious agents of such a Christian Enlightenment. There is incidentally an instructive contrast with contemporary England, where the wide curriculum that was beginning to appear in Bengal was still very unusual in elementary schools." Even the very act of mastering English, wrote Alexander Duff, must make "the student . . . *tenfold less* the child of Pantheism, idolatry and superstition than before."[9]

It is this simultaneous coding of (Western) knowledge itself as rational and Hinduism as something that was both a religion and a bundle of superstitions that launched the career of a certain kind of colonial hyper-rationalism among Indian intellectuals who self-consciously came to re-gard themselves as modern. Of course, there have been important In-dian intellectuals both before British rule and after—Rammohun Roy and Swami Dayanand Saraswati and even the nationalist scientist J. C. Bose would fall into this category—who strove, not unlike many intel-lectuals in European history, to develop dialogues between science and religion.[10] But research on how these heritages have influenced the na-ture of modern academic knowledge formations in India is still in its early stages. The self-image of modern Indian secular scholarship, par-ticularly the strands that flowed into Marxist social history writing, not only partakes of the social sciences' view of the world as "disenchanted," but even displays antipathy to anything that smacks of the religious. The result has been a certain kind of paralysis of imagination, remarkable for a country whose people have never shown any sense of embarrassment about being able to imagine the supernatural in a variety of forms.

To be sure, these developments in India shared something of the spirit of the eighteenth-century Enlightenment in Europe to the extent that, for all its internal diversity, the Enlightenment "meant repudiation of the irrational and the superstitious": "Insofar as it was concerned with social and political questions, the 18th century Enlightenment . . . pro-duced a great variety of mutually incompatible ideas. . . . For all this, nevertheless, there were points on which people with any claim to being enlightened were agreed in every country. Particularly, Enlightenment meant the repudiation of the irrational and the superstitious. . . . To be superstitious was to believe in the supernatural."[11]

Historians today are generally more sensitive to the diversity within the Enlightenment. Nor would they be unaware of the many connec-tions forged in Europe between science and religion. But what propa-gated itself among modern Indian intellectuals was something like—to take Preserved Smith's expression somewhat out of context—"the pro-paganda of Reason," which equated modernity with the possession of the scientific outlook and ignorance with superstition—as, indeed, Smith himself did in his own book on the Enlightenment.[12] The secular ratio-nalism of the Indian intellectual carried with it an aggressively hostile at-titude toward religion and everything that the practices of Hinduism—whether in the context of kinship, life-cycle rituals, or public life—seemed to sanctify.[13]

Why this came to be so is a long, involved, and, on the whole, unre-searched story. The problem is not the so-called alienation of the secular intellectual in India from the country's religious elements. The Hindu Right often makes this criticism of the Left, and Sarkar is quite right to reject it.[14] The problem is, rather, that we do not have analytic categories in our aggressively secular academic discourse that do justice to the real, everyday, and multiple connections that we have to what we, in becoming modern, have come to see as nonrational. Tradition/modernity, rational/nonrational, intellect/emotion—these untenable and problematic binaries have haunted our self-representations in social-science language since the nineteenth century.

Andrew Sartori's work on the nineteenth-century Bengali Orientalist and Indologist Rajendralal Mitra has recently drawn our attention to this problem. As Sartori shows, the split between the analytic and the affective is something that is itself produced by the colonial discourse and that marks forever the speech of the colonized intellectual. Sartori has given us a telling example of this phenomenon from the colonial period. He quotes Mitra, writing in the 1870s, on the custom of "blood sacrifice" in ancient India. The Orientalist in Mitra no doubt saw this custom as barbaric and uncivilized. However, this ancient practice was in no sense antiquated in Mitra's own times. And Mitra himself had had some personal exposure to it. Yet he categorized his own, lived connection to the ritual as part of his affective, rather than rational or reasoning, self. In a memorable passage at the end of an essay discussing the custom, he wrote: "The offering of one's blood to the goddess [Kali] is a medieval and modern rite. . . . The last time I saw the ceremony was six years ago when my late revered parent, tottering with age, made the offering for my recovery from a dangerous and long-protracted attack of pleurisy. Whatever may be thought of it by persons brought up under a creed different from that of the Indo-Aryans, I cannot recall to memory the fact *without feeling the deepest emotion for the boundless affection* which prompted it" (emphasis added).[15]

This strong spirit of hostility between the rational and the affective, or between reason and emotion, characteristic of our colonial hyperrationalism, has generally afflicted Indian Marxist historians' attempt to understand the place of the religious in Indian public and political life. What else is this but an unreflexive (re)statement of the struggle of the Enlightenment with superstition? Reason and truth on the side of democracy and humanism, faith—a "tissue of superstitions, prejudices and errors," as a famous philosopher of the Enlightenment put it—on the side of tyranny.[16]

This conflict, for Sarkar, structures the whole narrative of Bengali modernity. He traces it "right through the nineteenth century from the days of the Atmiya Sabha and the Dharma Sabha [the 1820s]" and sees it "continu[ing] at the heart of the Swadeshi movement just as in the [Bengal] 'renaissance' which had preceded and prepared the way for it":

"Insofar as the Swadeshi age saw a determined though not entirely successful effort to give the national movement a solid mass basis, the period can be regarded as a sort of test for the relevance of these opposed
ideological trends in the work of national awakening."[17] This is Enlightenment rationalism, indeed, but now (re)visiting the history of the colonized as a modernist dogma and wreaking intellectual havoc in its trail.
Sarkar's failure to give us any insights into the religious that constantly
erupts into the political in Indian modernity is not a personal failure. It
is a failure of hyperrationalism, a failure that marks the intellect of the
colonial modern. It occurs within a paradigm that sees science and religion as ultimately, and irrevocably, opposed to each other.

It is no wonder, then, that, to Sarkar and many other secular historians of India, modernity in India has seemed "grievously incomplete."[18]
The 1970s Marxist critique of colonial India argued, as one respected
historian put it, that "alien rule and modernity are never compatible"
and deduced, therefore, that what India had received as a legacy of the
colonial period could be characterized only as "enclaves" of modernity:

> There were indeed variances in western European early modern
> developments . . . on a comparative scale. Yet each particular pat-
> tern in western Europe was clearer and more spontaneous, and
> where foreign interference could be resisted, more *secular* and *ra-
> tional* than conditions in the previous period. . . . What is nor-
> mally described as modernity represents the superstructure of a
> given culture, whose economic base is the emergence of capital-
> ism. It is unrealistic to define a superstructure without its base, to
> expect the fruits of modernity without the uneven development
> and hardheaded exploitative practices of a European modernity
> which often [in places like India] came to terms with feudal rem-
> nants . . . and which took to colonialism for maintaining progress
> in its capitalist development.[19]

This language of a "base and superstructure" Marxism was representative of what would have passed for common sense in Indian Marxist
historiography of the 1970s. For the purpose of this discussion, however, I wish to highlight what this statement shares with Sarkar's understanding of what it meant to be modern. True, modernity born in Europe had been productive of colonialism in India, but it still had a
discernable "progressive content" that was diluted in the colony because
of underdevelopment (remember that this was also the period of dependency theory). This progressive content had in part to do with "the rational outlook," "the spirit of science," "free inquiry," etc. "It is possible," wrote Barun De, "that some future historians . . . might put the

19th and early 20th centuries at the end of a medieval period of uncertainty, instead of the beginning of the modern period, which still awaits us in the third world."[20]

"Modernity still awaits us"—this is the refrain of the hyperrational colonial modern. Why should modernity still await us in India, more than two hundred years after its career was launched in India by European imperialism? How long does it take for an Indian to become modern? This historiography never entertained the possibility that what we had, warts and all, was, indeed, our modernity. Historians were prone to think that what India possessed as a result of colonial modernization was only a bad version of something that, in itself, was an unmixed good. The blame, it was decided, lay with colonialism. Colonialism stopped us from being fully modern. Scholars would repeat Barun De's lament: we are incompletely modern. Sumit Sarkar would open his *Modern India*, published a decade after Barun De's essay, on this elegiac note: India's is a story of a "bourgeois modernity" that is "grievously incomplete."[21] The mourning will speak through Susie Tharu and K. Lalitha's impressive and sensitively edited collection *Women Writing in India:*

> Scholars who have questioned . . . a linear or progressive understanding of history claim that the liberal ideals of reformers [of women's condition] could not have been realised under the economic and political conditions of colonial rule, and warn against applying such simple, linear narratives of progress to the study of nineteenth century India. What appears as retrogressive in nationalism was not a conservative backlash, but the logical limits of reformist programmes in a colonial situation that would never, as Sumit Sarkar writes, allow more than a "weak and distorted" caricature of "full blooded" bourgeois modernity, either for women or for men.[22]

The Enlightenment's story of the struggle of science/rationalism against faith/religion—which in Europe produces all kinds of hybrid solutions—gets repeated in India without attention to the process of translation and the resultant hybridities.[23] For both sides of the equation are violated in translating them from the European context into our past and present practices. The history of our hyperrationalism is not the same as that of Enlightenment rationalism, and the practices that we gather under the name *religion* do not repeat the history of that European category of thought. Such translations are by definition hybrid or incomplete. It may precisely be an irony of any modernist understanding of modernity that we are constantly called on to study with the purest of categories that which is necessarily impure and hybrid, to treat translations that are necessarily incomplete as though their incompleteness is nothing but a hurtful betrayal of history.

An attitude of incredulity toward the metanarratives of the European Enlightenment, however, moves us from the register of lament to that of irony. But, while that is only the first step, it prepares us for opening up our histories to other possibilities, some of which I will consider in the final section of this essay.

UNREASONABLE ORIGINS OF REASON

Salman Rushdie's *Midnight's Children* contains a subplot that illustrates how the problem of force or coercion may arise in the conversation between the so-called modern and the nonmodern and, indeed, how strategies of domination emerge as a necessary move to bring to a close arguments in this conversation that cannot be settled through purely rational procedures. It is significant that the subaltern of this particular narrative of modernity should be a woman.

Adam Aziz, the European-returned medical doctor who is also the grandfather of the narrator, Saleem Sinai, inaugurates a nationalist project in his domestic life when he marries Naseem Ghani. As a modern person, Aziz knows that women in Islam/tradition have been confined/unfree. He instructs his wife "to come out of purdah" and, as a demonstration of his will, burns her veils, saying: "Forget about being a good Kashmiri girl. Start thinking about being a modern Indian woman." Naseem, later the Reverend Mother of Saleem Sinai's description, the daughter of a Muslim landlord, is from the beginning portrayed as tradition herself.

Readers of the novel will recall that, when Adam Aziz first encountered her as a patient in a conservative/traditional Muslim family, she could be examined only through a seven-inch hole in a bedsheet held over her body with only the relevant part of her body made visible. The doctor fell in love with this fragmented body and discovered only after their wedding the formidably traditional heart that beat within it. Their mutual incomprehension starts with their lovemaking, when, on their second night, Aziz asks her "to move a little": "'Move where?' she asked. 'Move how?' He became awkward and said, 'Only move. I mean, like a woman . . .' She shrieked in horror. 'My God what have I married? I know you European-returned men. You find terrible women and then you try to make us girls be like them! Listen Doctor Sahib, husband or no husband, I am not . . . any bad woman.'"[24]

The battle continues throughout their marriage, Aziz conducting it from the position of the knowing, willing, and judging subject of modernity. His modernizing political will sometimes expresses itself in the form of physical force. He physically throws out of the house the Muslim *maulvi* (a religious teacher) whom the Reverend Mother had appointed for their children's religious education, the only element in the children's education that was her choice. The reason he gives to his wife in defense of his action will probably warm the heart of every "secular-rationalist" Indian: "He was teaching them [the children] to hate, wife. He tells them to hate Hindus and Buddhists and Jains and Sikhs and who knows what other vegetarians."[25]

The Reverend Mother is in the position of the classic subaltern of many modernist narratives. The reasonableness of the doctor's position is never self-evident to her. So the battle goes on in the lives of the Reverend Mother and her husband, a battle organized around mutual incomprehension. This mutual incomprehension is what, one could argue in Aziz's defense, drives both the good doctor and his wife to their respective desperate measures.

If I were to read this part of the novel as an allegory of the history of modernity, historians would object. It would be said that this allegory, powerful because it ran such a strong black-and-white binary of tradition/modernity right through the story line, was not true to the complexities of real history (which historians are fond of picturing in the color gray). A historical narrative could have gone differently and might not have been structured by such a strong opposition between the modernizer and the yet to be modernized. In such possible alternative accounts, the Reverend Mother might, in fact, have needed Aziz as an ally against other patriarchal authorities, her father, or a possible mother-in-law and could have been more amenable to his suggestions. Similarly, the peasants held down by tyrants might seek out the help of the modern in their own struggles. And what if, through their own agency, the subaltern discovered the pleasures of the modern: of the autonomous self, of interiority, of science, of technology, of post-Enlightenment rationalism itself? In such historical recall, the coming of Enlightenment rationalism would not be a story of domination. Have not the critics of the modern state had it said to them that the people actually want the state or the critics of modern medicine that the people, once introduced to modern medicine, actually want it?

Granted, but then what is the relation between Rushdie's story and the history of modernity? Rushdie's is an allegory of the *origins* of modernity. It tells us about the beginnings of the historical process through which women in the Aziz family became modern. This process was not benign, and that is not an unfamiliar tale to historians of modernity, even in the homeland of the Enlightenment, Western Europe. The door by which one enters citizenship or a nationality always has a *dur-wan* (gatekeeper)—himself usually only partially admitted to the rites of equality—posted outside. His job is to be mean, to abuse, bully, insult, and exclude, or to humiliate—even when he lets you in. The fact that one is often ushered into modernity as much through violence as through persuasion is recognized by European historians and intellectuals. The violence of the discourse of public health in nineteenth-century England directed itself against the poor and the working classes.[26] The process by which rural France was modernized in the nineteenth century was described by Eugen Weber as something akin to "internal colonization."[27]

Derrida discusses the same problem from within the experience of being French. "As you know," he writes, "in many countries, in the past and in the present, one founding violence of the law or of the imposition of the state law has consisted in imposing a language on national or ethnic minorities regrouped by the state. This was the case in France on at least two occasions, first, when the Villers-Cotteret decree consolidated the unity of the monarchic state by imposing French as the juridico-administrative language and by forbidding . . . Latin. . . . The second major moment of imposition was that of the French Revolution, when linguistic unification took the most repressive pedagogical turn." Derrida distinguishes between "two kinds of violence in law, in relation to law . . . : the founding violence, the one that institutes and positions law . . . and the violence that conserves, the one that maintains, confirms, insures the permanence and enforceability of law."[28]

These are known facts and are probably features of the history of modernity anywhere. The question is, What is our relation, as intellectuals, to these two kinds of violence in Indian modernity? It is easy to see that an intellectual's attitude to the first kind of violence—the founding one—is determined largely by his or her relation to the second. For Eugen Weber, for instance, the fact that something like an "internal colonization" was needed to make peasants into Frenchmen arouses no ire, for the end result has been good for everybody. "The past," he writes, "was a time of misery and barbarism, the present a time of unexampled comfort and security, of machines and schooling and services, of all the wonders that are translated into civilization."[29] Beginnings, however ugly, do not matter for Weber—they cannot act as a site from which to develop a critique of the present (as Foucault teaches us to do with his genealogical method)—for he tells, and believes in, a story of progress. His teleology saves him from having to be critical. The pain of the nineteenth-century peasant is not his own. It is a wound over which time has formed a scab; it does not bleed anymore.

Where can we, historians of a Third World country like India, where the distinction between the founding and the preserving modes of violence in the functioning of the law is hard to sustain, anchor such facile optimism?[30] The process of making *peasants* or individuals into *Indians* takes place every day before our eyes. It is not a process with a single or simple characteristic, nor is it without any material benefits to the people involved. But, were we to convert particular benefits, which often do create problems in their turn, into some kind of a grand narrative of progress, it would leave us with a few important and nagging problems. If a certain kind of colonizing drive is inherent to the civilizing-modernizing project, and if one were, in one's point of view, to side uncritically with this project, how would one erect a critique of imperialism? Weber's solution to this problem does not solve anything: he says, in effect, that it may be all right to practice colonialism on one's own people if the process brings in its train prosperity for all. But that is getting the story back to front, for the assumed purpose of this colonialism, in Weber's schema, was to make real the category *one's own people*. One cannot assume into existence at the beginning of a process what the process is meant to produce as its outcome. If Weber's sentiment has any political validity in France today, it means only that the colonizing process succeeded in achieving this end, popularizing the story of progress (although that would be taking a Whiggish view of that history).

Let me repeat my point once more: if it is true that Enlightenment rationalism requires as its vehicle the modern state and its accompanying institutions—the instruments of governmentality, in Foucault's terms— and if this entails a certain kind of colonizing violence anyway (however justifiable the violence might be from a retrospective point of view), then one cannot uncritically welcome this violence and at the same time maintain a critique of European imperialism in India except on some kind of essentialistic and indigenist ground (e.g., only Indians have the right to colonize themselves in the interest of modernity). In the 1970s, Marxist historians in India and elsewhere—seeing themselves as inheritors of the European Enlightenment yet wanting to distance themselves from the fact of European colonialism—tried out another solution. By fusing Marxism with dependency theory, they sought to fetishize colonialism into a distinct socioeconomic formation, inherently productive of underdevelopment. The demise of dependency theory has robbed us of that ground. Frankly, if Enlightenment rationalism is the only way in which human societies can humanize themselves, then we ought to be grateful that the Europeans set out to dominate the world and spread its message. Will our self-proclaimed rationalist and secularist historians say that?

HISTORY AS DEMOCRATIC DIALOGUE WITH THE SUBALTERN

The task is not to reject ideas of democracy, development, or justice. The task is to think of forms and philosophies of history that will contribute to struggles that aim to make the very process of achieving these outcomes as democratic as possible. How do we make the subalterns genuinely the subjects of their history? Surely not by assuming a position in which the ideal nature and shape of modernity is decided from the very beginning by historians or philosophers as intellectuals. That would be inviting the subaltern to a dialogue in which his position was secondary from the very beginning. I come now to what to me is the hardest part of my argument, not least because I myself have not practiced what I am about to preach. I am trying to think my way toward a subaltern historiography that actually tries to learn from the subaltern. And I am also trying to transcend the position that the early *Subaltern Studies* project took as its point of departure.

Let me go back to one of the fundamental premises of this essay. I do not deny the immense practical utility of Left-liberal political philosophies. One cannot perform effectively in the context of modern bureaucracies—and, therefore, one cannot access the benefits that these institutions are capable of delivering—if one is not able to mobilize one's own identity, personal or collective, through the languages, skills, and practices that these philosophies make possible. The very idea of distributive justice requires that these languages and competencies—of citizenship, of democracy, of welfare—be made available to all classes, particularly those subordinated and oppressed. It means that, whenever we, members of the privileged classes, write subaltern histories—whether we write them as citizens (i.e., on behalf of the idea of democratic rights) or as socialists (desiring radical social change)—a certain pedagogical drive comes into play. We write, ultimately, as part of a collective effort to help teach the oppressed of today how to be the democratic subject of tomorrow.

Since pedagogy is a dialogue, even if it is only the teacher's voice that is heard—as Barthes once said, "When the teacher speaks to his audience, the Other is always there, punctuating his discourse"—the subaltern history that is produced in this manner is dialogic.[31] But, by its very structure, this dialogue is not democratic (which is not to say that it is *not* of use to the subaltern). To be open-ended, I would argue, a dialogue must be genuinely nonteleological; that is, one must not presume, on any a priori basis, that whatever position our political philosophy/ideology suggests as correct will be necessarily vindicated as a result of this dialogue. For a dialogue can be genuinely open only under one condition: that no party puts itself in a position where it can unilaterally decide the final outcomes of the conversation. This never happens between the modern and the nonmodern because, however noncoercive the conversation between the transcendent academic observer and the subaltern who enters into a historical dialogue with him, this dialogue takes place within a field of possibilities that is already structured from the very beginning in favor of certain outcomes.

In pedagogical histories, it is the subaltern's relation to the world that ultimately calls for improvement. The *Subaltern Studies* series was founded within this gesture. Guha's insurgent peasants, for instance, fall short in their understanding of what is required for a comprehensive reversal of the power relationships in an exploitative society.[32] And this was exactly the position of the man who gave us the category *subaltern*. For Antonio Gramsci, readers will recall, *subaltern* named a political position that, by itself, was incapable of thinking the state; this was a thought to be brought to that position by the revolutionary intellectual. Once the subaltern could imagine / think the state, he transcended, theoretically speaking, the condition of subalternity.

While it is true that Gramsci developed a dialogic Marxism that aimed to take seriously what went on inside the heads of the oppressed, he was clear on what the subaltern lacked. His words bear repetition: "The subaltern classes, by definition, are not united and cannot unite until they are able to become a 'State.' . . . *The history of subaltern social groups is necessarily fragmented and episodic.* There undoubtedly does exist a tendency to (at least provisional stages of) unification in the historical activity of these groups, but this tendency is continually interrupted by the activity of the ruling groups. . . . In reality, even when they appear triumphant, the subaltern groups are merely anxious to defend themselves" (emphasis added).[33]

As I have already indicated, histories written in this pedagogical-dialogic mode are in fact inescapable. We live in societies structured by the state, and the oppressed need knowledge forms that are tied to that reality. Indeed, this must remain one entirely legitimate mode of producing subaltern histories. Yet the problem of undemocracy remains in the structure of this dialogue. Can we *imagine* another moment of subaltern history, one in which we stay—permanently, not simply as a matter of political tactic—with that which is fragmentary and episodic? *Fragmentary,* not in the sense of fragments that refer to an implicit whole, but in the sense of fragments that challenge, not only the idea of wholeness, but the very idea of the fragment itself (for, if there were not any wholes, what would fragments be fragments of?).[34] Here, we conceptualize the fragmentary and the episodic as those which do not, and cannot, dream the whole called *the state* and must, therefore, be suggestive of knowledge forms that are not tied to the will that produces the state.

Couched thus, my question sounds utopian. For the subaltern who abjures the imagination of the state does not exist in a pure form in real life. The subaltern classes around us are as invested in the benefits of modern institutions as are any other class, and it is only reasonable for them to be so. Nor would it be realistic to argue that the peasant and other oppressed classes as such are incapable of either comprehending or embracing ideas of a whole such as the state.

I am simply using the quotation from Gramsci to point to a possible and alternative theoretical horizon. Imaginations of the whole, in that quotation, belong to a certain understanding of politics. These are statist understandings, understandings in which the subaltern classes—indeed, their very position of subalternity—are read as such telling figures of misery and privation that the violence and undemocracy of the state looks like a small price to pay for the attainment, ultimately, of a more just social order. The pedagogical drive in histories written out of this position aims to instill or incite in the subaltern class (or its representatives) a desire to participate in this political imagination. But an element of undemocracy remains in that, in the Gramscian formulation at least, the imagination of the state (and other forms of the whole) has to be brought to the subaltern classes from outside themselves, for they are, "by definition," as Gramsci put it, incapable of such imagination, being always kept divided by the ruling classes. How do we make the politics of politicizing the subaltern more democratic?

The quotation from Gramsci suggests one obvious line of thinking. Howsoever divided, the "historical activity" of the subaltern classes always has, Gramsci reminds us, "a tendency to . . . unification." One way toward subaltern forms of democracy would be to foster this tendency and ground the modern state in it. This would be one legitimate line of thinking.

Gramsci's statement, however, also allows us to consider a contra-Gramsci perspective. It helps us ask a question that Gramsci does not ask. What would happen to our political imagination if we did not consider the state of being fragmentary and episodic as merely disabling? If a totalizing mode of thinking is needed for us to imagine the state theoretically, what kind of political imagination and institutions could sustain themselves on the basis of a thought that joyously embraced the idea of the fragment? If the statist idea of the political defined the mainstream of political thought, then here may be an alternative conceptual pole to it: an idea of the political that did not require us to imagine totalities.

There are difficulties here: most thought about social justice entails the idea of equality in one form or another. The state is often idealized as an instrument for enforcing equality. What kind of (modern) social justice would one envisage as one embraced the fragment? The question is at the same time legitimate (from a perspective committed to notions of equality) and not legitimate (for a radical embracing of the fragment as political-philosophical starting point would mean that we would not answer such questions in an a priori and systematic manner).

I do not pretend to have all the answers to the questions that come up here, but thinking the fragment radically changes the nature of the political agent whom we imagine. The subaltern, on this register, is no longer the citizen in the making. The subaltern here is the *ideal* figure of the person who survives actively, even joyously, on the assumption that the statist instruments of domination will always belong to somebody else and never aspires to them. This is an *ideal* figure. No actual member of the subaltern classes would resemble what I imagine here. The question is, Are there moments in the life practices of the subaltern classes that would allow us to construct such an agent? The Buddhist imagination once saw the possibility of the joyful, renunciate *bhikshu* (monk) in the miserable and deprived image of the *bhikshuk* (beggar). We have not yet learned to see the spectral doubles that may inhabit our Marxism-inspired images of the subaltern.

To go to the subaltern in order to learn to be radically fragmentary and episodic is to move away from the certitudes that operate within the gesture that the knowing, judging, willing subject always already knows what is good for everybody, ahead of any investigation. The investigation, in turn, must be possessed of an openness so radical that I can express it only in Heideggerian terms: the capacity to hear that which one does not already understand.[35] In other words, to allow the subaltern position to challenge our own conceptions of totalities, to be open to the possibility of our thought systems, with all their aspirations to grasp things in their totality, being rendered finite by the presence of the other: such are the utopian horizons to which this other moment of *Subaltern Studies* calls us.[36]

What will history written in this mode look like? I cannot say, for one cannot write this history in a pure form. The languages of the state, of citizenship, of wholes and totalities, the legacy of Enlightenment rationalism, will always cut across it. I was only pointing to a utopian line that may well designate the limit of how we are trained to think. But this does not mean that this limit does not exist at all. We know about its existence indirectly, when we come across historical evidence that does not easily fit our categories. To open ourselves to such disruptive histories would require us seriously to grant our social life a constant lack of transparency with regard to any one particular way of thinking about it. This is no ground for the rejection of Enlightenment rationalism. It is rather to be secure in the knowledge that investigative procedure embodying this rationality gives us only a partial hold on our lives—and that too through necessary, much-needed, yet inevitably poor translations.

Sarkar's fear that a critical understanding of our intellectual inheritances from the European Enlightenment would only help the "fascist" Hindus is based on some spurious assumptions. Granted that European fascism drew on a certain spirit of disenchantment with post-Enlightenment rationalism, but from this the reverse does not follow. One cannot argue on this basis that every critique of post-Enlightenment rationalism must end up being fascist. If one could, we would have to count strange candidates among our list of reactionaries, and among them would be such different people as Gandhi and Weber and, for our times, not only Michel Foucault but Jürgen Habermas as well. These thinkers remind us that to critique post-Enlightenment rationalism, or even modernity, is not to fall into some kind of irrationalism. As Lydia Liu has recently remarked in her discussion of Chinese history, "The critique of modernity has always been part of the Enlightenment legacy from the Romantics, Nietzsche, Marx and Heidegger to Horkheimer, Adorno, Foucault, Derrida and even Habermas."[37]

It is also true that the experience of fascism has left a certain trauma in leftist intellectuals in the West. They have ceded to the fascists all moments of poetry, mysticism, and the religious and mysterious in the construction of political sentiments and communities (however transient or inoperative). Romanticism now reminds them only of the Nazis. Romantic nationalism in India has left us with another heritage exemplified by the life experiments of such stalwarts as Gandhi and Tagore. It would be sad if we ceded this entire heritage to the Hindu extremists out of a fear that our romanticism must be the same as whatever the Europeans produced under that name in their histories and that our present blunders, whatever these are, must be the same as theirs in the past. What, indeed, could be a greater instance of submission to a Eurocentric imagination than that fear?

THREE Modernity and the Past

A Critical Tribute to Ashis Nandy

Whatever else it may mean for those who do not explicitly set out to intellectualize, a self-conscious embracing of modernity has since the middle of the nineteenth century posed a question to the Indian intellectual. What does one do with or about those practices of the past that seem undesirable but that apparently refuse to die? Consider the undemocratic and cruel practice of caste discrimination or the practice of sati (self-immolation by widows) among upper-caste Hindus in India. It is far from certain that these practices are extinct even in educated milieus (sati, of course, being far, far less common than caste discrimination). Or try and imagine the numerous instances of everyday incidents when people in the subcontinent invoke the supernatural, whether in newspaper columns on astrology or in the cause of a political movement.

All academic intellectuals in India—like intellectuals in many other Third World countries— would have grown up with such practices. These experiences may form the innocent stuff of childhood memories. But they may also be not so innocent after all. Tradition takes a murderous form when the supernatural event of images of the god Ganesh drinking milk gets a political interpretation justifying a militantly Hindu and anti-Muslim political movement or when astrology or indigenous medicine acts as an excuse for sheer commercial exploitation of the needy or the poor.

This experience of being a modern intellectual in an India in which undesirable practices from the past seem to help produce deformities in the modern gives that modernity a peculiar edge. The intellectual has an ambivalent relation to the past, whether this past is embodied in rural India or in one's older relatives. This can be seen in the problem of defining *tradition*. Should *tradition* include all the past? Or should it include only those bits of the past that meet with our approval today? Should the aim of education be to educate people out of the practices that are contrary to the principles of modernity, to move them away from activities or ideas that scientific rationality, democratic politics, and modern aesthetics find disturbing, if not downright repulsive?

Only rarely have Indian intellectuals addressed this problem in a self-conscious manner, although it often erupts in what they write about the past. In the brief span of this short essay on Ashis Nandy, who, more than anybody else in India, has drawn our attention to the questions that the very idea of *tradition* poses to all modernizers/cultural critics of the subcontinent, I will endeavor to show how the question with which I began—the problem of the undesirable past—configures itself in Nandy's work.

Much of Nandy's admirable and powerful critique of modernity strikes me as somewhat decisionist in spirit. By *decisionist*, I mean a disposition that allows the critic to talk about the future and the past as though there were concrete, value-laden choices or decisions to be made with regard to both. The critic is guided by his or her values as to what the most desirable, sane, and wise future for humanity should be and looks to the past as a warehouse of resources on which to draw as needed. This position is connected to but attitudinally different from the revolutionary-modernist position—that of early Ambedkar, for instance, in his polemic against Gandhi about the (de)merits of caste—in which the reformer seeks to bring (a particular) history to nullity in order to build society up from scratch. Many modernizers have talked about scrapping the past altogether. Nandy's position, by contrast, is respectful of the past without being bound by it. It uses tradition but in a way that is guided by the critique of the present that it has developed.

In discussing Gandhi—in many ways, the person who comes closest to his idea of a wise political leader—Nandy names his position *critical traditionalism*. Critical traditionalism, according to Nandy, is different from uncritical adulation of past practices, a position that he finds illustrated in the writings of the Anglo–Sri Lankan intellectual Ananda Kentish Coomaraswamy. For Coomaraswamy, says Nandy,

> Tradition remains homogeneous and undifferentiated from the point of view of man-made suffering. His defence of the charming theory of *sati*, for example, never takes into account its victims, the women who often died without the benefit of the theory. . . . Such traditionalism reactively demystifies modernity to remystify traditions. . . . Likewise, one may concur with Coomaraswamy that the untouchables in traditional India were better off than the proletariat in the industrial societies. But this would be an empty statement to those victimized by the caste system today. When many untouchables opt for proletarianization in contemporary India, is their choice merely a function of faulty self-knowledge? . . . I am afraid Coomaraswamy's traditionalism, despite being holistic by design, does not allow a creative, critical use of modernity within traditions.

Nandy's positive examples are those of Gandhi and Tagore, arguably the two best products of Indo-British cultural encounter. Nandy sees Tagore's novel *Gora* as pointing to "another kind of tradition which is reflective as well as self-critical, which does not reject or bypass the experience of modernity but encapsulates or digests it." Gandhi he names as someone who "represented this concept of critical traditionalism aggressively."[1]

Clearly, then, scholars who have accused Nandy of practicing some kind of atavistic indigenism have read him incorrectly. His position is, indeed, different from that of the revolutionary modernizer, but it is also different from that of a so-called nativist. Critical traditionalists are critical of post-Enlightenment rationalism as an overall guide to living, although they do not reject science in toto: "The critical traditionalism I am talking about does not have to see modern science as alien to it, even though it may see it as alienating. . . . Such traditionalism uncompromisingly criticizes isolation and the over-concern with objectivity, but it never denies the creative possibilities of limited objectivity. Ultimately, intelligence and knowledge are poor—in fact, dangerous—substitutes for intellect and wisdom."[2]

This limited appreciation of objectivity leads to a theory of resisting enslavement to the discipline of history. "Liberation from the fear of childhood," writes Nandy in critiquing modern conceptions of life stories of humans, "is also liberation from the more subtly institutionalized ethnocentrism towards past times." By *ethnocentrism*, he means the process whereby, in the name of objectivity, the historian mobilizes voices from the past for fighting projects that are modern and contemporary. What makes the enterprise ethnocentric for Nandy is the fact that, unlike the native informants of the anthropologist, these voices cannot talk back or argue with the historian: "Elsewhere, I have discussed the absolute and total subjection of the subjects of history, who can neither rebel against the present times nor contest the present interpretations of the past."[3] The point receives elaboration in an essay on Gandhi:

> Critics of objectification have not often noticed that the subjects of "scientific history" are subjects irrevocably and permanently. . . . [T]here can be no transference, no real dialogue, perceived mutuality or continuity between the historian and his subjects from the subjects' point of view. The historian's subjects are, after all, mostly dead. . . . One wonders if some vague awareness of this asymmetry between the subjects and the objects, and between the knowers and the known, prompted Gandhi to reject history as a guide to moral action and derive such guidance from his reading of texts and myths. . . . Gandhi, like Blake and Thoreau before him, defied this new fatalism [i.e., the idea of historical laws] of our times.[4]

Myth for history, tradition for modernity, wisdom and intellect for science and intelligence—Nandy's choices are clear. But they are, in my sense, decisionist. They do not share the same ground with those of the Marxist or liberal revolutionary, for they are neither about a completely willful rejection of the past nor about viewing history as a process of dialectical overcoming of the past. Nandy's choices may even sound conservative (in the good sense of the term). But one would be mistaken to see Nandy as anything but a modern intellectual. For decisionism, even of his kind, entails the same kind of heroic self-invention that has characterized the modern in Europe.[5] The theme of choice, albeit backed up by the notion of wisdom rather than that of scientific objectivity, and in particular the continual construction in his writings of an object called *the future*, an object without which Nandy's critique of Western modernity would have no meaning, tells us that we are listening to an intellectual who takes his bearings in the world from concerns that are unmistakably modern.

I want to suggest that what makes Nandy's critique of modernity truly interesting and powerful is a particular tension that sometimes breaks the surface in his writings. It is a tension between the decisionist, heroic strand and certain other possible positions with regard to the past that do share the voluntarism of the critical traditionalist. These other positions are not subject to the mutually exclusive binary of historical law (modern fatalism) versus mythopoeic fables. Nor do they offer us immediate choices about how to live, mainly because these are positions that do not assume complete transparency of the object of investigation, whatever that object may be—society, culture, tradition. In these positions, one gives up the assumption that more research or intelligence will help us dispel the opacity in the object itself. Even the warmth of respect that the critical traditionalist displays toward the past does not dissolve the mist of perception here any more than does the light of scientific reason. It is at these points that Nandy's sensitivities cease to suggest solutions such as critical traditionalism and become instead an invitation to deepen our questions. I say this in a spirit of gratitude, for it is, unfortunately, a rare moment in current Indian scholarship when, instead of rushing to suggest that solutions are just around the corner if only we would listen to the right-minded analysis, an intellectual actually allows the question to gather depth.

I see such a moment emerging in a controversial essay that Nandy wrote in the course of the debate on sati that ensued in India after Roop Kanwar, a young woman from the village of Deorala near Jaipur in Rajasthan, killed herself by becoming a sati in 1987. (The question of her agency is, naturally, hotly debated—albeit irresolvable.) Nandy's was an angry essay. The debates between Nandy and his supporters, on the one hand, and some secular liberals and feminist intellectuals, on the other, were heated exchanges in which each side sought to classify and abuse the other. Thus, Nandy called his opponents "Anglophile, psychologically uprooted Indians"; and they retaliated by writing about "attempts, usually from anti-Marxist, neo-Gandhian positions, to re-establish the difference between us and them (the West) by taking a stand against the values of the Enlightenment (reason, science, progress) using a rhetoric of anti-colonial indigenism."

Nandy himself mentions—with justifiable relish—some of the criticism that his essay received on publication: "It was read as directly supporting *sati* and some, not knowing that I was not a Hindu, even found in it indicators of Hindu fanaticism."[6] The labels traded were and are unhelpful. We have to argue against Nandy, for example, that no Indian, however much an Anglophile, is thereby rendered an instance of a culturally "uprooted" person. Anglophilia has existed in India as a phenomenon of contemporary Indian culture. It is, culturally, as legitimate as any form of orthopraxy. Being Westernized is one way of being Indian. Similarly, it is patently absurd to suggest that Nandy could have been in any way abetting the practice of sati. Even the few quotes from his writings that I have used here make clear how unfair that charge is.

For me, the interesting moment in Nandy's reflections on sati comes when he recognizes an element of duality in the attitude that intellectuals like Rabindranath Tagore, Abanindranath Tagore, and Ananda Coomaraswamy displayed toward the phenomenon of sati. They, Nandy found, were appreciative of the values for which the practice was meant to stand in quasi-mythic, idealized representations of the past while (as in the case of the Tagore family) they fought against the real practice in their own times. This innovative distinction between the mythic sati and the historical sati is grist to Nandy's mill of critical traditionalism. It underwrites his injunction that, once modernity has arrived and has inserted everybody in historical time, one should approach the myths of the past respectfully and use them to fight historical battles for a more just society. He writes: "This differentiation between sati in mythical time and sati in historical time, between sati as an event (*ghatana*) and sati as a system (*pratha*), between the authentic sati and its inauthentic offspring, between those who respect it and those who organize it in our times, is not my contribution to the understanding of the rite. These distinctions were already implicit, for instance, in the writings of Rabindranath Tagore, who was an aggressive opponent of sati as practised in contemporary times, yet respectful towards the ideas behind it."[7]

At first sight, this may look like a vindication of Nandy's strategy of critical traditionalism. Yet the essay is interesting because the strategy actually breaks down in other places. How can one completely separate a positive interpretation of sati from a critical rejection of the action of becoming sati? Why would such an interpretation not be an indirect and unintended way of legitimating the act itself? How would one completely separate myth from history? Why is a tradition entitled to respect even when one does not agree with it? Its popularity is no clear answer. Any strategist-politician in a political system where numbers matter must reckon with that which is genuinely popular. But this does not mean that the popular practice is respectable. One can perform, effectively but instrumentally, the language of respect in order to mobilize the masses. Nandy is not an advocate of the cynical or instrumental use of respect. Nor do I read him as recommending the language of politeness that many—not all—anthropologists use, which, in effect, says to the native, "Yes, I respect your beliefs, but they are not mine." This kind of respect is as shallow as the instrumental kind and, as we know, is often replaced by arrogance when the proverbial push comes to shove.

Some of Nandy's answers to the question why the tradition (as distinct from the practice) of sati is to be respected are couched in terms of the desire not to be alienated. He asks: "What does one do with the faith of millions of Indians that the soil that received the divided body of Sati constitutes the sacred land of India?" Once again, there seems to be no reason why a minority position, which is the only place from which reformers can begin, must be described as alienated. One can empathize and still genuinely disagree. If the answer is in terms of a humanist plea for respect for different life worlds, then it is not clear how that answer would suit the strategy of critical traditionalism for it must be remembered that the aim of this strategy is eventually to build a more just society, as Nandy explains repeatedly in his *Traditions, Tyranny, and Utopias.* There is no guarantee that the life world that one respects will truly bend itself to such a project.

Nandy recognizes a problem here, but the recognition is not yet explicit. His critique of the violence of the extreme modernizers is persuasive. Yet the grounds for the respectful attitude that he recommends toward tradition are not clear when we are confronted with a cultural monstrosity such as sati. Because he does not yet explicitly confront the issue that the past has produced at this point for his problematic—how to combine a respectful attitude toward tradition with the search for the principles with which to build a more just society—the dilemma breaks out into a plethora of practical, policy-related questions. Commenting on the ambiguities and impracticalities contained in a bill recently passed in the Indian parliament—with assistance from feminists—banning any kind of glorification of sati, Nandy launches into a series of powerful but rhetorical questions:

> How far can or should glorification of sati go? . . . Does the new law mean that children will not read about or admire Queen Padmini's self-chosen death in medieval times? Does it mean that that part of the Mahabharata which describes Madri's sati will now be censored? What about Rabindranath Tagore's awe-inspiring, respectful depiction of sati and Abanindranath Tagore's brilliant invocation of the courage, idealism, and tragedy of sati in medieval Rajasthan? Do we proscribe their works too . . . ? What about Kabir . . . who constantly uses the "impulse to sati" as an image of surrendering one's ego to God[?] . . . Does one ban the celebration of Durga Puja or, for that matter, Kalidasa's *Kumarasambhava,* [since] both celebrate the goddess who committed sati? Do we follow the logic of the two young activists who were keen to get the Ramayana declared unconstitutional? . . . That these questions may not in the future remain merely theoretical or hypothetical is made obvious by the fact that the Indian History Congress felt obliged to adopt a statement critical of the TV Ramayana in its 1988 convention.[8]

Behind these questions lies a larger issue: How does a modern intel-lectual think about the way a culture may have elaborated a series of val-ues for itself from practices of cruelty and violence? Sati is one example; blood feud could be another. Here, I am deliberately avoiding Nandy's more practical formulation of the question, What does one do? and ask-ing instead, How does one think? Doers will have to answer their ques-tions practically, in terms of the specific historical opportunities available to them, and that is why the options of a Tagore or a Coomaraswamy may not be available to us (although this is no reason for not considering their examples carefully). Besides, my location in the United States makes it pretentious for me to consider the practical question. But, as an academic-intellectual from India, I can join Nandy and his colleagues in the shared project of thinking about India.

In answering this question, I take my cue from a perceptive remark of Nandy's. "Every culture," he says, "has a dark side": "Sati in the *kali yuga* is an actualization of some of the possibilities inherent in the darker side of India's traditional culture, even if this actualization has been made possible by the forces of modernity impinging on and seeking to subvert the culture. After all, the tradition of sati exists only in some cul-tures, not in all; the kind of pathological self-expression displayed by some cultures in South Asia is not found in other parts of the world."[9]

Nandy's use of the word *dark* is obviously related to his use of the word *pathology*. I grant him that use, although I will note that it is just as normal for human beings to contract a disease as it is for them to seek a cure (i.e., to seek restoration to some kind of a normal, although not necessarily normalized, body). One might think of cultures in similar terms. Whether modern or not, cultures will have pathological aspects, just as Nandy argues, and some of our choices may be between patholo-gies.

But I want to read the work *dark* in its more literal sense. Dark is where light cannot pass; it is that which cannot be illuminated. There are parts of society that remain opaque to the theoretical gaze of the mod-ern analyst. Why a history of cultural practices will seize on a particular practice—especially a practice of cruelty and/or violence—and elabo-rate many of its own themes around it is a question that cannot be an-swered by the social sciences. It is also in this literal sense, then, it seems to me, that cultural practices have a dark side. We cannot see into them, not everywhere.

In saying this, then, I oppose the liberal modernists, whose investiga-tive methods, not only treat the investigator as transparent, but also as-sume that society itself is such a transparent object that they can look into its heart and find an explanatory key (in class, patriarchy, technology). My point is that societies do not exist in an object-like fashion. We analysts construct them as analyzable objects. What exist out there are translucent at best. Beyond a certain point theory cannot see. And where theory cannot see is where we live only practically. (None of this denies the heuristic value of class, patriarchy, or technology in social analysis. But clarity of a constructed model is not the same as clarity of the object for which the model stands.)

But this position also obliges me to modify Nandy's strategy of critical traditionalism in one important respect. If it is true that I do not entirely see into society, then it follows that I cannot use tradition in a completely voluntarist or decisionist manner. To the extent that I am self-consciously modern, Nandy's strategy may provide an ethic of living and of working for a more acceptable future. But the past also comes to me in ways that I cannot see or figure out—or can see or figure out only retrospectively. It comes to me as taste, as embodied memories, as cultural training of the senses, as reflexes, often as things that I do not even know that I carry. It has the capacity, in other words, to take me by surprise and to overwhelm and shock me.

Faced with this, I cease to be the self-inventing hero of modern life. As happens in the relation between humans and language, I am to some extent a tool in the hands of pasts and traditions; they speak through me even before I have chosen them critically or approached them with respect. That is why, it seems to me, that, in addition to the feeling of respect for traditions, fear and anxiety would have to be the other affects with which the modern intellectual—modernity here implying a capacity to create the future as an object of deliberate action—relates to the past. One never knows with any degree of certainty that a sati will never happen again or that an ugly communal riot will never again break out. It is out of this anxiety that the desire arises in the breast of the political revolutionary to scrap the past, to start from scratch, to create, as they say, the new man. Out of the same fear may even arise the attitude of respect.

But pasts retain, as Derrida says, a power to haunt.[10] They are a play of the visible and the invisible; they partially resist discursivity in the same way that pain resists language. My theory, then, always somewhat gropes and, as in all cases of speculation, takes a leap in the dark. And, where theory cannot see, I can live only practically, the future ceasing to exist as an object of analytic consideration (while it can always be the subject of poetic utterance). Decisions, which have this factor of darkness built into them, cannot, therefore, be based on any ground of certainty that would justify the infliction of suffering on others in the name of progress.

This is the burden of Nandy's critique of modernity, and with it I concur. At the same time, I would argue that an acknowledgment of the opacity of the world makes critical traditionalism less voluntarist than I found it to be on my first few readings of Nandy. A commitment to a future that we want to work out in advance makes us anxious, at least in principle, about the past in ways that are peculiar to the modern. As moderns, we may, therefore, want to defy the past and reduce it to nothing. That, as I have said, is the path of the revolutionary, and it is open to much of Nandy's critique. Alternatively, we may want to respect the past and relate critically, as Nandy so superbly explains, to tradition. The problem with this choice, it seems to me, is that it overstates the autonomy that we have with respect to the past. To live with a limited sense of autonomy is to accept pragmatism as a principle of living.

PART TWO

PRACTICES OF MODERNITY

FOUR *Khadi* and the Political Man

Are values in public life always a matter of conscious choice? An affirmative response to this question is at least implicit in much that is written on public life and its requirements. I do not, as such, question this assumption. There are good reasons for advocating consciously held values in the practice of public life in any modern country. But this essay, which is a historian's discussion of values in Indian public life, focuses on the phenomenon of the historical survival of shared values, beliefs, and desires in what people do rather than in what they say. It is important to explain this point.

India now has a recognizable public life made up of all the ingredients that one would consider standard for the construction of the public sphere: a representative democracy, the rights of free speech, and an active fourth estate. This public life produces, in everyday discussions, its own interpretive system and categories for measuring its own quality. One such key category, perhaps one of the most frequently used in discussions of Indian political life, is *corruption*. Like any other moralizing category, *corruption* has many meanings and associations, both conscious and unconscious. However, my purpose

51

here is not to explore its semantic range. I simply want to begin by identifying a particular semiotic of *corruption* that, for Indian politicians (usually men), has something to do with their bodies.

There is a strong Gandhian semiotic that still circulates in Indian public life and marks the public man—the politician—out from others. The most general uniform for the respectable public servant in India is the safari suit; for the politician, however, it has been, from the time before Independence, white *khadi*, the coarse, homespun cotton that Gandhi popularized in the 1920s. Its symbolism, as intended in the official/ nationalist rhetoric, is clear. The white of *khadi* symbolizes the Hindu idea of purity (lack of blemish, pollution), its coarseness an identification with both simplicity and poverty; together, they stand for the politician's capacity to renounce his own material well-being, to make sacrifices (*tyag*) in the public/national interest. *Khadi* indicates the person's capacity to serve the country.

Gandhi's own gloss on *khadi*, provided in 1921, mobilized all these meanings and added, in a characteristic nationalist touch, some essential Indianness as well: "I know that many will find it difficult to replace their foreign cloth all at once. . . . In order, therefore, to set the example, I propose to discard at least up to the 31st of October my *topi* (cap) and vest, and to content myself with only a loin cloth and a *chaddar* (shawl) whenever found necessary for the protection of the body. . . . I consider the renunciation to be also necessary for me as a sign of mourning, and a bare head and a bare body is such a sign in my part of the country."[1]

Gandhi also claimed that this divestment aligned him, symbolically, "with the ill-clad masses. . . . [I]n so far as the loin cloth also spells simplicity let it represent Indian civilization."[2] Emma Tarlo has quite rightly pointed out that it would be a mistake to assume that there was only one meaning to *khadi* and that that meaning was available to every Indian in a transparent way. She adduces many pieces of evidence from the writings of Gandhi and his followers to suggest that there was confusion about, as well as criticism of, the significance of *khadi* in Gandhi's own time.[3] *Khadi*, she argues, worked practically for our nationalist politicians because various kinds and designs of *khadi* could be used, not only to express different understandings of its meanings, but to make social distinctions visible as well.

There is a telling and humorous story about this in the history of the nationalist movement in Bengal. The story involves the Bengali novelist Saratchandra Chattopadhyay and the nationalist leader Sarat Bose and their respective attitudes toward *khadi*. When he was a member of the Bengal Provincial Congress Committee, Sarat Bose preferred to wear *khadi* that was fine, stylish, and easy on the body, while another member of the committee, Anilbaran Ray, wore, as a symbol of his devotion to the cause of *swadeshi* (economic nationalism), *khadi* that was heavier, coarser, and harsher and, hence, harder to wear. This difference led to animated exchanges among other members of the committee, who were often highly critical of Bose's sartorial preferences. The story goes that, referring to this differential use of *khadi* among nationalists of the same rank, and using the language of homeopathy, which became popular in Bengali nationalism, Saratchandra quipped one day: "You see, we have all different kinds here. A little variety is a good thing. Anil[baran Ray] is the *mother tincture* [of *khadi*], while Sarat [Bose] is *two hundred per cent dilution,* don't you understand?"[4]

Today, the joke is different. The attainment of independence and the marginalization of any practice of Gandhian politics have made *khadi* less a matter of conscious discussion. While *khadi* persists, its meanings have lost the richness of the times of struggle against British rule. It now represents either thoughtless habit or—if the decision to wear *khadi* is clearly conscious—callous hypocrisy. The image of a political leader from a 1994 issue of the magazine *Sunday* captures the close association that people now see between the donning of *khadi* and the illegal acquisition of wealth.[5] It documents something about the routine cynicism with which we now read the *khadi* that adorns the body of the political man. Thus, *khadi,* once described by Nehru as "the livery of freedom" and by Susan Bean as the "fabric of Indian independence,"[6] now stands unambiguously for the reverse of its nationalist definition. The *khadi-*clad politician is usually seen today as "corrupt," *khadi* itself as a dead giveaway, as the uniform of the rogue, as something like the hypocritical gesture of one who protests too much.

In terms of the semiotic of *corruption* in modern Indian public life, then, there already exists a reading of *khadi*—no longer as "purity" and "renunciation," but now as "corruption" and "thievery." Given that bribery is commonplace in Indian public life, this interpretation is more than reasonable—especially considering the pretense, in which politicians regularly engage, of making public their annual incomes and the value of their estates (much was made of this after Mrs. Gandhi's death) or of announcing, on the assumption of ministerial office, that they will accept only one rupee per month in salary. The hypocrisy of the gesture is only too transparent. Therefore, we cannot contest the semiotic that allows us to interpret *khadi* as shameless hypocrisy.

I agree with that reading. Yet it does not explain why *khadi,* or at least the color white, remains the most visible aspect of a male Indian politician's attire. The question is, Why does such a transparently hypocritical gesture persist even today? Why do politicians do that which fools nobody? In other words, if I assume that the hypocrisy of *khadi* is visible to everybody, then its (effective) purpose cannot be to deceive people into thinking well of the wearer. What has been read as a transparent gesture of hypocrisy must, then, because of its persistence, be amenable to another reading. I will, therefore, read the Indian politician's uniform, *khadi*, as if it were not meant to convince, as if it were meant (possibly unconsciously) to serve an entirely different purpose.

Let me clarify this point. Of course, it is true that—in the same way in which we are always half conscious of things that we do through habit—when a politician wears *khadi*, he is aware of what he is doing. But, just as we do not consciously control all the messages carried by all our actions, the politician wearing *khadi* is not always aware of all the messages that he is communicating. Consider the Hindu action of worshiping a god or goddess. There are many rituals involved in a *puja* (worship) that have neither literal nor scriptural meaning. Yet they are not meaningless—even if their meaning cannot be verbalized. And we communicate these meanings when we practice these rituals—even if we are unaware of those meanings and, therefore, have no control over them.

One may view the ritual wearing of *khadi* by male Indian politicians in a similar manner: not as conscious and hypocritical (one can, I think, reasonably assume that no one would opt for a course of action that communicates precisely that which he is seeking to hide), but as a series of messages circulating in public life but not intentionally communicated. This can happen only if certain notions about *khadi* or about politicians wearing white are common and ingrained enough to be in circulation in the public consciousness. In other words, just as one can decode social or cultural convention, reading it as a highly condensed statement of some social ideal (whether consciously held or not), one can in the same way decode the conventional wearing of *khadi* by politicians—by asking what kind of notions about the ideal form of public life (since politics is, broadly speaking, rules for conducting a society's public life) are embodied in the wearing of *khadi*.

Khadi is my excuse for thinking about alternative constructions of the values of public life—and, in particular, about ways in which heterogeneous possibilities are both opened up and closed off—in the modernity that is the legacy of colonial rule. What is of interest here are alternatives to the kinds of public life that capital—lately, multinational capital—have helped us think. While speaking of alternatives, I have no as-yet-unrealized or unrealizable future in mind. We are talking about alternative practices of modernity as they are lived now, at this moment of history. These alternatives, as we imagine them, are not autonomous of or separate from mainstream politics. We can describe them only through an act of reading certain everyday practices constitutive of the mainstream. What makes this exercise legitimate is the fact that existing interpretations of why so many male Indian politicians wear *khadi* or white are inadequate, as I have already explained. What is argued here is that, while *khadi* may legitimately be read as merely an Indian instance of a problem that is a universal feature of modern politics—the corrupt politician—its continuous use by men in Indian public life also sustains another reading, one that addresses desires for alternative constructions of the public sphere, constructions that illustrate the heterogeneity of cultural practices that gives Indian modernity its sense of difference.

If there is to be a condensed imagination of alternative public life to be read through the *khadi*-clad body, it cannot but be an imagination strongly tied to Gandhian politics. And, here, one last word of qualification is in order. Although much of what I discuss could be extended to women active in public life, I contemplate mainly the figure of the male politician. There are two reasons for this: First, although there is a history of women politicians wearing *khadi* or cotton saris in political life, studying their case would require us to focus more attention on differences in the way in which men and women operate in the Indian political sphere. Second, the majority of India's dominant politicians are still, alas, men. Also, as will become clear in what follows, a critical part of the argument connects *khadi* to an analysis of the cultural location of the middle-class male body in Indian public life under British rule. My expression *the body* refers to an abstracted, generalized body. But the body discussed here is male because an Indian woman could not have used and exposed her body as a symbol in the same way in which Gandhi did.

THE BODY OF THE PUBLIC MAN: THE COLONIAL CONTEXT

There is a reason for beginning with the question of the body. For the use of the body was central to the way in which colonialism operated, the British being the first to introduce the idea that the body and character were intimately connected. The Gandhian understanding of *khadi* must be placed squarely within the semiotics of the body in British colonial rule in India and the possibilities thus unfolded. Colonial modernity was fundamentally concerned with domination. The British use of the body in constructing a modern public life in India reflected that relation. In creating a public culture based on the theme of racial superiority, however, the British conflated character and physical strength, claiming to have an excess of both, unlike Indians.

The idea of character itself, it seems to me, was connected with corruption in late-eighteenth-century political thought. It must be remembered that the rapacious practices of the employees of the East India Company in the mid- to late eighteenth century at the time of Lord Clive—*baksheesh* (payment to expedite service), *nazar* (token tribute), and other kinds of interaction that the British saw as graft—were rationalized in England as the result of the enfeebling effect of Indian culture on the character of the Englishman in India.[7] Lord Cornwallis's appointment in the late 1780s as governor-general of Fort William in Calcutta was made on the assumption that only blood that was both blue and English was capable of maintaining character in public life in the face of all the temptation to corruption that India offered the European fortune seeker. To evolve soon afterward from this assumption was the colonial doctrine that the English/British body in India must be seen as the seat of such character and that in such an embodied practice of superiority lay the everyday guarantee of the permanence of British rule.

The projection of European physical superiority came to be seen as essential to the exercise of authority in colonial Indian public life. One aspect of this superiority was the assumed greater strength of the male European body. Numerous anecdotes and other kinds of evidence attest to this. Stories of Indians in India being forcibly prevented from sharing with Europeans the same public space—whether a train compartment or the white part of a city—abound in nationalist memories of British rule.[8] They formed a genre of their own in our schoolbooks. The whole history of modern physical training in India is rooted in the nationalist construction of modern imperial rule as an experience in direct physical humiliation.[9] The body was, thus, central to the projection of European political strength in India.

The study of history, biography, and literature—forms of modern knowledge introduced early by the British—helped popularize in India this connection between character, the body, and modern public life. The Hindus had no tradition of writing secular histories, and, while the Muslims had the art of historical chronicling, this did not amount to studying history in the post-Renaissance sense of that activity. The British introduced this particular imagination and genre of writing to India. The early histories written of India by European missionaries, administrators, and educators were often judgments on the character of old Indian rulers. For reasons of convenience, this process will be illustrated with some examples from the history of Bengal before discussing Gandhi again. That the last independent *nawab* of Bengal, Siraj-ud-daulah, was a venal, corrupt, and profligate character—whose defeat at the hands of the British was, therefore, a matter of natural justice—was regarded for a long time by Bengali historians, who began by translating

European texts, as the chief moral lesson of our eighteenth-century history.[10]

The consumption and production of modern Bengali literature, first drama and then novels, were deeply influenced by the idea that the function of literature was to reproduce variety in human character. A telling example of this is the nineteenth-century Bengali poet Michael Madhusudan Dutt's attempt to portray heroes in his blank-verse epic *Meghnadbadh Kavya* (1861)—an outlandish effort since the Indian epics, the *Ramayana* and the *Mahabharata,* are not centered around the idea of the hero in quite the same way as the major European epics are. As the following quotation from a later Bengali literary critic shows, the consumption of the *Meghnadbadh Kavya* has also been in terms of appreciation of character: "Ram and Laksman are two of the noblest figures in Indian mythology, but in Madhusudan's poem they are utterly devoid of valor and honor. . . . In the *Ramayana,* Meghnad is killed in the battle-field and in fair fight, but in Madhusudan's poem he is unarmed and engaged in worship in a temple when Laksman appears clad in celestial armor and kills him in cold blood. . . . We wonder whether we are reading a heroic or a mock-heroic poem."[11]

Biography, of course, was another important area of writing that was meant to instill in young Indian men (and, later, women) the idea of character. The first attempt to disseminate biographies of eminent public men among Indian/Bengali schoolboys was a book called *Jibancharit* (1849) by the nineteenth-century Bengali social reformer Iswarchandra Vidyasagar—a translation of a popular Victorian text by Robert and William Chambers, *Exemplary Biography.* It promoted discipline, the formation of regular habits, punctuality, and obedience. Being a translation of European material, however, it soon gave rise to the criticism that Indian boys needed Indian examples to follow, and a series of attempts by Indian authors to indigenize the field of modern biography soon followed.[12]

Finally, there was the question of physical strength, the training of the body to be strong, a subject increasingly popular in nationalist discourse in the second half of the nineteenth century. One whose statements inscribed this message into the nationalist memory was the nineteenth-century nationalist Hindu monk Swami Vivekananda, who, as is well-known, asserted that young Indian boys would do themselves a service if they concentrated more on playing football (soccer) than on reading the *Gita.* For the swami, the absence of physical health was an index of social degradation. As Tapan Raychaudhuri puts it: "Vivekananda identified better food as one cause of the westerners' generally better health. Climate and better living conditions were other contributory factors. But the most important reason, in his understanding, was the practice of late marriage. It explained why in Europe a man was still considered young at forty and a fifty-year-old woman not described as old. By contrast, a Bengali was past his youth at thirty."[13]

There was, however, a critical difference between British imperial and Indian nationalist understandings of the category *character* as applied to public life. Whereas the British saw it as something embodied and, therefore, inherited—a ruling-race argument—nationalists saw it as a universal and, hence, translatable idea, a collection of precepts and techniques that could be learned and, therefore, made into an object of pedagogy. Vidyasagar's *Jibancharit,* for instance, saw nothing problematic in presenting to Indian schoolboys an assortment of "characters" taken at random from world history. Thus, schools became a critical site for acquiring character—textbooks, classrooms, playing fields, and gymnasiums became the arenas where character was both discussed and imbibed.

THE BODY AND GANDHI'S DESTRUCTION OF THE PRIVATE

Gandhi's understanding of the body of the public man cannot be discussed in isolation from this colonial dynamic. It is easy to see that his early experiments with meat eating were fundamentally influenced (if not inspired) by a nationalist question that troubled many Asian cultures in the nineteenth century: Were the Europeans stronger because they ate beef? (Indeed, so many non-European nationalists have asked this question, and thereby promoted the eating of beef, that one might be tempted to ask, Is the cow the worst victim of European imperialism?) Gandhi, thus, records the arguments of a meat-eating friend that convinced him to try goat:

> A wave of reform was sweeping over Rajkot at the time when I first came across this friend. He informed me that many of our teachers were secretly taking meat and wine. He also named many well-known people . . . as belonging to the same company . . . and he explained it thus: "We are a weak people because we do not eat meat. The English are able to rule over us, because they are meat-eaters. You know how hardy I am, and how great a runner too. It is because I am a meat-eater. Meat-eaters do not have any boils or tumours, and even if they sometimes happen to have any, they heal quickly."

Gandhi goes on to quote a "doggerel of the Gujarati poet Narmada" that was popular "amongst us schoolboys." The verse captures the colonial nationalist understanding of the role of the body in the construction of political power:

> Behold the mighty Englishman
> He rules the Indian small
> Because being a meat-eater
> He is five cubits tall.[14]

Many of the colonial—indeed, modern—concerns about character, however, were to remain with Gandhi. He accepted and advocated the need for discipline and integrity in public life. Observers have commented on the determination with which he submitted himself to the tyranny of the clock. His management of public money with scrupulous honesty also owes something to modern notions of the public and of the accountability of the public man.[15] His lifelong interest in both public health and civic consciousness also marks him out as quintessentially modern.[16]

But the critical move that set him apart from both imperialists and (other) nationalists was the way in which he eventually came to separate the question of character, not so much from the body, as we shall see, as from the issue of sheer physical strength, where the imperialists as well as many of the nationalists had located it. Instead, Gandhi grounded the question of the character of the public man in what we would regard today as the issue of sexuality, in overcoming the power of the senses. This is what gives the Gandhian political body its special charge.

Let me summarize the Gandhian argument about the relation between the body and nonviolence.[17] Aggression, Gandhi seems to be saying, is inseparably connected to male lust. (Gandhi saw female sexuality as passive.) Nonviolence involved love toward all and depended critically on one's capacity to destroy self-love. One's sexual desires are at the core of one's self-love; therefore, nonviolence requires a joyful acceptance of celibacy. Gandhi often made a model, for both men and women, of the ideals of sacrifice and suffering: "Hinduism will remain imperfect as long as men do not accept suffering . . . [and] withdraw their interest in the pleasures of life."[18] There was, to his mind, a direct relation between this "withdrawal from pleasure" and *swaraj* (self-rule), his word for freedom: "The conquest of lust is the highest endeavor of a man's or a woman's existence. And without overcoming lust, man cannot hope to rule over self; without rule over self, there can be no Swaraj. . . . No worker who has not overcome lust can hope to render any genuine ser-

vice to the cause of the harijans [Gandhi's name for the so-called un-
touchables], khadi, cow protection or village reconstruction. Great
causes like these . . . call for spiritual effort or soul force. Soul force
comes only through God's grace and never descends upon a man who is
a slave to lust."[19]

Sexuality forms a complex theme both in Gandhi's life and in descriptions of it, including his own. That Gandhi was haunted by his own sexuality is a point made by many observers, particularly those looking at
his life from a psychoanalytic angle, the most famous being, of course,
Erik Erikson.[20] And, of course, gossip columnists and authors of sensa-
tionalist histories have been fascinated by his descriptions of the experiments that he conducted in old age to test his self-control. So it is by
now a commonplace to find Gandhi obsessed with sexuality.[21] I am not
concerned with the clinical accuracy of such assessments, for I am not
competent to judge what constitutes obsession. Besides, it is clear from
the available literature that Gandhi's ideas about sexuality and celibacy
were influenced by many different sources. There were at work Indian-
Hindu practices and ideals of asceticism and abstinence (*brahmacharya*)
and of sacrifice (*tyag*) and other such notions. As Gandhi himself wrote
on the technique of fasting in a chapter on *brahmacharya* in the autobiography: "It may be said that extinction of the sexual passion is as a rule
impossible without fasting, which may be said to be indispensable for the
observance of *brahmacharya*."[22]

What I intend to do here is to move away from the question of
whether Gandhi's detailed discussion of the problem of his sexuality
constitutes, clinically speaking or otherwise, an obsession on his part.
That is not relevant to my attempt to read in the Gandhian representation of the body a semiotic system of (alternative) modernity. For the
purpose of my analysis, I will read as confessional what is commonly seen
as obsessive in Gandhi. Once we do this, we will see in clearer outlines
the alternative conceptions of public life that Gandhi articulated and of
which *khadi* now acts as an extremely condensed statement.

Gandhi's is, in fact, the only confessional autobiography ever to be
written by a prominent Indian public leader, and it shares much with the
tradition of Augustine and Rousseau. Not only does Gandhi adopt from
certain monastic strands in Christianity the idea of a universal love that
can be fostered only by destroying all traces of self-love (sexuality) in
oneself, but he also uses a Christian confessional technique—central, as
Foucault would remind us, to the construction of the modern subject—
to narrate himself in the public sphere (his autobiography was written in
part to fill the pages of his weekly magazine, *Navajivan*). One can, in-

deed, read his obsessive descriptions of his guilt-ridden sexual experiences as so many confessions of his sins.

But there remains one very interesting difference between a Christian confessional autobiography and Gandhi's. On this difference hinges a critical part of my argument. A confession, argues William Spengemann in discussing Augustine, makes the work of self on self visible to a higher self, an all-knowing God. Confessions are narrations of self-knowledge addressed to a being who knows everything anyway.[23] Gandhi's confessions are, interestingly, not called that; rather, they are described as provisional results of ongoing experiments. The addressee of Gandhi's narration, the higher being to whom the work of self on self is being revealed, is, thus, no all-knowing self, the word *experiment* carrying within itself an inexorable connotation of openness and uncertainty. Gandhi makes it quite clear that God is not the addressee of his autobiography; in this sense, his autobiography is not confessional. "There are some things which are known only to oneself and one's Maker," he writes, adding: "These are clearly incommunicable. The experiments I am about to relate are not as such. But they are spiritual, or rather moral."[24]

In thus shifting the addressee from the register of Christian godhood, Gandhi converts the confessional into a mere technique and orients it toward a secular engagement, the task of building a modern public life. In so doing, however, he constructs a new modern subject of political and public life, one who has been neither theorized nor deconstructed in European thinking. The gaze that Gandhi invites on himself, the gaze to which he exposes himself, is relentless. "Watch me closely," was his instruction to those who wanted to study him. He deliberately shunned any idea of privacy. When the anthropologist Nirmal Bose sought his permission to study him close-up in the 1940s, Gandhi said: "One should actually see me at work and not merely gather from my writings." On another occasion, the instruction was even more forthright: "You have drunk all that I have written. . . . But it is necessary that you should observe me at work. . . . I have called you to my side. You must examine if it was dictated by self-interest. Self-interest may be of two kinds, one is entirely personal, and the other is in relation to what one stands for. . . . Examine my motives carefully."[25]

Gandhi, thus, shunned the idea of privacy—sleeping naked and completely asexually with others was one of his experiments in this regard. Nothing in his life was to be hidden from public gaze. Everything was open to observation and narration. Not that there could not be a private Gandhi, but, whatever the private man was, it was not for narration to others: "Things which are known only to oneself and one's Maker . . . are clearly incommunicable." Gandhi marks here the emergence of a modern whose difference from the European/Christian modern is measured precisely by this statement. The interiority of the European modern subject—the interiority that pours out in novels, autobiographies, diaries, and letters—contained within itself a secularized version of what one once confessed to God.[26]

The European modern is born on this condition—that the private be narratable—and, in that sense, the private self of the European exceeds or transcends the body. The European private, one might say, is a "deferred public." Give it time, and the private of the European becomes available for public consumption in many different forms of narration or representation. The Gandhian private is nonnarratable and nonrepresentable. Not that it does not exist, but it is beyond representation, and it dies with the body itself. In one stroke, as it were, Gandhi, thus, collapsed the distinction between the private and the public on which the theoretical side of the political arrangements of Western modernity rest.

CONCLUSION

The Gandhian modern was, thus, in a relation of both affinity and tension with the modernity of the citizen of European political theory. With the latter, the Gandhian modern shares a concern for public health, freedom of speech and inquiry, and civic awareness. Yet it does not fulfill the condition of interiority that the discourse of rights both produces and guarantees for the citizen of the modern state.

Three lines of tension are easily detected: First, the idea of a completely narratable public life and a completely nonnarratable private one corresponds to the idea of a completely transparent government—"Examine my motives carefully," as Gandhi said. The modern state, however, cannot ever fulfill this requirement—*national security, political intelligence,* etc., are its watchwords. Second, the moral claim to representation does not go with the idea of politics as a profession. The Mother Teresas are not politicians in our everyday understanding, whereas, in Gandhian modernity, such a distinction would be difficult to sustain. Third, the relation between the Gandhian construction of the public sphere and the logic of capital accumulation is not straightforward, for, if public life valorizes renunciation as a supreme value, how would one write acquisitiveness into a universal model of the human being?

I read the *khadi* that adorns the body of the "hypocritical" Indian politician as a condensed statement of this tension between an untheorized and increasingly unacknowledged subject of colonial modernity—to which I will now apply the collective appellation *Gandhi*—and the actual rapacity of Indian capitalism. For our capitalist practices promote values quite the opposite of those that Gandhian politics taught us to desire. Those desires have receded, but not disappeared, from Indian public life. We do not think about them, but we do, in a manner of speaking, practice them, however perversely, in our politicians continuing with the collective habit of still sporting *khadi* or some metonymic substitute for it. This cultural statement, however, does not belong to the order of intentional or conscious transactions. To read *khadi* as a conscious statement of intent can, as mentioned earlier, only lead us to see it as ritualistic and hypocritical.

That reading is not invalid, but it carries a post-Protestant understanding of rituals as "empty." The fallacy here is of the same order as the one that Slavoj Žižek discusses in his *The Sublime Object of Ideology*—the reduction of ideology to conscious intentions and beliefs. Žižek argues against the idea that "a belief is something interior and knowledge something exterior"; rather, he says, "it is belief, which is radically exterior, embodied in the practical, effective procedures of people." The point is repeated in his discussion of the law: "Belief, far from being an 'intimate,' purely mental state, is always *materialized* in our effective social activity: belief supports the fantasy which regulates social reality."[27]

What appears in Žižek as theory may be recognized as a home truth of the Hindu tradition. Within that tradition, the so-called rituals have never been empty, for they have always been nonsubjective and nonintentional means of communication. There is, thus, a question of (practiced) belief involved in the wearing of *khadi*. This question is both logically and culturally valid, although the reduction today of the Gandhian alternative to what looks like an empty ritual is understandable, for the qualities that Gandhi demanded of the public man do not, as I have explained, sit easily with the logic of capital accumulation. The condition of Gandhi's success was colonial rule. The very fact that, except during moments of limited devolution of power, the actual instruments of government belonged to the colonizers allowed Indian nationalists to fabricate for themselves arenas—outside the sphere of formal institutional politics—that could act as the theater for the self-expression of the Gandhian modern. With the dawn of Independence, Indian capitalism and democracy have developed their own distinctive characteristics, different from both the tenets of Gandhian politics and those of European classical writings on either of these phenomena.[28]

Yet the survival to this day of the Gandhian uniform—for all the historical mutations that it has undergone—cannot be explained as just an empty or hypocritical ritual, for we would then have to think of the Indian voters as enormously gullible. I have, therefore, read it as the site of the desire for an alternative modernity, a desire made possible by the contingencies of British colonial rule, now impossible of realization under the conditions of capitalism, yet circulating insistently within an everyday object of Indian public life, the (male) politician's uniform. I do not think that *khadi* convinces anybody any longer of the Gandhian convictions of the wearer, but, if my reading of it has any point to it, then its disappearance, were that to happen, would signify the demise of a deeper structure of desire and would signal India's complete integration into the circuits of global capital.

FIVE Of Garbage, Modernity, and the Citizen's Gaze

Until Salman Rushdie and his followers arrived on the scene and made the intellectual ferment of modern India more visible to the outsider, India remained, in the dominant grids of Western perceptions, a place of "heat and dust" where the Europeans had once founded a resplendent raj. To heat and dust was often added another familiar list: crowds, dirt, and disease. Continuous with all this was a conception of an Indian nature that highlighted Indians' capacity to remain blind to the unwholesome aspects of their public places.

A recent example of this perennial theme in discussions of what Indians might do in public is the way in which V. S. Naipaul begins his *India: A Million Mutinies Now.* True, this book represents Naipaul's second thoughts on India and does capture some of the movements that India causes in the souls of its people. Nevertheless, Naipaul's travelogue begins by offering the reader a path that has been beaten into familiarity now for at least a century and a half: "Bombay is a crowd. . . . Traffic into the city moved slowly because of the crowd. . . . With me, in the taxi, were fumes and heat and din. . . . The shops, even when small, even when dingy, had big, bright signboards. . . . Often, in front of these shops, and below those signboards, was just dirt; from time to time depressed-looking, dark people could be seen sitting down on this dirt and eating, indifferent to everything but their food."[1]

It would be unfair, however, to think of this perception as simply Western. What it speaks is the language of modernity, of civic consciousness and public health, even of certain ideas of beauty related to the management of public space and interests, an order of aesthetics from which the ideals of public health and hygiene cannot be separated.[2] It is the language of modern governments, both colonial and postcolonial, and, for that reason, it is the language, not only of imperialist officials, but of modernist nationalists as well. Lord Wellesley's street policy for Calcutta, minuted in 1803, embodies this connection between order, public health, and a particular aesthetics of the cityscape. He wrote: "In those quarters of the town occupied principally by the native inhabitants, the houses have been built without order or regularity, and the streets and lanes have been formed without attention to the health, convenience or safety of the inhabitants. . . . The appearance and beauty of the town are inseparably connected with the health, safety and convenience of the inhabitants, and every improvement . . . will tend to ameliorate the climate and to promote and secure . . . a just and salutary system of police."[3]

These sentiments were echoed in European writings on India throughout the nineteenth century. M. A. Sherring's 1868 description of Banaras in terms of its "foul wells and tanks" with their "deadly" water breeding cholera and fever, the "loathsome and disgusting state" of its temples where offerings decomposed rapidly from "the intense heat of the sun," the "stagnant cesspools, accumulated refuse and dead bodies of animals" crowding its "narrow streets," can now be read, not simply as realist prose, but also as evidence of a particular way of seeing.[4]

While this way of seeing is no longer exclusively European, its main bearers in nineteenth-century India were, no doubt, the Europeans themselves, whose modernist categories *public* and *private* were constantly challenged by the ways in which Indians used open space. In the many different uses to which it was put, the street presented, as it were, a total confusion of the private and the public. People washed, changed, slept, and even urinated and defecated in the open. As a traveler to India put it in the nineteenth century: "As to any delicacy about taking his siesta, or indeed doing anything in public, nothing is farther from the Hindoo mind, and it is a perpetual source of wonder and amusement to see the unembarrassed ease with which employments of a personal nature are carried on in the most crowded streets."[5]

The scene of the bazaar added yet another side to this perception of the Indian character: ever-present dirt and disorder. "Filthy drains," "disgusting" sellers ("corpulent to the last degree"), crowded and noisy lanes, people, birds, "goats, dogs and fowls," all worked together to produce the effect of a nightmare: "The whole seems at first more like some strange phantasmagoria, the imagery of a hideous magic lantern or a bewildered dream, than like a sober, waking reality." To this Indian chaos was opposed the immaculate order of the European quarters, where "pleasant squares," "white buildings with their pillared verandas," and "graceful foliage" lent, to European eyes, a "fairy-like loveliness" to "the whole scene."[6]

If these pictures seem tainted by Orientalism, let us remember that they are by no means outdated. We need only recall the time when Naipaul still wrote—out of his own (historic) wounds, he explains in *India: A Million Mutinies Now*—in a tone that made many see him as a brown Englishman. According to his *An Area of Darkness* (1965): "Indians defecate everywhere. They defecate, mostly beside the railway tracks. But they also defecate on the hills; they defecate on the river banks; they defecate on the streets; they never look for cover. Indians defecate everywhere."[7]

These accusations have hurt nationalists no less than the sights themselves have. Gandhi himself once commented acidly on the national character that expressed itself on Indian streets. "Everybody is selfish," he said, "but we seem to be more selfish than others": "We do not hesitate to throw refuse out of our courtyard on to the street; standing on the balcony, we throw out refuse or spit, without pausing to consider whether we are not inconveniencing the passer-by. . . . In cities, we keep the tap open, and thinking that it is not our water that flows away, we allow it to run waste. . . . Where so much selfishness exits, how can one expect self-sacrifice?"[8]

Nirad Chaudhuri's autobiography presents the problem, in sarcasm mixed with irony, as a cultural puzzle. In sharp contrast to the "extremely tidy" interiors of Bengali households—"the mistress or mistresses never permitted the slightest displacement of any object from its place"—remained their habit of rubbishing the outside. Oblivious to the classist and sexist biases of his statement, Chaudhuri describes this phenomenon as "the most complete [case of] non-cooperation between the domestic servants and the municipal sweepers": "The streets were regularly watered, swept and even scrubbed. But while the street-cleaning ended by about six o'clock in the morning and three in the afternoon, the kitchenmaids would begin to deposit the off-scouring exactly at quarter past six and quarter past three. Nothing seemed capable of making either party modify its hours. So little piles of waste food, ashes, and vegetable scraps and peelings lay in individualistic autonomy near the kerb from one sweeping time to another."[9]

Both Gandhi's and Chaudhuri's are nationalist comments deploring the absence of a citizen culture on the part of the people. They are also at the same time attempts (employing very different rhetorical devices) to inculcate in their hypothetical Indian readers a sense of civic life and public interest. Yet, as we all know, Indian history bears a constant testimony to a gap that persists well into the present day between the modernist desires inherent in imperialist/nationalist projects of social reform—and I shall later argue the complicity of the social sciences as well in this—and popular practices. The complaint about popular blindness in India toward dirt and disease has not lost any of its force (although, as a slander on some eternally condemned Indian character, it no longer circulates much).

Nita Kumar's sensitive—and, in the present context, understandably somewhat coy—ethnosociology of the artisans of Banaras reports this blindness: "These same galis [lanes] are notorious among visitors for being dark, narrow, tortuous, filthy and even dangerous. . . . None of the Banarasis themselves ever described their galis as any of these things. . . . Queries about their rather 'unsanitary conditions' could elicit no response because these ideas seemingly fell outside Banarasis' conceptions of their city. . . . Most ignore the matter altogether, as they do most government officers. . . . Men often told me that one aspect of the overall friendliness and convenience of the city was that they could urinate wherever they liked. This, I realized after months of unwilling observation, was not an exaggeration."[10]

While Kumar is careful to distance her prose from that of the public-health inspector by putting quotation marks around *unsanitary conditions,* and while she reports, perceptively and with good humor, a mismatch between, say, the modernist view of the city and the urbanism of the Banarasi, her description of the *galis,* of the supposed incapacity of the Banarasi to respond to questions of sanitation and health, invests the modernist complaint (about popular blindness to these questions) with a certain degree of objectivity. This is precisely the objectivity of the outsider, which is the only position from which an aggressively modernist observer can speak on this subject. (It matters little for my argument whether the particular speaker is white skinned or brown.) As Thompson says of the passage from Naipaul quoted earlier: "Only the outsider can see that all of India is the Indian's latrine. It is all too easy as an outsider to spot the Indians' conspiracy of blindness."[11]

I should clarify, however, that, unlike Thompson, I do not by *outsider* mean a non-Indian person. The outsider here is the observer who does not inhabit the conceptual or theoretical framework of the actor whom he or she observes. It is the observing position that I have tagged here as *modernist,* and I shall return later to the question of the relation between modernism and ethnosociology.

My aim in this essay is to contest and critique these modernist readings of uses of open space in India by opposing to them certain structuralist speculations based on a preliminary, and by no means exhaustive, study of some of the relevant historical and anthropological material. I am aware of the limitations of structuralist methodology and also of that which arises from the somewhat ahistorical character of my argument. This essay is in the nature of a beginning, with all the tentativeness that beginnings entail. A deeper and more convincing analysis would no doubt need to locate the argument in a more historically grounded context.

I should also clarify that a major aim of this exercise is methodophilosophical. It is to show, through a critical reading of some aspects of Kumar's otherwise excellent ethnosociology, that, when it comes to questions relating to health, that is, to life rather than death, the nonbourgeois subaltern citizen is always already condemned in our social science, however sympathetic the stance of our ethnography. As social scientists, we align ourselves with those who want to build citizen cultures. The moral consequences of wanting to do otherwise can, as some of Kumar's most honest remarks betray, be excruciatingly painful.

LOCATING DIRT: SOME STRUCTURALIST SPECULATIONS

Since I have allowed myself the speculative freedoms of a structuralist, I shall begin by taking a leaf out of Mary Douglas's celebrated book on dirt and start with the proposition that the problem of dirt poses, in turn, the problem of the outside.[12] For, whether we are talking about radioactive waste from the industrialized countries or the waste of a household or village in India, the dirt can go only to a place that is designated as *outside.* It is this problem of the outside that I want to explore in this section of the essay. Let us begin with the problem of household rubbish.

The fact that the dirt goes out of the house implies a boundary between the inside and the outside. This boundary does not simply delineate a hygienic space where cleanliness is practiced. Housekeeping is also meant to express the auspicious qualities of the mistress of the household, her Lakshmi-like nature that protects the lineage into which she has married.[13] As outsiders who must be received into the bosom of the patrilineal and patriarchal family, women are particularly subject to the rituals of auspiciousness. For, in this conception, the outsider always carries "substances" that threaten one's well-being. The "negative qualities and substances that may afflict persons, families, houses and villages," as Gloria Goodwin Raheja has recently noted, are seldom "one's own": they achieve their "entry" through lapses in the performance of auspicious actions. "All forms of inauspiciousness are said to originate in entities and events that are 'different' and 'distant' from the person or other afflicted entity," writes Raheja; "they are alien."[14] Auspicious acts protect the habitat, the inside, from undue exposure to the malevolence of the outside. They are the cultural performance through which this everyday inside is both produced and enclosed. The everyday practice of classifying certain things as household rubbish marks the boundary of this enclosure.

Nirad Chaudhuri's cultural puzzle thus contains themes that, I suggest, pervade Indian popular culture. The figure of the outsider as troublemaker was strongly conveyed by the Santal term *diku* so prominently used in the rebellion of 1855.[15] In the Munda country, jealousy, which is seen as corrosive of communal bonds, is attributed to mischievous outsiders.[16] Hatred of people conceived of as outsiders is a universal feature of so-called ethnic conflict in India and elsewhere.[17] Correspondingly general is the practice of enclosing a place as a gesture of protection. The more-enduring boundaries—such as the wall of a fort city or a *mohalla*—of course also signify ownership and authority, but that is not a point that I will pursue here.[18] The general connection, however, between the *mohalla* and the insider/outsider division of identity is widely accepted in the literature.[19]

Our nonmodernist ways of handling disease are replete with these themes of the enclosed inside and the exposed outside. Only a few examples are necessary to make the point. Whitehead's well-known study of the village gods of south India makes several connections between boundaries and their protective power. "The boundary-stone of the village lands is very commonly regarded as a habitation of a local deity, and might be called a shrine or symbol with equal propriety," writes Whitehead. The propitiation of the cholera goddess at Iralangur (Trichinopoly district) or of Pedamma, an epidemic goddess of the Telugu country, involved, in both cases, symbolic enactments of the village boundary. In the former case, it was the duty of a washerman to place, at the end of the propitiation ceremony, the offerings to the deity "at the point where his village border[ed] on the adjoining village": "The deity is thus propitiated and carried beyond the village limits. The villagers of the adjacent village in their turn carry the *karagam* [the offerings] to the border of the next village, and in this way the baleful influence of the goddess is transferred to a safe distance." The worship of Pedamma also included activities that ritually inscribed village boundaries.[20]

Catanach has written of Punjab villages where, during the plague scare of 1896–98, "the village site [was] surrounded with a circle of stakes, with demons' heads roughly carved on top to serve as supernatural guardians."[21] More contemporary evidence comes from Ralph Nicholas's study of the smallpox goddess Sitala in southwestern Bengal, where worship rituals include the taking out of processions that circumambulate the village "planting flags where paths cross the village borders, or otherwise bounding the village before her [Sitala's] *puja* is begun."[22] Diane Coccari has studied similar processes in urban Banaras—the Bir *babas* who act as boundary gods of neighborhoods: "The deity is described as 'the god' or 'the protector of the neighbourhood.' . . . There are hundreds of Bir . . . shrines in the city. . . . Like the village deities, the urban Bir control the boundaries of their domains, especially with regard to the exit and entry of the intangible agents of illness, misfortune and disease."[23]

If the house, thus, is only an instance of a theme general to South Asia—an inside produced by symbolic enclosure for the purpose of protection—what, then, is the symbolic meaning of the outside, which can, indeed, be rubbished?

To answer this question, I shall take the bazaar as the paradigmatic form of the outside. The bazaar, the street, and the fair (*mela*), it seems to me, have for quite some time formed a spatial complex in India. Streets, for good or bad, all too often become, effectively, bazaars, and *melas* combine the different purposes of pilgrimage, recreation, and economic exchange.[24] I take the bazaar as a space that serves the needs of transportation as well as those of entertainment and the buying and selling of goods and services. I am aware that there have been different kinds of bazaars in India, going by different names (*hats, mandis, ganjes,* etc.), and varying in their functional specializations.[25] I also ignore the interesting problem of connections between the bazaar and the structures and relationships of power in its vicinity.

The bazaar of which I speak is obviously an abstraction of certain structural characteristics that, to my mind, define the experience of the bazaar as a place. Everyday linguistic practices involve and permit such an abstraction—in the Bengali language, for instance, the word *bajar* (bazaar) is often used in a metaphoric way to represent an outside to *ghar-shangshar* (the way of the householder, i.e., domesticity); thus, prostitutes are called *bajarer meye* (women of the bazaar) to distinguish them from *gharer meye* (housewives or women of the household). In this analysis, *bazaar* is the name that I give to that unenclosed, exposed, and interstitial outside that acts as the meeting point of several communities. It should also be clear by now that the division inside/outside involves a metaphoric use of space for the purpose of making boundaries, however transient these boundaries may be. Actual spatial arrangements may embody this division, but the cultural practices productive of boundary markers cannot be reduced to the question of how physical space is used in particular circumstances.

Structurally speaking, in my terms, then, the bazaar or the outside is a place where one comes across strangers. And, if, as I have argued, strangers, being outsiders, are always suspect and potentially dangerous, it is only logical that the themes of familiarity/unfamiliarity and trust/mistrust should play themselves out in many different aspects of the bazaar. All "economic" transactions here—bargaining, lending and borrowing, buying and selling—are marked by these themes. The cultural material uncovered in Jennifer Alexander's study of the bazaar (*pasar*) in rural Java will not surprise those used to the marketplaces of South Asia (for the bazaar is obviously an institution belonging to a much larger culture zone than the subcontinent alone). Protestations of honesty, for example, are a recursive feature of bargaining talk. The copperware seller in Alexander's extended recording of a particular case of haggling repeats several times:

> I'm not lying.
> If you can discover a repair there's no need to pay!
> How could I lie to you and your daughter!
> I'm not lying to you!
> Yes, [the seller's mother says,] she's not lying to you. I swear it!
> If I am lying to you, don't buy another one.
> I'd be extremely ashamed if I was lying to you, truly![26]

In these transactions, often conducted in terms of weights and measures that are only approximate, the economic cannot be separated from the social, for prices reflect the concern with trust and familiarity. As Ostor observes in his study of a Bengali bazaar: "Regular customers do not need to haggle, but those who are mainly strangers or out-of-towners."[27] In other matters, too, the social remains a prominent part of the economic. In a group of rural markets in Gujarat studied in the late 1950s, the owners of *hat* (market) lands, it was reported, "generally levied fixed charges" once "the traders . . . [became] accustomed to the place and the people." Even the bonds of credit forged in these (predominantly tribal) markets followed the lines of familiarity and acquaintance: "[The cloth merchants] . . . maintained close and intimate ties with the

influential sections of tribal society [their customers and debtors]. . . .
They made it a point to attend social occasions like marriage, death, illness, etc. in these tribal households. Interestingly, when these households purchased cloth for wedding occasions from their shops, these
traders invariably gave them [a tribal wedding party] one meter of cloth
and a cash amount of Rs 1.25. They said that this gift is from their
side. . . . This is a time-honoured practice among cloth merchants in
the hats."[28]

That familiarity reduces risk in economic transactions is obvious.
What I want to highlight is the way in which kinship categories are used
in the bazaar in this making familiar of the strange, in this process of taming, as it were, the potentially malevolent outsider. "Most commonly
men of the bazaar, are *dada* [older brother] and *bhai* [brother] to each
other," writes Ostor. "In the bazaar *bhai* expresses a continuing relationship and enjoins a code of conduct."[29] Alexander reports a similar
practice from her *pasar* in Java: "Kinship terms are the most common
mode of address and usage is governed by age. *Bakul* [the seller] addresses
most male adults as *pak* (lit. father) and females as *bu* (lit. mother), young
women as *mbak* or *yu* (lit. older sister) and young men as *mas* or *kang*
(lit. older brother)."[30]

Not surprisingly, then, unlike the modern marketplace, the bazaar
(i.e., the outside) is geared to the production of social life.[31] Unlike its
modern counterpart, it privileges speech. The physical organization of
shops in the bazaar encourages, as Anthony King has observed, "visual"
and "verbal" inquiry and helps convert the former into the latter.[32] The
centrality of speech and linguistic competence to the economic transactions of the bazaar is also underlined in S. P. Punalekar's study of the Gujarat market. "The cloth merchants," reports Punalekar, "knew and
spoke fluently in tribal dialects," for they feared that, without this skill,
they "[would] be in the dark about what they [the tribals] [were] commenting among themselves: about price, quality or about myself [the
merchant]."[33]

The street or the bazaar, thus, serves the "multiple purposes" of "recreation, social interaction, transport and economic activity."[34] Many
observers have noted this. Ostor, for example, writes: "Drinking tea,
chewing *pan* [betel leaf] and smoking, the men discuss everything from
business, to theatre and rituals. . . . Newspapers are read and exchanged,
radio news broadcasts are heard and interpreted."[35]

In contrast to the ritually enclosed inside, then, the outside, for which
I have used the bazaar as a paradigm, has a deeply ambiguous character.
It is exposed and, therefore, malevolent. It is not subject to a single set of
(enclosing) rules and rituals defining a community. It is where misce-

genation occurs. All that do not belong to the inside (family/kinship/community) lie there, cheek by jowl, in an unassorted collection, violating rules of mixing: from feces to prostitutes. It is, in other words, a place against which one needs protection.

Some of the devices meant to provide such protection are bodily and personal, ranging from the mark of *kaajal* (collyrium), which little children are given to protect them from the evil eye, to *subh naam* (auspicious name), which all upper-caste Hindus use in dealing with outsiders and formal situations. Often, the community-forming rituals of enclosure are themselves replicated in the bazaar. Shopkeepers will use their own rituals for marking the area of the shop as enclosed space. Some of these strongly resemble housekeeping activities: worshiping a deity (Ganesh rather than Lakshmi since Ganesh is the lord who removes obstacles); sweeping with a broomstick the area of the street immediately adjacent to the front of the shop.[36] The more permanent traders in a particular bazaar sometimes even develop a sense of community and patronize a single bazaar temple.[37] Speech and face-to-face interaction have to do, as we have seen, with overcoming the mistrust of the outsider in a space where transactions are contingent on trust. The inside/outside dichotomy, therefore, is a matter of constant performance in the exchanges of the bazaar.

The duality of this space is inescapable. It harbors qualities that threaten one's well-being (strangers embody these qualities). Yet it provides a venue for linkage across communities (linkages with strangers). Speech and direct interaction produce such solidarity. The bazaar or the *chowk* is, as Freitag has noted, often the most public of arenas in Indian cities—*public* in the sense of "publicity"—and has, for that reason, hosted traditionally colorful religious/political spectacles involving large numbers.[38] The connection between the *chowk*, the bazaar, and the spectacle of public events is also drawn by Kumar in her study of Banaras.[39] And Guha has recently drawn our attention to the importance of rumors, that is, speech par excellence, in the political mobilization of peasants.[40] Spaces like the bazaar are, as Guha shows, central to the dissemination of rumors, which goes some way toward explaining why riots or rebellions often start in the bazaar.

Ambiguity and risk are, thus, inherent to the excitement of the bazaar. Punalekar's survey of tribal markets in the Surat-Valsad area gives a striking example of this. Here, people who specialize in providing entertainment at the bazaar are often those who are trusted the least. "Acrobats, rope walkers, snake charmers, singers and mimics," as well as owners of performing monkeys and bears, gamblers, and others who performed in these bazaars, all were, Punalekar notes, often strangers to

particular markets. Belonging to the poorest sections of the bazaar pop-
ulace, these entertainers "moved from one hat to another" without "a
regular schedule," not only thereby violating the codes of familiarity and
trust, but also deriving from this violation itself the mysterious attrac-
tions of their presence as strangers.[41]

It is, therefore, easy to see why roaming the streets of the neighbor-
hood is a pleasurable activity for most Indian men. (I say *men* advisedly,
for the pleasure is gendered even when it is not class specific.) As Kumar
says of her Banarasi respondents: "In their free time, they like to indulge
in *ghumna-phirna:* to stroll in the galis, wander in the bazaars, hang
around the ghats, visit temples, take in the ambience of the evening
lights, crowds, bustle, and activity. But if you ask them what they like to
do *best* in their free time, it is, to go *outside.*"[42] Or, as Raj Chandavarkar
says of the textile workers of Bombay: "Street life imparted its momen-
tum to leisure and politics as well. . . . Thus, street entertainers or the
more 'organised' tamasha players constituted the working man's theatre. The street corner offered a meeting place."[43] The bazaar or the
street expresses through its own theater the juxtaposition of pleasure
and danger that constitutes the outside or the open, unenclosed space.
The street is where one has interesting, and sometimes marvelous, en-
counters. Even when nothing out of the ordinary happens, the place is
still pregnant with possibility. And such pleasures are, by nature, trans-
gressive because they are pleasures of the inherently risky outside.

DIRT, CAPITALISM, AND THE LOGIC OF CITIZENSHIP

This analysis is admittedly partial and incomplete. To refine it, I would
need to accommodate within my argument the subtle and critical distinctions that have been made in different regions of India between, say,
the road and the bazaar. I have also ignored differences between different kinds of bazaars or between different kinds of pathways. Nor have I
paid attention to the very distinctive constructions of communal space
that the caste system, with its varied rules of purity and pollution, can
create. Studying the roles assigned in Indian villages to castes associated
with dirt would be of particular relevance in this regard. Also, the idea of
the outside would have been modified by the kinds of changes in the experience of public space that British rule created. Besides, as movements
such as "temple entry" or "breast cloth" agitations in south India in the
late nineteenth century and the early twentieth would suggest, the decline of landlords' private control over roads must have brought to many
a new sense of public space. In a fascinating analysis of Muslim reactions
to British rule in north India, for instance, Faisal Devji has recently

drawn our attention to a newly emergent sense of the public as expressed in a couplet by Ghalib:

Neither temple nor mosque, neither door nor threshold
It is the public road we are sitting on,
why should any rival dislodge us?[44]

I grant these changes. But the question of garbage has raised for me the question of the outside, and I have argued that, structurally speaking, the space that collects garbage is the one that is not subject to a single set of communal rules. It is the space that produces both malevolence and exchange between communities and, hence, needs to be tamed through the continual, and contextual, deployment of a certain dichotomy between the inside and the outside. This need to be tamed is what makes the outside exciting, albeit in unpredictable and dangerous ways.

Both the colonialists and the nationalists were repelled by what they saw as the two predominant aspects of open space in India: dirt and disorder. "The market-place," an Englishman said of the colonial Philippines, "is always dirty and disorderly."[45] This colonial perception was guided by two kinds of fear, political and medical. Politically, the bazaar was seen as a den of lies and rumors, *bazaar gup*, through which the ignorant, superstitious, and credulous Indian masses communicated their dark feelings about the doings of an alien *sarkar* (government).[46] The bazaar or the *mela* was the place where conspiracies and rebellions were plotted and carried out. It was where riots began and spectacles of blood and gore were played out before large numbers of interested eyes. Medically, as David Arnold, Veena Talwar Oldenberg, and other scholars have shown, places where Indians collected in great numbers were seen as threats to European health in India.[47] A major aim of public-health measures in colonial India was to control the spread of epidemics from fairs, bazaars, and pilgrimage centers. The theme of public order is, of course, common to both the political and the medical sides of this perception. As Foucault remarked in *The Birth of the Clinic*, "A medicine of epidemics could exist only if supplemented by a police."[48]

The nationalists' ideology was not the same as that of the raj. Their project was to convert the colonial state into a full-fledged modern state (ignoring, for the moment, the anarchist strain in Gandhi). Chaudhuri is acutely aware that, while British rule "conferred subjecthood on us," it "withheld citizenship."[49] His bourgeois sensibility is hurt at the absence of civic consciousness in Calcutta. Gandhi's, similarly, is a call for more citizen-like behavior: keeping the roads clean; turning taps off in the public interest.

Notwithstanding these important differences, both the imperialist and the nationalist reactions have one element in common. They both seek to make the bazaar, the street, the *mela*—the arenas for collective action in pre-British India—benign, regulated places, clean and healthy, incapable of producing either disease or disorder. They both present a new definition of the public, one that has often been at odds with the other forms of community that have historically come into being in these communal spaces. The British wanted to control these spaces because they were concerned about the health of the Europeans, especially of those in the British Indian army.[50] For the modern state, and, hence, for the nationalists—at least in terms of their ideals—good public health is a basic condition of existence, for there is no vigorously productive and efficient capitalism without a healthy workforce and increased longevity. And the latter, in turn, require disciplined, regulated public places.[51]

People in India, on the whole, have not heeded the nationalist call to discipline, public health, and public order. Can one read this as a refusal to become citizens of an ideal, bourgeois order? If that question is guilty of reading intentions into popular culture, let me put the problem another way. The cultural politics of transforming open spaces into public places requires a certain degree of divestment of pleasure on the part of the people. The thrills of the bazaar are traded in for the convenience of the sterile supermarket. Old pleasures are now exchanged for the new pleasures of capitalism: creature comforts, an insatiable obsession with the body and the self (the pleasures of privacy), and the mythical freedoms of citizenship.

When capitalism has not delivered these cultural goods in sufficient quantities—and Indian capitalism has not—the exchange of old pleasures for new remains an understandably limited exercise. In this situation, state action (in the arena of open space), directed at the preservation of public health or interest, will often take the form of a violent, intrusive, external force in the lives of the people. It is not coincidental that the statement of Wellesley's introduced early in this essay moved easily between the ideas of urban beauty, public health, and efficient policing in defining a street policy for colonial Calcutta. *Halla,* a colonial practice—continued by the national government—of sudden, violent police action aimed at clearing streets of hawkers and vendors (whose presence is proscribed by law), has, for years, served to illustrate this phenomenon.

It is, of course, the nationalist desire for a strong nation-state that makes certain European practices the universal rituals of public life in all countries. However, for people who, for diverse historical reasons, are yet to participate in this collective desire, this universality hardly ever has the status of a self-evident fact. The battle between their sensibility and the academic observer's is often one between the nonbourgeois peasant-citizens and those who want to inhabit a bourgeois-modern position, and, in this war, analysis is not neutral.

At the end of her book, in an impressive spirit of self-criticism that indicts the rest of the work, Nita Kumar offers a very telling story. She calls it "The Limits of Ethnosociology." I want to consider this story in bringing this essay to an end. "As my research proceeded," writes Kumar,

> I found myself understanding my informants and their world with progressive sensitivity, and paradoxically, also understanding how this world should be shunned and condemned as "lower-class" and "backward." . . . The dilemma became partly clear to me on the death of one of my favourite informants, Tara Prasad. . . . [H]e passed away of mysterious ailments, regarding which, including the exact symptoms, and even the location, whether in the chest or the stomach or the legs, his family was frustratingly vague. This was of course the same "vagueness" glorified by my informants in other contexts, and by me in subsequent reporting of these contexts. It was however clear that he had fallen victim to . . . poverty and ignorance. . . . He had been killed by the filthy galis and mohallas of Banaras; the very same which are extolled by indigenous Banarasis as beyond any considerations of stench and garbage. . . . I clearly reach the limits of ethnosociology here, for death matters to him and his family in a different way than it does to me, and I have no sympathy for their way.[52]

This is a rare moment of honesty, one in which the ethnosociologist, committed, by her training, to understanding the "natives" on their own terms and without prejudice, confronts the political responsibility of that commitment. Should such subaltern citizens have the freedom to die in their ignorance, or should we intervene with our knowledge and the police? Let us follow Kumar to the very end of her journey: "I do not care for my informants' lifestyle in the way they do. I want them to live longer, enjoy better health, earn more, beget fewer children, and, out of place as it sounds, learn of modern science. I do not know how best their culture can be encouraged to coexist with such development, but, however it does happen, a precondition will be a knowledge of this culture in itself."[53]

In this battle of the bourgeois moderns versus the subaltern citizens (those who have not imbibed a bourgeois outlook on matters of public health and personal hygiene), the violence of Kumar's dilemma reveals to us the purpose of our knowledge. It is, not to adjudicate, but to write epitaphs for the gravestones of dying and defeated concepts and practices, to help preserve them as objectified knowledge. This objectified knowledge is what Kumar calls *a knowledge of this culture in itself.* To do anything else would be untrue to our own concerns for prolonging life, the fear of death and the desire for preservation on which modernity is founded. This is why, as Rey Ileto has remarked in the context of the Philippines, "nationalist writers . . . find it impossible to interrogate the established notion that among the blessings of American colonial rule was a sanitary regime which saved countless Filipino lives."[54]

Can modern knowledge transcend this concern with prolonging lives? I suggest that it cannot but that we can at least recognize it as the (historical) condition within which we speak and ask of Kumar's dilemma, How is the subject of this quandary produced? Through what historical process of subject formation did long life, good health, more money, small families, and modern science come to appear so natural and God given?

Kumar's dilemma is too real to be trivialized. And I have no easy answers. In my younger and more citizenship-minded days, I once told a nine- or ten-year-old boy in Calcutta not to throw rubbish in the street. "Why not?" he asked, as he proceeded to throw the rubbish anyway. "I suppose you like to think that we live in England, don't you?" This essay is a troubled and overly delayed response to that defiant question.

SIX Governmental Roots of
Modern Ethnicity

There is an Indian character in *The Satanic Verses* who says (and I imagine here the "Indian" shaking of the head and a heavy upper-class Delhi accent): "Battle lines are being drawn in India today, secular versus religious, the light versus the dark. Better you choose which side you are on."[1] It is precisely this choice that I am going to refuse in this analysis. I want to explore instead some of the complex and unavoidable links that exist in Indian history between the phenomenon of ethnic conflict and the modern governing practices that the British introduced in India as the historical bearers of Enlightenment rationalism.

This is not an argument against liberal values or against the idea of modernity as such. But shadows fall between the abstract values of modernity and the historical process through which the institutions of modernization come to be built. It is true that, at this moment, there do not seem to be any *practical* alternatives to the institutions of capitalism and the modern state in India. In all our actions, we must take into account their reality, that is, their theoretical claims as well as the specific histories through which they have developed in India. But it is, nevertheless, important that we create an Archimedean point—at least *in theory*—in order to have a longer-term perspective on our problems. Today's understanding of what is practical need not constitute our philosophical horizon; if we let it do so, we submit, even inside our heads, to what already exists. The short review that I shall present here of the history of modern governmental practices in India is offered in the spirit of a dictum by a great thinker of the European Enlightenment (in reproducing it, I reverse the order of his statement): "Obey, but argue as much as you want and about what you want."

If a pristine form of liberalism (the Indian word is *secularism*) is one danger besetting the analysis of contemporary racism in India, the other danger is that of Orientalism, sometimes indistinguishable from claims that India can be understood only on Indian, or, better, Hindu, terms. The possibility that the current conflicts in India between Hindus and Muslims or between the upper and the lower castes may be, in a significant sense, a variant of the modern problem of ethnicity or race is seldom entertained in discussions in the Western media, both Hinduism and caste being seen, not altogether unreasonably, as particular to the subcontinent. Even serious and informed scholars are not immune to the tendency. Klaus Klostermaier's knowledgeable survey of Hinduism, published from New York in 1989, warns us against understanding Hindu politics on anything but Hindu terms: "Political Hinduism, I hold, cannot be understood by applying either a Western-party democratic gauge or a Marxist-socialist pattern. Its potential has much to do with the temper of Hinduism, which was able throughout the ages to rally people around causes that were perceived to be of transcendent importance and in whose pursuit ordinary human values and considerations had to be abandoned."[2]

Even when the problems are placed in an international framework, as in some passages of V. S. Naipaul's recent *India: A Million Mutinies Now*, what one gets is a patronizing pat on the back, a view of history somewhat reminiscent of what Hegel said about India in his lectures on the philosophy of history: "Hindoo political existence presents us with a people but no state." This, for Hegel, meant the worst kind of despotism and a necessary absence of history: "It is because the Hindoos have no History in the form of annals (*historia*) that they have no History in the form of transactions (*res gestae*); that is, no growth expanding into a veritable political condition."[3]

Naipaul's Hegelianism is neither conscious nor sophisticated. He simply reproduces the idea that an awakening to history is the condition for democracy. For him, therefore, all the ethnic ferment in the Indian scene is simply a sign of the youth of India's historical consciousness; with time will come the maturity that nations with an older sense of their history presumably possess: "To awaken to history is to cease to live instinctively. It was to begin to see oneself and one's group the way the outside world saw one; and it was to know a kind of rage. India was now full of this rage. There had been a general awakening. But everyone awakened first to his own group or community; every group thought itself unique in its awakening; and every group sought to separate from the rage of other groups."[4]

Within India, too, the same law of oversight rules, for racism is thought of as something that the white people do to us. What Indians do to one another is variously described as *communalism, regionalism,* and *casteism,* but never as *racism.* There are, of course, particularly Indian twists to this story, and it is also true that modern racism, properly speaking, has social-Darwinist connotations and should not be conflated with ethnic prejudice. Yet, for me, the popular word *racism* has the advantage of not making India look peculiar. A relative of mine wanting to sell a plot of land near Calcutta was recently told by the local Communist leaders that he could, indeed, sell his land, but not to Muslims. How is that any different, I would want to know, from an English landlady asking, on being told on the phone the name of a prospective tenant, "Is that a Jewish Kahn or a Pakistani Khan?" (both varieties being, to the landlady's mind at least, undesirable).

In focusing on the theme of contemporary Indian ethnic intolerance, I will argue that the experiment of nation making in India shows how modern problems of ethnicity cannot be separated from modern means of government and communication. My emphasis, in other words, will be on the way in which the development of a modern public-political life in India has called into being constructions of both Hinduism and caste that do not admit of such simple binary distinctions as Salman Rushdie's character invokes: secular/religious; liberal/fundamentalist; nationalist/ communal.

But first let me try to anticipate and forestall a few misunderstandings. It is not my intention to deny the traditions of violence that existed in India before British rule. There are recorded instances of Hindu-Muslim tensions during the precolonial period. Historians and anthropologists are agreed that the brahmanic claim to ritual supremacy was seldom accepted without challenge by other social groups, including those whom we know as the *untouchables.* Citing examples from the period between the seventh and the twelfth centuries of Hindu sects destroying Buddhist and Jaina monasteries and sometimes killing the monks, the eminent historian Romila Thapar has usefully reminded us that the "popular belief that the 'Hindus' never indulged in religious persecution" is simply untrue.[5]

This ancient history is something that I neither discuss nor deny in this essay, for my point is different. Something has fundamentally changed about both Hinduism and caste since British rule and particularly since the beginning of the twentieth century. The change can be crudely but simply described using the example of caste. We know from anthropologists and historians of the so-called caste system that there were no strong systemic rules guiding caste identity; this could be a matter of negotiation between individuals and groups. Marriage rules and rules of commensality could change within one's own lifetime or over generations, depending on factors such as social, economic, and geographic mobility. In other words, caste society operated as a nonstandardized system, and rules guiding caste transactions would have required a sensitivity to context.

Just as the British sought to give India a standardized legal system, they also attempted to fix and officialize collective identities (such as caste and religion) in the very process of creating a quasi-modern public sphere in India.[6] The concept and the institutions that make up the public sphere—a free press, voluntary associations, avenues for uncensored debate and inquiry in the public interest—are modern Europe's intellectual and practical gifts to the people whom they considered less fortunate than themselves and at whose doors they arrived as civilizing imperialists. My point is that modern problems of Hinduism and caste are inseparable from the history of this modern public life in India, which the British instituted and the nationalists preserved in what they thought were the best interests of the country.

MODERN GOVERNMENTAL PRACTICES IN INDIA: A BRIEF HISTORY

British rule in India lasted from 1757 to 1947, a little short of two hundred years. The most fundamental and far-reaching innovation that the British introduced to Indian society was, in my view, the modern state— not a nation-state, for that was what the nationalist movement created, but a modern state nevertheless. One symptom of its modernity was that its techniques of government were very closely tied to techniques of measurement. From surveys of land and crop output to prospecting for minerals, from measuring Indian brains (on behalf of the false science of phrenology) to measuring Indian bodies, diets, and life spans (thus laying the foundations of physical anthropology and modern medicine in

India), the British had the length and breadth of India, its history, culture, and society, mapped, classified, and quantified in detail that was nothing but precise even when it was wrongheaded. The most dramatic examples of this governmental concern with measurement were the decennial Indian censuses, the first of which was published in 1872. Since the British did not go to India in search of pure knowledge, all these studies were produced in the cause and in the process of governing India, and it is this pervasive marriage between government and measurement that I take as something that belongs to the deep structure of the imagination that is invested in modern political orders.[7] Without numbers, it would be impossible to practice bureaucratic or instrumental rationality.

This is not to say that premodern government had no use for numbers. The Mughals gathered statistics on produce, land, and revenue, among other things. William the Conqueror ordered the survey that resulted in the Domesday Book (1086). Historians of demography talk about ancient censuses conducted in such distant and disparate places as China, Rome (the word *census* itself being of Latin origin), and Peru. But this information was, on the whole, haphazardly collected and seldom updated with any regularity.

The systematic collection of statistics in detail and in specific categories for the purpose of ruling seems to be intimately tied to modern ideas of government. The history of the very discipline of statistics carries this tale. The word *statistic* has, etymologically speaking, the idea of statecraft built into it. The *Shorter Oxford Dictionary* tells us that, "in early use," statistics was "that branch of political science dealing with the collection, classification, and discussion of facts bearing on the condition of a state or community." Gottfried Achenwall, who, as Ian Hacking informs us, was the first to coin the word *statistics*, intended it to imply a "collection of 'remarkable facts about the state.'"[8] While the census itself is an old idea, the first modern census was, according to some scholars, taken in the United States in 1790 and the first British census in 1801. The Indian censuses were not to appear until late in the nineteenth century, but the East India Company caused quite a few regional censuses to be taken before that period.

Measurement is central to our modern ideas about fairness and justice and how we administer them—in short, to the very idea of good government. Foucault has emphasized in several places—especially in his essay on "governmentality"—how this has been critically dependent on "the emergence of the problem of population" in the eighteenth century and, therefore, connected to the development of the other important science of the same period, that of economics.[9] Benthamite attempts to use law for social engineering—the idea, for instance, that punishment should be in proportion to the crime committed or the utilitarian aim of devising a society that maximizes the pleasure of the maximum number of people—all speak a language borrowed from mathematics and the natural sciences (not surprisingly, given the connection between Enlightenment rationalism and scientific paradigms). The 1790 American census had to do with the idea of proportionality in the sphere of political representation. Ideas of *correspondence, proportionality,* and so on mark Rousseau's thoughts on equality. Without them, and without the numbers that they produced, the equal-opportunity legislation of our own period would be unworkable. A generalized accounting mind-set is what seems to inhabit modernity.

As the representatives and the inheritors of the European Enlightenment, the British brought these ideas to India. It is, in fact, one of the ironies of British history that the British became political liberals at home at the same time as they became imperialists abroad. British policy in India was forever haunted by this contradiction. While the British would not grant India full self-government until 1947, they were often concerned about being fair to the different competing sections that, in their view, made up Indian society, sections that they had identified early on on the basis of religion and caste. A count made of the population of Bombay in 1780, for instance, divided the population into "socio-religious communities."[10] In the eighteenth century, British amateur historians often portrayed India as a society weakened by its internal religious and caste divisions, an understanding shared later on by Indian nationalists themselves.

Understandably, then, categories of caste and religion dominated the censuses that the British undertook in India. At every census, people were asked to state their religion and caste—in marked contrast, as the American historian Kenneth Jones has pointed out, to what the British did at home. Religion, says Jones, was never an important category in the censuses conducted in Britain during the period between 1801 and 1931. Only once, in 1851, were the British asked about religious affiliation, and answering the question was optional.[11] Counting Hindus, Muslims, Sikhs, and untouchables, then, became a critical political exercise, particularly in the twentieth century, as the British began to include Indian representatives in the country's legislative bodies in very measured doses.

What made the census operations critical was that, in trying to be fair referees, the British made the process of political representation "communal": seats in the legislative assemblies were earmarked for different communities according to ideas of proportionality. Nationalists like Nehru and Gandhi abhorred this process and the ideology that governed it, namely, *communalism,* a word that still leads a stigmatized existence in India and works as a surrogate for *racism.*[12] They pointed out, with some justice, that it was invidious to treat untouchables as a community separate from the Hindus.

A language-based definition of political communities would have seemed more natural to them, but post-Independence Indian history has shown that language is no surer a guide to ethnic identity and inter-ethnic peace than is religion. Heads have, since the 1950s, been regularly broken in the subcontinent over linguistic issues, the liberation war of Bangladesh in 1971 being only a dramatic example of the process. Political leaders of the Muslims and the untouchables, on the other hand, felt much happier going along with the British-devised arrangements until the final decade before Independence and Partition. Of particular importance in the Indian story is the category *scheduled caste*— which the British coined in 1936 (and the government of India has retained)—so called because it referred to a schedule of particularly disadvantaged castes that was drawn up for "the purpose of giving effect to the provisions of special electoral representation in the Government of India Act, 1935."[13] It represents a pioneering attempt at affirmative action.

Historians and political scientists studying modern India have recently made several attempts to understand what happened to ethnic identities through this process of a quasi-modern, albeit colonial, state instituting, through modern means of measurement, a structure of political representation tied to notions of proportionality. What, in other words, did the census do to identities? Historians and anthropologists of colonial India have reported a social process akin to what Ian Hacking calls *dynamic nominalism:* people came to fit the categories that the colonial authorities had fashioned for them. Hacking explains dynamic nominalism thus:

> You will recall that a traditional nominalist says that stars (or algae or justice) have nothing in common except our names ("stars," "algae," "justice"). The traditional realist in contrast finds it amazing that the world could so kindly sort itself into our categories. He protests that there are definite sorts of objects in it . . . which we have painstakingly come to recognise and classify correctly. The robust realist does not have to argue very hard that people also come sorted. . . . A different kind of nominalism—I call it dynamic nominalism—attracts my realist self, spurred on by theories about the making of the homosexual and the heterosexual as kinds

of persons or by my observations about official statistics. The claim of dynamic nominalism is not that there was a kind of person who came increasingly to be recognized by bureaucrats or by students of human nature but rather that a kind of person came into being at the same time as the kind itself was being invented. In some cases, that is, our classifications and our classes conspire to emerge hand in hand, each egging the other on.[14]

The Indian political scientist Sudipta Kaviraj has pursued a similar argument with regard to the history of "communities" in pre-British and British India. In pre-British India, says Kaviraj, communities had "fuzzy" boundaries; in British India, they became "enumerated."[15] By *fuzzy*, Kaviraj means vague boundaries that do not admit of discrete, either/or divisions. Census or official enumerations, however, give us discrete kinds of identities even if particular identities change, as, indeed, they often do, over time. For the purpose of affirmative action, a scheduled-caste person is a scheduled-caste person is a scheduled-caste person.

The distinction that Kaviraj draws is parallel to one that Hacking draws in his attempt to find a path somewhere between the epistemological obstinacies of the nominalist and the realist positions: "It will be foolhardy . . . to have an opinion about one of the stable human dichotomies, male and female. But very roughly, the robust realist will agree that there may be what really are physiological borderline cases, once called 'hermaphrodites.' The existence of vague boundaries is normal: most of us are neither tall nor short, fat nor thin. Sexual physiology [i.e., the categorical structure of sexual physiology] is unusually abrupt in its divisions."[16]

The kernel of Kaviraj's argument is that the post-Enlightenment governing practices that the British introduced in India and that entailed counting collective identities in an all-or-nothing manner enabled people to see and organize themselves in the light of these categories. I shall quote here at some length Kaviraj's own gloss on these terms as all my knowledge of Indian history as well as my lived experience of India compel me to agree with him. Kaviraj writes:

> Communities were fuzzy in two senses. Rarely, if ever, would people belong to a community which would claim to represent or exhaust all the layers of their complex selfhood. Individuals on suitable occasions could describe themselves as *vaisnavas*, Bengalis or more likely *Rarhis, Kayasthas*, villagers and so on; and clearly although all these could on appropriate occasions be called their *samaj* [society/community] . . . their boundaries would not coincide. . . . [Their identity] would be fuzzy in a second sense as well.

To say their community is fuzzy is not to say it is imprecise. On the appropriate occasion, every individual would use his cognitive apparatus to classify any single person he interacts with and place him quite exactly, and decide if he could eat with him, go on a journey, or arrange a marriage into his family. It was therefore practically precise, and adequate to the scale of social action. But it would not occur to an individual to ask how many of them there were in the world, and what if they decided to act in concert.[17]

I would like to modify Kaviraj's incisive analysis in one respect, however. The movement from fuzzy to enumerated communities did not represent a complete change of consciousness. In their everyday lives, in negotiating the spheres of friendship and kinship, say, Indians, like human beings everywhere, are comfortable with the indeterminacies of ethnic identities and share none of the tenacity with which social scientists and governments hang on to the labels that inform their sense of both analysis and action. Yet the very existence of administrative categories of ethnicity—whether one is looking at the international level or at developments within a country—suggests a modern, public career for ethnic tags, a national identity being its highest form. It is, of course, within this sphere that the identity of being Indian or Hindu or Muslim or scheduled caste takes on a new political meaning. This meaning resides alongside, and is interlaced with, the more fuzzy sense of community.

The late-nineteenth-century censuses and other similar institutions, then, reconstituted the meaning of *community* or *ethnicity* and gave Indians three important political messages, all of which are entirely compatible with liberal political philosophy as we know it. These messages were (1) that communities can be enumerated and that in numbers lies political clout; (2) that the social and economic progress of a community can be measured, in the case of Indian censuses, in terms of share in public life (education, the professions, employment, etc.); and (3) that this enables governments and communities to devise objective tests for the relative backwardness or otherwise of a community.

Indians were quick to learn the art of participation in this public sphere. They learned, as we all do when we want to take advantage of equal-opportunity legislation, that modern governments have limited intelligence and that their principles of distributive justice require simple, homogeneous, sharply delineated identities, the kinds that passports bear. While identities can proliferate and have a tendency to do so under the pressure of the politics of democratic representation, the sense of multiple identities that propels individuals in their everyday-ness is too complex for the rules that govern the logic of representation in modern public life, where identities, however numerous and internally differentiated they may be, must each remain distinct and discrete in the competitive race for goods and services that the state and civil society may offer. It is this pressure, which is essentially the pressure that modern political orders produce, that led many Indian leaders to profess simplistic, homogeneous ethnic identities in public life, disregarding all the heterogeneity and diversity of Indian social practices. These were categories by which few leaders actually lived their private lives.

When we look back now at India in the 1870s and 1880s, it becomes clear that the era of modern, competitive, governmentally defined ethnic identities familiar to us in liberal democracies had already arrived. The peculiarity of colonial Indian history lay in the fact that these identities were based on religious categories because of a certain degree of reification of these categories by the British. (But, even if the British had picked language as a mark of distinction in this multilingual country, the result would have been the same.) By the 1890s, Hindu and Muslim leaders were quoting census figures at each other to prove whether they had received their legitimate share of benefits (such as employment and education) from British rule. The rise of modern caste consciousness shows a similar concern for the measurement of "progress" in public life. The famous anti-Brahman "manifesto," produced in Madras in 1916 by members of the non-Brahman caste in forming a new political party, owed its rhetorical force to the statistics that the government had collected to demonstrate a Brahman monopoly of the civil service.[18]

Demography was pressed into the service of such ethnic jealousies between Hindus and Muslims or between castes by several authors who used the censuses to make their points. One example of this process, discussed by Kenneth Jones, is a set of articles published by a Bengali author, U. N. Mukherji, in 1909 (a time in Indian history when the Muslims were being given reserved seats in the legislature by the British). In this series, entitled "A Dying Race," Mukherji used the census data from the period 1872–1901 to demonstrate, to the satisfaction of many Hindus, "that within a given number of years all Hindus would disappear from British India." In doing this, writes Jones, Mukherji "was actually following the lead of M. J. C. O'Donnell, Census Commissioner of Bengal for 1891, who had calculated 'the number of years it would take the Hindus to altogether disappear from Bengal if Muhammadan increase went on at the rate it was doing.'"[19]

Let us put aside for the moment what to our ears may sound racist in these remarks. My point is that the social assumptions on which the classification and organization of census figures rested were fundamentally modern: they showed India to be a collection of communities whose progress or backwardness could be measured by the application of some supposedly universal indices. That is exactly how the modern world of nation-states is structured: it is a united but internally hierarchized world where some countries are described as measurably—or should I say im-measurably?—more advanced than others. This structure of relations has the nature of what scientists call *fractals* or self-similar patterns: it is capable of reproducing itself at many different levels—between nations, between modern ethnic groups, between perceived races, and so on. It is what constitutes the liberal idea of competitive pluralism. As the French historian Lucien Febvre once reminded us, as an idea it has been with us since the second half of the eighteenth century.[20] It was packed into the idea of *civilization,* a word that the French started to use in the 1760s and that soon found its way into the English language to provide the no-blest justification for England's work in India.

The word *civilization* has long since fallen out of favor—we preferred to talk about *progress* in the nineteenth century and *development* in the twentieth—but the idea of a united world with an internally articulated hierarchy measurable by some universally agreed on indices has remained with us. How strongly the Indian middle classes internalized this idea is suggested by the following quotation from a Bengali book of morals that was published in Calcutta about 140 years ago for consumption by children. Notice how the world is seen as both one and hierarchic, the observable differences in standards of living between countries being—to make a conscious gesture toward the idea of measurement—propor-tional to their "total national efforts": "Countries where people are averse to labor . . . are uncivilized. The Aboriginals of America and Aus-tralia as well as the Negroes are still in this state. They live in great hard-ship without adequate food and clothes, and they do not save anything for bad times. . . . The Germans, the Swiss, the French, the Dutch, and the English are the most industrious nations/races [*jati*] of the world. That is why they enjoy the best circumstances among all nations."[21]

Use of such language today would be offensive, but there is a homol-ogy between what this children's primer said and the sensibility that makes of the modern industrialized nations a model for the rest of the world to follow. We all partake of this sensibility, and I am no exception. All I am saying is that this sensibility, what we hold to be common sense with respect to these matters, is undergirded by the mechanisms of the modern state and the universal requirements of governmentality, the same mechanisms that influence our constructions of competitive blocs of ethnicity in the public sphere. Hindus, Muslims, the scheduled and lower castes of India, both during and after British rule, have, in a sense, done no more than apply this sensibility to their public, political lives.

ETHNICITY AND / OR THE NATION: AN IRONIC PERSPECTIVE

But, of course, they have done more than that. Were India simply a place where ethnicity is contained within the liberal structure of competitive pluralism, it would not have made news, and I would not be discussing it today. Ethnic strife in India has resulted in the deaths of hundreds of thousands in the past hundred years. Recent skirmishes in Assam, Punjab, and Kashmir have been particularly deadly. What, then, is the difference between the recent Western and the contemporary Indian experience of ethnicity?

What the difference is came to me forcefully in 1989 when I received a (form) letter from the Australian prime minister encouraging me to become an Australian citizen. In that letter, the prime minister went to some trouble to spell out what it means to be an Australian. It is not the color of your skin, or your religion, or the language that you speak that makes you an Australian, he said. It is believing in freedom of speech, in freedom of association, in everyone having "a fair go," etc. This letter prompted me to subject myself to some imaginary tortures—of the Geoffrey Robertson kind.[22] For example, I asked myself, If this is all there is to being an Australian, then what would be my proper patriotic response if Australia ever went to war with a nation that professed the same liberal values but was much better equipped to protect them and, hence, by definition, to protect my Australianness as well? (Of course, a Margaret Thatcher would argue that a liberal-democratic country would never start a war and that the question is, therefore, moot!)

A little reflection made it clear that the prime minister was speaking in a historical context that afforded him one rare luxury: he felt no pressure to spell out what made Australians different from other people. The letter was, by implication, relegating cultural difference to the sphere of the personal. If pressed, a liberal would no doubt tell me that—as the British Muslims who burned *The Satanic Verses* at Bradford were often reminded—ethnicity can find a place in public life so long as its expression is in conformity with the core values of the nation (as defined by the state). Ethnicity functions here under the aegis of equal-opportunity principles, in the form of a pressure group—in my case, an Indian Association that demands things like time slots on Australian public radio or funding for community schools as part of liberal-pluralist multiculturalism.

As Talal Asad has shown in his discussion of the Rushdie affair, there are hidden demographic assumptions behind this position, particularly that of a continuous dominance of a European-derived, if not an English-speaking, majority.[23] Of course, one must also take into account particular Australian institutions—the welfare state, a relatively prosperous economy, the structure of the Australian Labor Party, the official policy of multiculturalism, etc.—that have historically played a role in managing ethnic conflict in public life. That Australia would be able to retain this multicultural tolerance of ethnicity in public life if the cultural dominance of its Anglo-Celtic or at least European majority were ever seriously threatened is far from certain.

Modern ethnic consciousnesses in India have been fashioned under circumstances in which the politics of cultural difference has been of preeminent value. The question of Indian unity has never been settled beyond doubt or disputation, nor has there been any one, culturally homogeneous and dominant majority ethnic group that could both dominate and effectively claim to represent all Indians (at least until Independence—one might argue that the Hindu extremist party, the Bharatiya Janata Party [the BJP], has been trying to develop such a position for itself, precisely by denying the heterogeneity that characterizes Hinduism). The British cobbled a political India together for reasons of administrative convenience. The nationality question was muddled from the beginning. In the public sphere that the British created, there was no one, universally agreed on "Indian" ethnicity. The struggle to produce a sense of cultural unity against the British made mainstream Indian nationalism culturally Hindu. The Muslim search for Pakistan emphasized Islam. The lower castes' struggle for social justice produced anti-Brahmanism. After Independence, in the 1950s and the 1960s, there were the tribal communities of the Nagas and the Mizos on the northeastern frontier of the country that had to be bludgeoned into becoming Indian.

The past fifteen or twenty years have seen an explosive combination of democracy and demography. The Indian population has almost trebled since Independence. The growth and diversity of the middle class may be judged from the fact that, while at Independence there was consensus that the number of important languages was fourteen, there are now daily newspapers published in more than seventy-eight languages.[24] This middle class has tasted consumerism, and the result has been an increased sense of competition in urban life. The secessionist movements in Kashmir and parts of the northeast have gained in strength in recent years. Caste—particularly the Indian policy of positive discrimination in favor of the lower castes—has often been an extremely contentious issue in public life. And the latest attempts by the extremist Hindu political parties to convert Hinduism into a strong, monolithic, and militant religion have given many Indian Muslims and Christians understandable pause.

Like the former Soviet Union, India remains in part, although only in part, an imperial structure held together by strong tendencies toward centralism. Unlike the former Soviet Union, however, those centralist tendencies exist within, and must work through, a democratic political structure that also gives the state more popular legitimacy and unity than the Stalinist states ever had. Indians have an investment in electoral democracy, as was proved by the acute popular resentment of the Emergency declared by Mrs. Gandhi during the period 1975–77. Yet the ideological scene has changed.

This centralizing tendency was most powerfully expressed in the ideology of Jawaharlal Nehru, which represented some kind of consensus among the political elite. This ideology, called in India *secularism,* drew heavily on the Western liberal heritage to argue for a separation between religion and the ideas that governed public life. In India, where a religious idiom and imagination had always been very strongly present, this ideology never described the actual culture of political practice. But, so long as the national leadership lay in the hands of a tiny elite reared in and respectful of the British traditions of politics, the everyday religiousness of Indian political culture could be kept separate from the decision-making boards of the government. The custodial nature of this elite was reflected in the unity of the Congress Party, in which Nehru always remained a Bonapartist figure.

The combination of demography, democracy, and political growth in India has ensured that the political elite is no longer tiny. There are no Bonapartist figures in India today. Nehruvian secularism, a close cousin of Western liberalism represented now by Marxists and the Left-liberals in India, is on the defensive (remember Salman Rushdie's character talking about the battle lines?).

Why this has happened will require a different analysis. But it should be clear from the preceding discussion that the problem of competitive and official constructions of ethnicity is a feature inherent in modern civil society. In the best of times, one expects to find lawful, bureaucratic means of resolving these tensions. Even then, the mobilization of ethnic sentiments always risks spilling over into racism in public places, as widely reported incidents of harassment of the Australian Muslims during the Gulf War would confirm. There are, however, other times in history when bureaucratic solutions lose their appeal. The difference here is not due to a total opposition between fascism and liberalism as political philosophies. The difference here is in historical context. Imagine the conflict between the Bengali Muslim sense of ethnicity and Pakistani nationalism in what was, before 1971, East Pakistan. Clearly, a model of pluralism that recommended that all signs of cultural difference be matters of private belief became untenable in that situation. Kashmir today represents, for many, a similar situation.

The point is that, as I have argued, the very structure of modern governmentality carries with it the seeds of competitive constructions of ethnicity. Whether those seeds will ever germinate and bloody conflict spring forth is a matter of the particular moment of history that one inhabits. This is not a counsel of despair. But it is a plea for our political analysis to be informed by a larger sense of irony.

Advocating the cultivation of a sense of irony about the civilizing narratives of modernity does not imply political passivity. The relation between philosophical positions and political action is seldom straightforward. Not only is there no alternative to action—we are condemned to act politically in this world whether we want to or not—but the subject who acts, and is mobilized to act in the face of events, is also more than an intellectual-philosophical subject. Action involves emotions, memories, tastes, feelings, will, and values—and these things have histories over which we have much less control than we have over our consciously thought out philosophical positions. I have been irreversibly conditioned by the histories of my childhood, my education, and my socialization (all influenced by British and nationalist critiques of Indian society) to be revolted by such practices as sati, female infanticide, human sacrifice, and *thagi*—to use the names by which British colonial discourse described (always inaccurately) and condemned Indian (yet another name) civilization—whatever my theoretical understanding today of their problematic histories. How, in what mode of action, this revulsion will express itself depends on particular situations and the opportunities that I read them as presenting.

What, then, is the relation between this critique and political or state policies that might be established to combat racism under conditions of modernization? First, this critique is about the limits of policy making under present institutional arrangements. I have argued that, given the connection between governmentality and measurement, both the modern nation-state and civil society necessarily set up certain competitive structures of identity through the very distributive processes over which they preside. The question, Distribution among whom? always takes identities for granted. Identities here are not seen as porous. In fact, identities are not measurable or enumerable except on the assumption that their boundaries are abrupt and not vague. In the language of distributive justice, identities represent, at any one point of time, some kind of narrative consensus in which everybody or every group knows who or what they are and this knowledge is shared by the institution that administers well-being.

In other words, the existing models of modern political and economic institutions handle the question of cultural difference in identity precisely by fixing and freezing differences into divisions that are not permeable (a Hindu cannot be a Muslim) and thus are amenable to measurement and enumeration. Even if we moved from the idea of allocative justice to that of procedural justice in the sphere of distribution, as John Rawls did in his classic *A Theory of Justice,* we would still have no way of handling differences in identities. Rawls's search for "justice as fairness," as readers of that famous text will know, led him to posit an "original position" (a perspectival position, really, as he himself explains) in which individuals met without any conception of their social or class locations—that is to say, as humans from whom all differences had been abstracted away.[25]

Even leftist intellectuals who try to modify Rawls's arguments in order to infuse a more self-consciously political life into his theory find it difficult not to universalize a distinction that is historically very particular, that is, the distinction between *public* and *private.* Chantal Mouffe's attempt to move away from the Rawlsian position of holding on to the idea of an original rational agreement and, instead, to ground democracy in a permanent state of disputation (since there can no longer be a "single idea of a substantial common good") is instructive in this regard. Pluralism here is seen as possible on the condition that the political is defined around a minimum shared agreement, that "the principles of the liberal-democratic regime *qua* political association"—"equality and liberty"—be defined as the "common political good." As Mouffe clarifies: "A liberal-democratic regime, if it must be agnostic in terms of morality and religion, cannot be agnostic concerning political values since by definition it asserts the principles that constitute its specificity *qua* political association, i.e., the political principles of equality and liberty."[26]

Where, then, will be the place for morality and religion in this (post)modern, socialist idea of liberal-democratic politics, one that accepts disputation as a foundation for democracy—or, indeed, for anything else that is not part of this minimum shared political good? Mouffe is clear on this: these ideas will exist as "private" belief, the sphere of privacy implicitly defined in such a way as to be incapable, by its very definition, of endangering the institutions that embody "the political principles of equality and liberty."[27]

What else can an intellectual thinking out of Indian history do but experience a sense of irony at what European political theory offers us?

On the one hand, there are the actually existing institutions that administer our lives both in India and outside. The very administration of (ethnic) identities by the actually existing civil-political institutions needs, as I have shown, the same fixed, discrete categories that racists of all colors use. The only difference is in idiom—bureaucracies use a certain impersonal, unemotional language, while racist mobilization in public life involves an explicit use of emotions as well—but this difference is superficial and depends on historical context. Governments will, in moments of crisis, use both.

On the other hand, whether arguing from a purely liberal position of a Rawls or a postmodernist, socialist position of a Mouffe, critics of these institutions cannot but resurrect the model of a human being who holds on to a cultural distinction between the public and the private as a condition for tolerance and pluralism. But is this distinction universal? Is it universal even in the West? Does *political emancipation* (I borrow the expression from the young Marx's essay "On the Jewish Question") require us to universalize the experience and skills of a particular group in modern European history? *Must* we all become humans who are able to objectify their relation to the supernatural, the divine, or the netherworld into stateable beliefs and who are able to categorize these beliefs as private?

The politics of being human differ between and within cultures. We are not impervious to one another, but that does not mean that the differences are not real. Some people in India possess the modern sense of privacy as it has developed in the history of the middle classes in the West. Many do not. The importance of kinship in Indian society suggests other paths of social change. If we swallowed a theory—hook, line, and sinker—that made tolerance and pluralism contingent on the idea of private belief, we would only move further away from our social realities than Rawls does from his by his theoretical maneuvering.

The writing of Indian history, then, must subscribe to two struggles. One is to document and interpret for contemporary needs the different practices of toleration and pluralism that already exist in Indian society, practices that are not critically dependent on the universalization of the distinction public/private. The other is to help develop critiques of already-existing institutions and the theoretical assumptions that lay behind them, for the struggle against the murderous and self-proclaimed Hindus of today must, in the long run, also be a struggle for new kinds of political and economic institutions for the management of public life—institutions that do not require for their everyday operation the fiction of cultural identities with fixed, enumerable, and abrupt boundaries. Nobody has the blueprints for such institutions, although we do know that two of the finest products of the Indo-British cultural encounter of the nineteenth century, Gandhi and Tagore, experimented with both facets of this struggle at different moments of their lives. If cultural and other kinds of differences are to be taken and negotiated seriously, then we also need institutions that can handle the fuzzy logic with which identities are built. The existing institutions in charge of producing and administering prosperity do not do that.

PART THREE

THE ETHICAL AND THE IN-HUMAN

SEVEN The Subject of Law and the Subject of Narratives

It is a problem of political thought that I want to confront in this essay. I use *confront* because the word carries the dual meanings of "being opposite to" and of "being face-to-face with." I want to test certain critiques of citizenship/rights/the state that some of us have been developing by bringing this spirit of opposition to the state/law/citizenship face-to-face with narratives and representations of cruelty/suffering to which most academics in the humanities would react precisely with citizenly outrage (recall Alasdair Macintyre's description of *indignation* as a very modern sentiment).[1]

The cruelty that I want to discuss is that often inflicted on Hindu widows of Bengali *bhadralok* families (*bhadralok* refers to respectable people of the middle classes). I could have chosen some other group (e.g., domestic servants) cruelty toward whom is often a licensed activity among the more privileged classes of India. But the widow in the *bhadralok* household is a figure of which, having grown up in a middle-class Bengali family, I have some personal—albeit, as a man, second-order—knowledge, and I can, therefore, bring my position as analyst into dialogue with my position as native informant.

There are, from my point of view, certain analytic advantages in making these moves. I personally react, as I expect my readers will, to these harrowing descriptions of oppression with a mixture of emotions: sadness and horror (that the familial and familiar structures of pleasure could harbor within them such everyday possibilities of cruelty) mixed with anger (I want to punish the oppressors; I think of the police, the law, the state!). Together with these emotions arise a desire and the will to intervene and do something (even if that something is only to produce a critique of the family as I know it). The state and the question of the law, thus, figure as part of my affect and desire. How do I square this reaction with my knowledge of the violence on which the nation-state and its laws are founded, the violence of the same modernity that teaches us to think of the law as the key instrument of social justice? (I realize that some people would argue that it is not the same modernity in every case, that there can be good and bad modernities. I am skeptical of these arguments, but let me leave it at this for the time being.)

Confront seems to be the right term. I recognize that my citizenly outrage on confronting Bengali widows' oppression has something in common with the reactions of nineteenth-century Bengali reformers like Rammohun Roy and Iswarchandra Vidyasagar—and their fellow travelers in other parts of the country, M. G. Ranade, B. M. Malabari, Viresalingam Pantalu, and G. Subramania Aiyer—who were moved, as the story goes, by the plight of the widows to act on the question and whose actions, endlessly retold in school histories, helped mold me in the cast of the citizen of a modernizing nation-state. I am modern in thinking that the answer to cruelty in family life is in rights, in law, and, therefore, eventually, in the legitimate violence of the state. What set the nineteenth-century reforms apart from anything that might have happened before the British ruled India was their protocitizenly character, for the instrument that these reformers used in their effort to stop this oppression was the colonial state and its power to legislate.

The state, however, is only part of the story. In Bengali public narratives of social reform, people like Rammohun or Vidyasagar are said to have confronted this cruelty in another sense, that is, not only in the sense of being hostile to it, but also in the sense of coming face-to-face with it, in knowing it with some degree of intimacy. Available accounts tell us of their coming across instances of cruelty within the world that they personally and concretely knew. Their recourse to an abstract and transcendent law was rooted in concrete emotions that sprang directly from their sense of personal involvement with someone who was a victim of domestic violence and/or cruelty.

Rammohun's revulsion toward the idea of sati (widow burning), we are told, first arose when he learned of a close female relative being forced to this fate by the men of the household: "The custom of burning widows with their husbands first roused his horror before he was much known. While he was at Rangpur in 1811, his brother Jugmohun died, when one of his widowed wives was burnt alive with him. Rammohun held this lady in high esteem, and the news of her cruel death gave such a shock to his feelings that [tradition has it] he took a vow never to rest till this inhuman custom was abolished."[2]

This seeing of the concrete is what I call being *face-to-face* here. Vidyasagar is legendary for the way in which he would allegedly cry at the sight of young or child widows. In the words of one of his biographers:

> Vidyasagar's naturally gentle and compassionate heart was moved at the sight of the tender-aged, young widows suffering rigorous hardships, and he firmly resolved to devote his life to the cause of the remarriage of these widows. . . .
>
> This resolution had sat deeprooted in his mind from his early years. It is said that Vidyasagar had a girl play-mate at Birsingha. He was very fond of her. After he had been separated from her, and had come down to Calcutta for education, she was married at an early age, but, in a short time, her husband died, and she was a widow. When Vidyasagar next went home during one of his college-vacations, he was deeply sorry to hear that his dear play-mate had been married and had lost her husband. He immediately called at her house to see her, and there learnt that she had not eaten anything that day, because it was the eleventh day of the moon (which is a day of fasting for Hindu widows). He felt so much commiseration for the little girl that he, there and then, resolved that he would give his life to relieve the sufferings of widows. He was at that time only 13 or 14 years old.[3]

In both Rammohun's and Vidyasagar's cases, then—at least in the Bengali recounting of their lives—this flow of compassion and up-welling of horror combined with their determination to get the colonial government to pass laws that they both thought would be the answer to the problem. (That they then mobilized *shastric* [scriptural] arguments is something that I do not discuss, for the problem thus raised—that of constructing tradition for a modern India—has been raised elsewhere.)[4]

One must separate the capacity for compassion, that is, the capacity to be horrified by cruelty and to be moved to action, from the historically particular solution of the law. We know that this capacity existed in India; contrary to some eighteenth-century European observers, the

Enlightenment had no monopoly on the idea of cruelty. The attempts of Akbar and other Muslim rulers to stop sati are well-known. There is also indirect but obvious evidence in the fact that most widows did not have to become satis. Similarly, we know of attempts before Vidyasagar's to get young widows remarried. It cannot, therefore, be argued that people had to wait for the coming of either the British or Western/modern ideas of cruelty in order to attain the capacity to be revolted by torture and oppression.

We should note, however, that Rammohun and Vidyasagar proposed significantly different solutions. Rammohun sought the solution in property (his position being that, if widows were given the right of inheritance, people would treat them fairly), Vidyasagar in remarriage (his position being that widows should be given a renewed claim on the male power of protection). Another way in which to view the difference is that Rammohun sought a proscriptive law (banning sati), Vidyasagar a permissive law (allowing remarriage).

Two types of history are being enacted here. First is the history of modernity, of the public sphere, of modern ideas of cruelty, which is encapsulated in the move toward legislation. Then there are the histories embodied in the feelings of compassion that Rammohun or Vidyasagar felt when personally confronted with the horrors of Bengali widowhood. These other histories are what they, or I, would share with others before and after them who felt horrified by torture but did not necessarily think of the law or rights as the remedy. I am not fixing for eternity these structures of feeling, nor do I want to equate law with history by suggesting that the nineteenth-century legal reforms represent a sharp divide in the history of our familial emotions, separating some "medieval" callousness from a "modern" sensitivity. I am simply applying something like a process of elimination. First there were pre-British histories and structures that were perfectly capable of producing compassion in people. What comes after the British is a specific connection between such sentiments and the more citizenly dispositions (including the desire to legislate). I want to isolate the two groups of histories to raise—but not necessarily solve—a problem about representation and political intervention.

In raising this problem, I use women's testimony rather than men's. What men—Rammohun or Vidyasagar—wrote was already addressed to the law. They provided the language in which the state could hear and understand, as well as intervene in, the expression of suffering. What women, on the other hand, wrote, is not always addressed to the state. It is true that testimony from the widows themselves does not in any way guarantee unmediated access to their experience of oppression. Deconstructionists have argued for a long time that voice is no indicator of direct presence. But the very act of listening to people orients us—opens us up—to their presence, however elusive the matter of *presence* may be from a philosophical point of view. This orientation is what I have called here the act of confronting suffering, of *facing*. Writing couched in the legal and universal language of rights and citizenship erases the history in which acts of facing the sufferer, confronting the scene of oppression, occur. Yet, without such a process of confrontation of oppression, the idea of the rights-bearing citizen cannot become a reality. I turn toward widows' own testimony in order to see how these testimonies were produced and collected in a specific period in Bengali history so that the widow could one day be subsumed into the figure of the citizen. For there to be an effective history of citizenship, the gesture of facing the particular, I argue, must supplement the fixed and universal gaze of the law. The recording of widows' voices—by publishers, readers, critics, investigators—allows us to see the many different social spaces from which the citizen-subject of modernity emerges in this particular history.

LISTENING FOR VOICES

While widows were and are part of the everyday experience of Bengali kinship and were made the subject of legal-social reform and fictional writing by progressive thinkers of the last century, there are very few generally available testimonies from the widows themselves. I discuss here a small number of cases—those of Saradasundari Devi (1819–1907) and Nistarini Devi (1832/33–1916), both of whom left autobiographies, as well as some others reported in Kalyani Datta's "Baidhyabya kahini" (Tales of widowhood), which consists of a few brief and anecdotal life histories collected in the 1950s and 1960s.[5]

There is, of course, no question of this small sample being in any statistical sense representative. Nor do I want to suggest that the sad stories discussed here would have been true of every Bengali widow. Widowhood has long been glorified in the patriarchal myths of Hindu Bengali middle-class culture as a path of extreme self-renunciation, and many widows have earned unquestionable familial authority precisely by subjecting themselves to the prescribed regimes (Rammohun Roy's mother herself being a well-known example). The nature of Bengali domesticity has also changed (influenced by such factors as women's education and entry into public life, the subsequent decline in the number of child brides, and the advent of the institution of the love match, among other things), a fact of which these cases and my analysis here do not take adequate account.

Yet there is no question that widowhood exposes women to some real vulnerability in a patriarchal, patrilocal system of kinship where they remain, until their sons marry and they achieve the status of mother-in-law, symbolic outsiders to the bonds of brotherhood that they enter as wives. Widowhood marks an absolute state of inauspiciousness in a woman (who has brought death to a member of the brotherhood). Potentially malevolent, she is considered to be an outsider who can be redeemed only by the lifelong performance of rituals of extreme atonement. This is particularly true of a widow who has no son to protect her. While the rituals of widowhood are glorified in the scriptures and in much of Indian literature as self-renunciation, and while they may, indeed, in many cases, express, on the part of the woman, a capacity for self-abnegation, the stories recounted here reveal the torture, oppression, and cruelty that often, if not always, accompanies the experience of widowhood. As a Bengali widow herself said: "A woman who has lost her father, mother, husband, and son has nobody else left in the world. It is only if others in the household are kind that a widow's life can be happy. Otherwise, it is like being consigned to a hell pit."[6]

Fundamentally, whatever their theological significance, the rituals of Hindu Bengali widowhood are aimed at achieving one effect: the denial (or renunciation) on the part of the widow of enjoyment or pleasure, whether material, physical, or emotional. The most obvious expressions of these rituals are remaining celibate, not eating meat, fasting frequently, and marking the body (by, e.g., not wearing jewelry, shaving one's head or wearing one's hair cropped, and wearing white saris with no, or just a black, border).

A graphic case of a woman robbed of her possessions is that of Indumati (born ca. 1872), a young widow of a zamindar (landlord) family who decided to live in Banaras on a monthly allowance from the estate and was cheated out of her inheritance. In Indumati's words (the accuracy of Kalyani Datta's reportage is not really an issue):

> I gathered that my monthly allowance was Rs 250. But the manager of the estate put only Rs 50 in my hand, saying that Rs 200 were being credited to my account in his office every month. . . . Six months had barely elapsed when my allowance began to shrink. Too many lawsuits [he pleaded], too much revenue unrealized. At last I defaulted on the house rent. The monthly allowance kept shrinking . . . until it reached the figure of Rs 10. I left the large room I had been renting for a room that cost Re 1. . . . In the early days I was highly conscious of the danger of pollution. I used to go about all twenty-four hours in a *tassar* sari, wearing rosary

beads, and carrying my [own] *kamandulu* [sacred water pot]. . . .
Now I eat at almshouses . . . [and] accept invitations from any-
one.[7]

The deprivation caused by the denial of pleasurable food is captured
in the testimony of one Gyanadasundari, whom Datta met sometime in
1965. A child widow who had, in fact, never met her husband, she was
sent to her in-laws to spend the rest of her life as a widow. "I entered the
kitchen," she says, speaking of her daily round of activities,

immediately after my morning bath [to cook for] this large family.
By the time I was finished, it would be late afternoon. A room full
of cooked food—I cannot describe how hungry the smell of rice
and curry made me feel. Sometimes I felt tempted to put some in
my mouth. But my [deceased] husband's aunt told me the story of
how once the wife of so-and-so became blind from eating stealth-
ily in the kitchen. Stories of this kind helped me control my
hunger. Every day I would pray to Kali: Mother, please take away
my greed. Perhaps it was through the grace of the goddess that I
gradually lost any appetite I had.

Widows, she added, were allowed only one meal a day, a meal that could
contain at most only a certain few fried vegetables: lentils, pulses, and
spinach. "Cauliflower, beetroot, eggplant," and "half the winter vegetables" were disallowed as "foreign."[8]

What stands out in these narratives is the close connection between
the cruelty that they exemplify and the question of entitlement to affec-
tion/protection in the Bengali extended family. Being a widow often
entailed a distinct loss of status and a consequent loss of this entitlement.
Nistarini Devi, a child widow of the last century who depended on her
late husband's brother for survival, reports how even the servants "followed my brother's wife" in treating her with disdain: "I was given no
food at night. If I asked the servant to chop some wood for me, he
would say: 'Do it yourself.'"[9]

The entitlement to affection/protection is, however, not in the nature of a general claim; it is not an entitlement to just anybody's affection
or care. Whether such a general claim can be sustained anywhere is de-
batable, but it is clear that the Bengali widow's testimony does not
evince a desire for the kind of treatment that, say, either the state or the
market can accord. The entitlement to affection is claimed from a particular, and in that sense irreplaceable, source—the late husband's family.
It should not, however, be assumed that the particularity of this claim
arises from a modern sense of individuality. The quality of affection/

protection sought has, in fact, very little to do with a modern, individualistic, "expressivist" construction of sentiment or affect, one in which the sentiments are characteristically regarded as deeply authentic and nonhypocritical expressions of one's own self.[10] The widows' discussion of entitlement to others' affection operates in the context of the kinship-based rules of emotional transactions in the extended family. The question of whether affection given is an expression of somebody else's deep individuality is foreign in this context. The demand for caring or tender behavior arises within kinship.

An example of this point can be found in Datta's relations with one of her informants. Datta last saw Indumati in 1955 in Kashi (Banaras). Indumati had, by then, reached the depth of her penury and was living in an institution. "I did not recognize her," says Datta:

> Our aunt, the wife of a zamindar family with a 50 percent share in the estate, sat naked in a dark room without windows, muttering curses aimed at . . . God. She could not see very well. Feeling helpless, I started yelling out my father's name and mine. She recognised me then and immediately started crying. . . . After a while, she asked me how long I had been in Kashi. When she realized that I had been there for twenty days and had come to see her only a day before my departure, her tears returned. "Here I am," she said, "hoping that I would [now] be able to shed some tears and spend some days in the comfort of your company, and all you offer me is this fake [perfunctory] sense of kinship. I don't even want to see your face." So saying, she turned her back to me.[11]

That the agent who withdraws affection/protection is a particular agent, and that it is this particularity that is a factor in the resulting distress, comes out clearly in the narrative of Saradasundari Devi's autobiography as well. When Saradasundari's husband dies, leaving her with young children (some of whom do not survive for long), her description of the hurtful treatment that she receives at the hands of her late husband's brothers represents an attempt to reinscribe her place within the network of her in-laws. The following quotation will clarify how property *as such*, that is, the simple fact of possession (which is something that the law can address), is less the issue here than is property as a language with which to express a domestic dispute about entitlement to affection and protection. Saradasundari writes:

> Within a fortnight of my husband's death, his (third) younger brother began to behave toward me in a hurtful manner. He forced his way into the room . . . where my husband slept and took

away the large bed he used. I cried, not out of greed for possessions, but at the way they began to treat me as soon as my husband
was gone. . . . He [her husband] had left some shawls in his
safe. . . . His younger brother took them all. . . . I asked if I could
keep a couple as mementos; he gave me only one. I said nothing
and avoided all arguments. My oldest daughter died within a year
of my husband's death. . . . I became absolutely restless with grief.
Close on the heels of this loss came my mother-in-law's death.
Struck such blows, one after another, I lost all sense of calm and
felt seized by a feeling of madness. I decided to leave for Sreek-
shetra [Puri].

I thought of ending my life. Nabin, my eldest son, said: "Mother
they will settle the property now, don't leave yet." I replied, "Whatever happens, and however unfortunate it may be, whether you
lose your property or not, I will not stay here." . . . I prayed to
God so that I might feel no sense of attachment.[12]

What hurts at this moment is nothing short of Hindu Bengali patriarchy and the utterly vulnerable place assigned to women within its phal-
locentric order. Becoming a widow meant the possibility of being exposed to this vulnerability. At the same time, the struggle to maintain
one's self-respect, to find a code of conduct proper to one's state of widowhood, entailed working through this structure. On the one hand,
then, Saradasundari is reminded by her brother-in-law's behavior that
she is, without her husband, what she was before her marriage, an outsider. She even seeks solace in this thought: "Why should I cry? I asked
myself. Why should I grieve if they took what belonged to *their* brother.
After all, these were not possessions I brought with me from my father's
household. But I also developed a fear over time. Where would I go if
they turned me out with my children?"[13]

At the same time, however, Saradasundari seeks to restore her standing as "auspicious wife" by fashioning herself in her autobiographical
narration as someone committed to the social standing of her husband's
family, even to the extent of actually resisting what would have been her
legal rights. Her husband's older brother divided up "all movable property" about the time she left for Puri. Her sons won part of their share
back later through court cases initiated by one of them, the famous Bengali social reformer Keshub Sen. Saradasundari writes: "Keshub said to
me . . . , 'Mother, if you want, I can get your and Krishnabehari's [an-
other son] shares, too, by getting a lawyer to write.' I replied, 'No. Is
money the most important thing? Should *your uncle* go to jail for the
sake of money? Let it be; there is no need [to claim the money] at pres-

ent'" (emphasis added).[14] What is at stake here is Saradasundari's relationship to this particular family, that is, her entitlement to *their* affection and protection. The family as such was not replaceable within that relationship.

Because it operated through the same connections that generated affection, this was cruelty that constantly proliferated both its agents and it victims. Consider the not uncommon case of a mother who, herself still married, finds herself forced to ensure that a daughter who has been both married and widowed while still a child, often without ever meeting her husband, observes all the rituals of widowhood. Gyanadasundari thus described her own experience to Datta: "How could I remember anything about my husband, dear? I never saw him more than two or three times. He killed himself by hanging within a few months of our marriage. When I was told the news, it did not make any sense. . . . My mother used to break down into tears if I ever wanted to eat fish [considered a great delicacy in the cuisine of riverine Bengal but not allowed widows] with my meal. So I stopped asking for fish. I cannot even recall now how fish tastes."[15]

Or consider the punishment that another mother took on herself when her daughter, a six- or seven-year-old child, became a widow. We have the story in Datta's telling: "Her mother used to feed her widows' food. The boys of the household would sit on another side of the room and be served fish. They said one day: 'How come you haven't got any fish?' Her mother pointed to fried lentil balls and said to her: 'This is your fish.' The mischievous boys would suck on fish bones and ask the girl: 'How come your piece of fish doesn't have any bones?' The girl would ask her mother, 'Mother, why doesn't my fish have any bones?' . . . The mother would later break off bamboo slips from baskets and stick them into the lentil balls, and the girl would proudly show them off to the boys [as proof that her fish had bones]. . . . It was long before she even realized the deception."[16]

NARRATIVE AND LAW

What kind of intervention is possible here? I will discuss two kinds, and they are not mutually exclusive. First, there is social intervention through the law (i.e., through legislation regulating social practice). Second, there is social intervention through narrative itself—biography, autobiography, and fiction.

The connection between narrative and social intervention has always been present in the history of our becoming modern. Kalyani Datta's search for widows' testimonies was itself inspired by fiction. According to her introductory statement: "Widowhood has figured endlessly in Bengali literature. . . . My interest in the lives of widows was aroused in my childhood as a result of meeting at close quarters characters in real life who resembled those encountered in stories and novels."[17] Widows, it has been pointed out, "play a significant role in the short stories and novels of Rabindranath Tagore," whose concern was not unconnected to nineteenth-century attempts at social reform.[18] Tagore himself sometimes saw fiction as his contribution to the same nineteenth-century project of social improvement that was embodied in colonial law. He wrote in a letter of 1894: "I have had this surprisingly happy thought in my head since yesterday. I decided after some deliberation that one may not necessarily succeed in being of direct use to the world even if one has the desire to be so. Instead, if I could simply accomplish what I was good at, the world might automatically derive some benefit. . . . Even if I did not achieve anything other than writing some short stories, they would at least cause me happiness and, if successful, provide some mental enjoyment to my readers as well."[19]

It would obviously be artificial to separate law from narrative, particularly when the administration of justice itself requires people to tell stories in court. Yet there are interesting differences between lawmaking as part of social/political intervention under (in this case, colonial) modernity and the production of narratives as an instance and instrument of such intervention. Rammohun sought a solution to the problem of cruelty to widows by giving them the right to inherit property, Vidyasagar by giving them the right to remarry. The classic problem of the *differend* separates the widows' narratives that we have considered here from the language of rights—the legal solution.[20] Because law is the embodiment of the "truth" of the theory of rights, one can argue that, between theory and suffering, that is, between the plaintiff and the victim, the *differend* would emerge. This is another way of saying that theory/law can never address the victim here in her own language as narrative does. Narrative places the reforming subject face-to-face with cruelty, alongside everyone else who faces the widow—the torturer, the mother, the in-laws, the children. Part of the argument here, then, concerns the inadequacy of theory to provide us with forms of intervention in our affective lives in ways that speak directly to the affects concerned.

To restate the question, Can theory that justifies the law-state combine ever provide us with a form with which to intervene in the politics of affection/cruelty? Can, for example, the welfare state (admittedly, a somewhat distant example in India's case) be the answer to the politics of familial cruelty that I have documented here?[21]

The law-state combine, or modern political philosophy itself, finds its justification in European Enlightenment thought. The problem with Enlightenment thought is not that it gives us visions of emancipation/ freedom that cannot be realized for everybody (this is, indeed, a problem—this is, in a sense, the problematic of distributive justice—but not a crucial theoretical one in this context as it produces, as a solution, only the noble, but predictable, effort to generalize the benefits to all). Situated in colonial modernities, our response is more complex. We cannot ignore the ideas of justice and freedom that are contained in the political theory of rights and citizenship, for, whether or not these rights can be enjoyed by all, the emancipatory visions underlying them form ethical horizons that, for all their problems of global claims and universalisms, shape all conversations within the academy, which remains my immediate audience. One always speaks within these visions.

Colonial histories, however, sensitize us to the paradox that has attended all historical attempts to ground in the violence of the modern state the Enlightenment thinkers' promise of happiness and justice for all. This paradox is the fact of imperialism, the fact that the modern state has always operated, whether inside or outside Europe, by producing its own colonized subjects whose consent to its rule is never won by pure persuasion; violence or coercion always has a role to play. Whether it is the law or theories of citizenship, they all work by abstracting and synthesizing identities and do not allow for the radical alterity of the other.

The Bengali widows' cry for affection is not a cry for general affection, that is, affection from anybody and everybody. The problem of the state is solved by a theory of general affection such as Gandhi's repressive, and remarkably Christian, doctrine of universal love. The very same entitlement that causes the widow to ask for affection from her in-laws makes her vulnerable to their acts of cruelty. The call is neither for rights nor for a self-denying universal emotion. As Levinas says: "The relationship between men is certainly the non-synthesizable par excellence. . . . Interpersonal relationship . . . is not a matter of thinking the ego and the other together, but to be facing. The true union or true togetherness is not a togetherness of synthesis, but a togetherness of face to face." He continues: "Politics must be able in fact always to be checked and criticized starting from the ethical. . . . This would be a responsibility [for the other] which is inaccessible in its ethical advent, from which one does not escape, and which, thus, is the principle of an absolute individuation."[22]

The hurtful and cruel withdrawal of affection, then, can take place only within relationships that bear this duality of which Levinas read the face as a classic expression. In other words, affection can be withdrawn only in those very particular networks that also allow it to be generated and given. What makes the hurt unbearable is that the giver of affection is not a generalizable, homogenized entity. In other words, it has none of the structure of abstract, general homogeneity that makes the question of the production-distribution of a commodity (think of Marx's notion of *abstract labor*) or even of such a bourgeois concept as *right* something amenable to the rule of either the state or the market. That is also why law or theory cannot address it directly as law itself is based on the idea of the abstract, general, homogenized citizen and his rights and duties.

Affection works on a contrary principle, that of radical individuation. Let me hasten to add that I am not necessarily universalizing any extreme form of individualism. The irreplaceable, concrete *other* whose affection is sought by the sufferer is not necessarily an individual in any modern sense. It could be, as I have said before, a concrete, specific kinship connection, a particular network of relationships that is addressed in the widow's complaint. Indumati's hurt at Kalyani Datta's behavior—visiting her only a day before she was to leave Banaras—was not dependent on Datta's individuality. The narrative of their meeting produces compassion here only if we imaginatively inhabit the affective field of kin relations within which Indumati and Datta met. Dialogic narrative, the telling of a story, whether biographical or fictional, thus works on the principle of the irreplaceable social rather than the general abstract social of the law or theory and, in this way, positions the reader face-to-face with the victim of cruelty whose face always carries the injunction: Thou shalt not kill. This is what makes narrative a political force in a sphere that law or theory can never reach. Let us listen to Levinas again:

> The face is exposed, menaced, as if inviting us to an act of violence. At the same time, the face is what forbids us to kill. . . . The first word of the face is . . . "Thou shalt not kill." It is an order. There is a commandment in the appearance of the face, as if a master spoke to me. However, at the same time, the face of the Other is destitute; it is the poor for whom I can do all and to whom I owe all. And me, whoever I may be, but as a "first person," I am he who finds the resources to respond to the call.[23]

Narrative, rather than theory/law, reproduces us as this first person. Tagore's letters and interviews explaining and justifying his literary efforts connect knowledge/intervention to themes of intimacy and love. Referring to his short stories as expressing a knowledge of Bengali lives, he spoke of the "intimate hospitality" that he had once enjoyed in the Bengal countryside. "People say of me," he complained in his old age, "'He is the son of a rich family, . . . what would he know of villages?' I can say that the people who say this know even less than I do. What do they know? Can one ever know from within the inertia of habit? Real knowledge comes from love. . . . I have looked at Bengal villages with unceasing love, and it is that that has opened the door of my heart."[24]

I do not mean to deny the importance of law and theories of citizenship. They help create new spaces for human struggles for dignity. Also, as I have already said, there was a certain complementarity in the social functions of the law and the novel in Bengali modernity. My purpose is to contemplate narrative, as distinct from abstract theory, as a form of political intervention. The law-state combine has a history, and it is the history of imperialism, of the arrogant invasion of the other. There may be particular contexts in which such invasion may, indeed, seem justifiable. In most cases, however, this invasion will produce intractable problems of ethics. The Gandhian solution of absolute love, on the other hand, works on the assumption of an abstract equality of human beings for whom love must be felt universally and equally. That this requires certain kinds of cruelty-torture—the renunciation of enjoyment both by the self and by others—is something borne out by Gandhi's life itself.

The politics of cruelty/tenderness takes us into face-to-face relations, where identities are radically individuated and therefore irreplaceable. Narrative points to a sphere of modernity that seems more compatible with the ethics of being face-to-face with the victim of suffering. Yet we build civil-political spheres on theories that view the social in terms of abstract, homogeneous units. While these theories do make formal equality possible either between commodities or between citizens, they will never be adequate to the demands of the politics of cruelty/affection that define and dominate the life processes of family and kinship. The question is, Can we imaginatively bring into being modern civil-political spheres founded on the techniques of the dialogic narrative even as we live and work through those built on the universalist abstractions of political philosophy?

EIGHT Memories of Displacement

The Poetry and Prejudice of Dwelling

emory is a complex phenomenon that reaches far beyond what normally constitutes a historian's archives, for memory is much more than what the mind can remember or what objects can help us document about the past. It is also what we do not always consciously know that we remember until something actually, as the saying goes, jogs our memory. And there remains the question, so much discussed these days in the literature on the Indian Partition, of what people do not even wish to remember, the forgetting that comes to our aid in dealing with pain and unpleasantness in life.[1] Memory, then, is far more complicated than what historians can recover, and it poses ethical challenges to the investigator-historian who approaches the past with one injunction: Tell me all.[2]

A set of essays that I propose to discuss here turns fundamentally on this question of the difference between history and memory. The essays were first serialized in the Bengali newspaper *Jugantar* beginning in 1950 and collected in 1975 in a book called *Chhere asha gram* (The abandoned village) under the editorship of Dakshinaranjan Basu, a journalist in Calcutta.[3] The names of the authors of the individual essays are not mentioned in the book, nor do we have any idea of the authors' age or gender, although one would suspect, from the style of writing, that, with one exception, they are men. The authors recount their memories of their native villages—sixty-seven in all from some eighteen districts in East Bengal. Written in the aftermath of the Partition, these essays capture the sense of tragedy that the division of the country represented to these authors. This attitude was more Hindu than Muslim, for, to many, if not most, of the Muslims of East Pakistan, 1947 was, not only about Partition, but also about freedom, freedom from both the British and the Hindu ruling classes.[4]

My aim is to understand the relation between memory and identity. And, in doing so, it is necessary to remember the context. There is no getting around the fact that the Partition was traumatic for those compelled to leave their homes, the experience being marked by forced eviction, physical violence and humiliation, and the sexual harassment and degradation of women. The Hindu Bengali refugees who wrote these essays were faced with making new lives for themselves in the difficult circumstances of the overcrowded city of Calcutta. Much of the story of their various attempts to settle down in the different suburbs of Calcutta is about squatting on government or privately owned land and about reactive violence by the police and propertyowners.[5] The sudden influx of thousands of people into a city where services were already stretched to their limits could not have been a welcome event. It is possible, therefore, that these essays were written in order to create a positive emotional response in the city toward the refugees.

It is clear, however, that the essays were committed to conveying a shared structure of Bengali sentiment through the grid of which the irrevocable fact of Hindu-Muslim separation in Bengali history and the trauma surrounding the event could be read. To re-create in print the air of sentimentality and nostalgia that pervaded the notion of the lost home was the task that these essays set themselves. Not surprisingly, therefore, they drew on modes that had already been used to portray the Bengali village, and, in particular, the villages of East Bengal, in Bengali literary and nationalist writings.

There is a particular aspect of these memories that concerns us here: the sense of trauma and its contradictory relation to the question of the past. The narrative structure of the memory of trauma works on a principle opposite to that of any historical narrative. At the same time, however, if memory is to be that of trauma, it must place the event, the cause of trauma—in this case, the violence accompanying Partition—within a past that gives force to the victim's claim. This past must be shared by the narrator and his audience. Yet it cannot be a historicist version of the past, one that aims to diffuse the shock of the traumatic by explaining away the element of the unexpected. Let me explain.

What makes a historical narrative—a narrative that leads up to the event in question, explaining why it happened and why it happened when it did—possible? The event itself must be open to explanation. What cannot be explained belongs to the marginalia of history—accidents, coincidences, and concurrences that, while important to the narrative, can never replace the structure of causes for which the historian searches.

Conceived within a sense of trauma and tragedy, however, these essays maintain a completely different relation to the event called *the Partition*. Their narratives do not lead up to it; it remains fundamentally inexplicable. Nothing here of the Hindu-Muslim conflict that historians find so useful in explaining the Partition—no trace of the by-now familiar tales of landlord-peasant or peasant-moneylender conflict to which historians of communalism in the subcontinent have normally turned to answer the question, Why did the Muslim population of East Bengal turn against its Hindu neighbors? Nothing, the narrators claim, could have prepared them for the ethnic hatred to which they were subjected in what they considered to be their homeland. The essays express a sense of stunned disbelief that something like the Partition could happen at all, that people could be cut off so suddenly and cruelly—and so completely—from the familiar world of their childhood.

The claim is, indeed, that what we have here is that which cannot be explained. The writers of these essays were all caught unawares by the calamity of the Partition. One refrain running through all the essays in *Chhere asha gram* is how inexplicable it all was—after years of peaceful and friendly coexistence, neighbors turned against neighbors, friends took up arms against friends. How did this come to pass?

This is the question that haunts *Chhere asha gram*. As the following quotations from it will show, not only was the Partition seen as inexplicable, but it was also seen as signifying the death of the social:[6]

> Dhirenbabu used to teach us history. . . . He had been the head-master of our Jaikali high school for the last few years. . . . Even a short time ago, I had heard that he was still in the village. I saluted his courage on hearing this. . . . But, to my surprise, he turned up in my office one day and told me about his plight. He and his companions were attacked by the friends of the very student who had advised him to leave while he still commanded respect. Eventually, he managed to extricate himself and his family in exchange for two

hundred rupees, thanks to some mediation by his favorite student, and crossed the Padma to come to Calcutta. But the simple-hearted teacher from a village school remained in a state of shock: What was this that had happened? How did it happen? All these questions crowded his mind. The age of Ekalabya is now in the womb of a bottomless past; we all know that it will not return. But still it was unthinkable that, in the land of the newly independent Pakistan, it is the guru who would have to pay the student. . . . Yet this happened, and who can tell if this will not be the permanent rule in the kingdom of shariat? (Bajrajogini, Dhaka; p. 7)

Hindus, Muslims, Sikhs, Christians, have always treated women with respect; what is this that happened today? (Shonarang, Dhaka; p. 57)

How could that land become somebody else's forever! Just one line drawn on the map, and my own home becomes a foreign country! (Binyapher, Mymensingh; p. 66)

True, my home is in a country to which I have no relation. The house is there, the village is there, the property exists, but I am homeless today. The suffering of somebody who has had to leave his home can be appreciated only by a person with a large heart. . . . Man, the son of the immortal one, knows no happiness to-day—pleasure, security, peace, love, and affection have also left the land with us. On all four sides exist the filthy picture of mean in-trigues. Where have the images of the olden days—of happy and easygoing people and villages—disappeared? . . . Who has stolen our good qualities? When will we be delivered from this crisis of civilization? . . . What happened was beyond the comprehension of ordinary human beings. By the time they could [even] form an idea [of the situation], the destruction was complete. (Sankrail, Mymensingh; pp. 88, 91)

Why was the innocence of the mind banished after so many days of living together? Why did the structure of the human mind change overnight? (Sakhua, Mymensingh; p. 101)

Who would have thought that the country would be engulfed in such a fire? Brothers fight and then make up with each other, but the common person had no inkling that the single spark of the day would start such a conflagration. (Kanchabali, Barisal; p. 122)

Who is the conspiratorial witch whose [black] magic brought death to the cordial social relations that were to be seen even only the other day? Why does man avoid man today like beasts? Can't we forget meanness, selfishness, and fraudulent behavior and retrieve [the sense of] kinship? . . . Was our kinship based on quicksand? Why would it disappear into such bottomless depths? (Rambhadrapur, Faridpur; pp. 155–56)

I am today a *vastuhara* [a homeless person] in this city of Calcutta. I live in a relief camp. Some in this camp have contracted cholera. A *vastuhara* child died of pox this morning when I received a handful of flattened rice. I do not dare to approach the "relief babu," who only gets into a rage if I try to say something. I do not ask why this has happened. . . . At the time of our leaving, I asked for [a loan of] the boat that belongs to the grandson of Nurshvabi without realizing that he also had turned against us. We tiptoed our way under the cover of darkness from Patia to Chakradandi. (Bhatikain, Chittagong; p. 194)

And our Muslim neighbors? For aeons we have lived next to them sharing each other's happiness and suffering, but did they feel the slightest bit of sadness in letting us go? Did it take only the one blow of the scimitar of politics to sever forever the kinship that had been there from the beginning of the eras? (Ramchandrapur, Sylhet; pp. 235–36)

On the day of the Kali *puja* [worship] we used to take care of the sacrificial goats, carefully feeding them leaves of the jackfruit tree and carrying them . . . and stroking them all day. But we never felt any pain at the moment when we pushed toward death these creatures that we had looked after with so much care all day. We were not old enough to explain then these contradictory qualities of the mind, but today it surprises me a lot to think about it. [But] isn't that what has happened all over Bengal? (Bheramara, Kustia; p. 293)

This very ascription of an inherent inexplicability to the event of the Partition is what gives these essays their pathos. They are more like the unwilling and uncontrollable recall of a victim overtaken by events and less like the reminiscences of one in narrative control. And this, I suggest, is the first important distinction to be noted between history and memory (for the Bengali *bhadralok,* the respectable middle classes) of the Partition in Bengal. History seeks to explain the event; the memory of pain refuses the historical explanation and sees the event as a monstrously irrational aberration.

These are undoubtedly essays written in the spirit of mourning, part of the collective and public grieving through which the Hindus who were displaced from East Bengal came to terms with their new conditions in Calcutta. Yet we must remember that this grieving was being publicized in print, perhaps in the cause of the politics of refugee rehabilitation in West Bengal in the 1950s about which Prafulla Chakrabarti has written in his *The Marginal Men*. This mourning had, therefore, the political task of garnering sympathy by speaking, at least in theory, to the entire readership of the Bengali press. One central concern of these essays was to generalize the sense of mourning over the Partition of Bengal. It was important to argue, therefore, that the loss of home was not something that affected only those who were actually displaced; the Bengali people as such had lost their home; nothing short of their sense of what it means to have a home had been called into crisis.

THE LANGUAGE OF HOMELESSNESS

There are two Bengali words for *refugee: sharanarthi*, meaning, literally, someone who seeks refuge and the protection (*sharan*) of a higher power (including God); and *udvastu*, meaning someone who is homeless, but homeless in a particular sense, the word *vastu* (home), a Sanskrit word of Vedic vintage, carrying a special connotation. Monier-Williams defines *vastu* as meaning, among other things, "the site or foundation of a house."[7] In Bengali, the word is often combined with the word *bhita* (or *bhité*), which is connected to the Sanskrit word *bhitti*, meaning "foundation." The idea of *foundation* is in turn tied to the idea of "male ancestry." And the result is that the combined word *vastuvita* reinforces the association between patriliny and the way in which one's dwelling or home is connected to the conception of foundation. One's permanent home is where one's "foundation" is (the subject of this imagination being, undoubtedly, male).

The Bengali language has preserved this sense of distinction between a temporary place of residence and one's foundational home, as it were, by using two different words for a house, *basha* and *bari*. *Basha* is always a temporary place of residence, no matter how long one stays there; one's sense of belonging there is transient. *Bari*, on the other hand, is where one's ancestors have lived for generations. When it comes to rituals marking life-cycle changes (such as marriage), middle-class Bengali Hindus of Calcutta often refer to the ancestral village in explaining where their *bari* is even if their *basha* bears a Calcutta address.[8] *Bari* is also interchangeable with *desh*, a word signifying one's native land.

An *udvastu*, then—the prefix *ut-* signifying "off" or "outside" or "raised" (evicted)—is someone who has been physically removed from his foundations. And, since this is not a desirable state, it can come about only through the application of force or through some grave misfortune. For the ability to maintain connections with one's *vastubhita* across generations is a sign of good fortune, a fortune that itself owes something to the auspicious blessing of one's ancestors.

This idea of *home* was extended during the course of the nationalist movement into the idea of the *motherland*, *Bengal* becoming the name of a part of the world made sacred by the habitation there of the ancestors of the Bengali people. To become an *udvastu* is, thus, to fall victim to an extreme curse. And, if this curse befalls people through no fault of their own, they deserve the sympathy and compassion of others.

This can, indeed, be taken as the language of self-pity. But, when a refugee spoke in this language, he spoke for the nation. "I recall," wrote one contributor to *Chhere asha gram*, "that about twelve years ago, when a household in our village lost their only son, Deben, my grandmother remarked in sadness, 'What a pity; there is nobody left to light the lamp at Sarada's *bhité* [this being an auspicious ritual of middle-class Hindu well-being]. Today, every Hindu family in East Bengal, even if they are blessed with sons, is bereft of people who might have lit the lamp at their *bhité*" (Dhamgar, Dhaka; p. 30).

To achieve this effect of speaking for the Bengali nation, the essays in *Chhere asha gram* have recourse to a particular kind of language, one that combines the sacred with the secular idea of beauty to produce, ultimately, a discourse about value. These are narratives that must demonstrate that something of value to Bengali culture as a whole has been destroyed by the violence of the Partition. The idea of *home* here must signify value. The native village is pictured as both sacred and beautiful, and it is this that makes communal violence an act of both violation and defilement. Muslim violence is seen here as an act of sacrilege against everything that stands for sanctity and beauty in the Hindu Bengali understanding of what home is.

There are four narrative elements that help achieve a mixture of the language of the sacred with that of aesthetics, thereby producing a modern idea of cultural value. The first element is patriliny, the ancestral connection, that which gives the native village its sacred nature. Worshiping the land of the village is equivalent to worshiping one's ancestors. The other three elements—the idea (and, hence, the relics) of antiquity, connections that the individual village may have had with recent nationalist history, and modern secular literary descriptions of the beauty of the landscape of rural Bengal—are all provided by the language of secular aesthetics, and all are identifiably modern in character. Taken as a whole, this is a combination in which the sacred can be separated from the aesthetic only with difficulty. But one thing is clear: what was seen as valuable is also what played into the politics of ethnicity. Nothing in this combination had anything much to do with the Muslim pasts of Bengal. Muslims are mentioned in these essays; indeed, their depiction is critical to the depiction of an idyll. But their traditions are not part of the sacred or of the beautiful. In the next three sections, I demonstrate these propositions by presenting further quotations from *Chhere asha gram*.

THE DISCOURSE OF VALUE I: ANCESTRY, PATRILINY, AND THE SACRED

The quotations that I have chosen to demonstrate the narrative association between the sacred and patriliny are, on the whole, self-explanatory. They require, therefore, only minimal framing. The village is variously seen as some form of a mother figure or mother goddess. This idea of the mother, often evoked in describing the writer's sense of attachment to the land, is not, however, a matriarchal conception. Fundamentally, these excerpts express the religious sentiment of *bhakti* (devotion). As I have discussed elsewhere,[9] Bengali nationalism—and nationalism in other parts of India—did make *bhakti* into a modern political sentiment. The activity often used for expressing that sentiment was *puja*, the act of worshiping. All the quotations that follow in this section express *bhakti,* and some produce the gesture of *puja* as well:

> In this urban life humming with the sound of work, a message of greeting from a friend reached me one evening. . . . He had just returned from [having spent some time in] the lap of the village in which we were both born. The question he asked as soon as we met was: "I have brought this ultimate treasure for you back from *desh;* can you guess what it might be?" . . . Eventually, he surprised all by handing over to me a clod of clay. This was from the soil of my *bhité,* the "Basu-house," sacred from the blessing of my father and grandfather. This soil is my mother. The sacred memory of my forefathers is mixed with this soil. To me this was not just of high value—it was invaluable. I touched this clod to my forehead. This is no ordinary dust. This clay is moist today with the blood that has been wrung out of Bengal's heart. (Bajrojogini, Dhaka; p. 1)

> For seven generations we have been reared on the affection and grace of this land; perhaps our yet-to-arrive progeny would have one day made this land their own. But that hope can feel only like a dream today. (Khaliajuri, Mymensingh; p. 73)

An obscure . . . village though it is, Gomdandi is a veritable part of historic Chattagram [Chittagong]. . . . Insofar as can be gathered from history, it is observed that my ancestor Madhabchandra Majumdar, exasperated by the oppression of the *bargi* [Maratha raiders], left Bardhaman for Chattagram nearly two hundred years ago and founded a settlement there in the village of Suchia north of the river Sankha. Sometime later . . . Magandas Choudhuri came to his farm in Gomdandi village and built a homestead there. . . . *The village that is more valuable than gold, where my forefathers had grown up for seven generations,*[10] where is that village lost today? Where is Gomdandi today, and where am I? (Gomdandi, Chittagong; pp. 195, 197)

But no friends stopped us, and no Muslim neighbor told us not to go, the day we, driven by the need to save our honor and life and with no fixed destination, left forever the sacred land of our place of birth where our forefathers for seven generations had had their *bhité*. (Ramchandrapur, Sylhet; p. 235)

We did not want to think that we might have to leave the village. Yet we had to leave and come away. Everybody did their last act of obeisance on the day of our departure—at the foot of the Tulasi tree [a sacred plant bringing well-being to the Hindu homestead], in the deity room, even at the door of the cowshed. My old aunt would not leave the threshold of the deity room; her tears and the sadness of the moment wetted my heart too. The village, associated with the many memories of my forefathers, was like a place of pilgrimage to me. On that last evening, I prepared myself for the departure with a respectful salute in the direction of the village, my mother. (Amritabazar, Jessore; p. 241)

I wonder, will it not ever be possible to go back to the lap of the mother we have left behind? Mother—my motherland—is she truly somebody else's now? The mind does not want to understand. (Dakatia, Khulna; p. 257)

THE DISCOURSE OF VALUE II: ANTIQUITY, HISTORY, AND NATIONALISM

It is understandable that the remembered village derives some of its value from the associations that it can claim with the nation's antiquity and with the anticolonial struggle. The point to note is how unselfconsciously this association becomes Hindu. Even this historical memory fractures along ethnic lines. Nothing in which the Muslims can take pride features in these accounts. The style of writing exhibited is undistinguished and predictable, but it derives from a recognizable genre— the literature on local history that Hindu Bengali authors began to produce from the late nineteenth century on.

Well-known and established scholars such as Haraprasad Shastri and Dineshchandra Sen were the intellectual godfathers of this tradition. As a general rule, Hindu landlords, small and big, funded these projects, while village local-history enthusiasts acted as so many research assistants.[11] Nationalist institutions like the Bangiya Sahitya Parishad stood at the apex of the process that produced these nationalist local histories of Hindu Bengali achievements.

The spontaneity of this effort bears testimony to the nationalism experienced by these scholars and their patrons. Mixing recent and ancient history with hearsay, archaeological evidence with mythical texts and stories, this literature produced a form of the past that was to be judged deficient by the more professional of historians.[12] Yet it represented the most popular form that the past took in the Hindu nationalist imagination.

The following quotations from *Chhere asha gram* represent the continuing hold of this tradition on the language of mourning used by the refugees:

> The name of Bajrojogini is unforgettable in the history of Bengal. . . . This is the place of birth of [the] ancient scholar Dipankar Srigyan Atish. . . . The historical village of Rampal next door—the seat of the Sena kings—is without any beauty today. . . . I had listened to speeches by the Congress leader Surya Sen at the time of [the] noncooperation [movement]. (Bajrajogini, Dhaka; pp. 3, 5)

> Sabhar, my village, is one of the main centers of commerce in the district of Dhaka. In her breast she carries centuries of indestructible history, fading skeletons of ancient civilizations. . . . It was here that the lamp of [learning of] Dipankar Srigyan was lit first; it was here that his education started in the house of the guru. Sabhar then was a city of supremacy, the capital of Raja Harishchandra, adorned with all kinds of wealth. (Sabhar, Dhaka; p. 10)

> Dhamrai, a place of pilgrimage. In the very ancient days the Sanskrit name was Dharmarajika. The modern name of Dhamrai was derived from the Pali name Dhammarai. Truly, the people of Dhamrai were mad about religion. But what is the result of so much cultivation of dharma? The people of Dhamrai are themselves without a *dham* [place]! (Dhamrai, Dhaka; p. 19)

The well-known educator Dr. Prasannakumar Ray and the once-famous doctor of Calcutta Dr. Dwarkanath Ray were both born in this village. It was in this village that Pandit Krishnachandra Sarba-bhauma, a logician of yore belonging to the whole of Bikrampur and the neighboring regions, lived in a thatched hut, teaching Sanskrit to the students of his *tol* [a traditional school for learning Sanskrit]. (Shubhaddhya, Dhaka; p. 42)

The history of my village is the history of peace. Its historical heritage makes it great. . . . It contains the ruins of the Buddhist period. . . . The successful women and men of this village come to mind. Some of the people from here have become famous professors, some ICS [Indian Civil Service officers], while some have gone to Europe as representatives of independent India. (Shonarang, Dhaka; pp. 54, 59)

Banaripara occupies a special place in [the annals of] all the political agitations, from the Swadeshi movement of 1905 to the non-cooperation and the civil-disobedience movements. The contribution of this village to the freedom struggle of the country is truly great. The sixteen-year-old Bhabani Bhattacharya, who gave his life to the hangman for trying to kill the then governor [Mr.] Anderson at a place called Lebong in Darjeeling in 1934, was an unselfish son of this village. (Banaripara, Barisal; p. 108)

My village has remained blessed and sacred ever since it received the touch of the sacred feet of Netaji Subhashchandra [Bose]. (Gabha, Barisal; p. 113)

It is said that it was during the reign of the emperor Shahjahan . . . that the Bosu family settled here. Under the protection of Kandarpanarayan, the *Bhuians* of Chandradwip, a great and civilized society grew up in the neighboring villages of Gabha, Narottampur, Banaripara, Ujirpur, Khalishakota, and so on. (Kanchabalia, Barisal; pp. 118–19)

Many, instead of going to Navadweep, would come to the world-conquering pandit of this village, Jagannath Tarkapanchanan. . . . I have heard that some of the stone images and stone inscriptions of Nalchira have found a place in the Dhaka Museum. (Nalchira, Barisal; pp. 141–42)

Navadweep, Bikrampur, Bhatpara—the place of our Kotalipara is inferior to none among these jewels of the crown of brahmanical knowledge in Bengal. (Kotalipara, Faridpur; p. 148)

This young Brahman named Rajaram Ray features as a footnote to the history of Bengal. By the sheer force of his arms, Rajaram . . . founded the settlement of this Khalia village. Gradually, his thatched hut was converted into a seven-winged palace. Only a fourth of that huge palace exists today. (Khalia, Faridpur; p. 164)

I have mentioned the copper inscriptions of Kumar Bhaskar . . . discovered only two miles away from our village. The Kushari River described in those inscriptions still flows past our village. . . . From this may be gauged the antiquity of the . . . villages in this area. (Ramchandrapur, Sylhet; p. 236)

Senhati is one of the famous villages of East Bengal. . . . There is a saying that Ballal Sena made a gift of this village to his son-in-law Hari Sena. . . . It was Hari Sena who named it Senhati. The book *Digvijaya-prakasha* says that Lakshman Sena established a town called Senhati near Jessore. . . . Be that as it may, we now no longer need history; Senhati today exists in its glory. I am a son of that village. That is what makes me proud. (Senhati, Khulna; p. 248)

The village is self-sufficient. Its name is Ghatabari. The little river Atharoda flows past it. A few miles away is Bhangabari, the birthplace of the poet Rajanikanta Sen. Raja Basanta Ray is the person whose name is unforgettable in the history of this village. . . . The ruins of his palace are still there in the village next door. (Ghatabari, Pabna; p. 277)

What I have heard about the history of the village is this. Sati, the goddess, killed herself on hearing Daksha [her father] speak ill of her husband [Shiva]. . . . One of the fifty-one pieces [of her body] fell on this obscure village Bhabanipur in north Bengal. (Bhabanipur, Bagura; p. 303)

Let me tell you the history of the name Boda. Budhraja built a big fort and a royal palace over two square miles. With the passage of time, a temple was built at the fort, the temple of the goddess Budheswari. . . . Gradually, the name was transformed in ordinary speech to Bodeswari, and from that came Boda. (Boda, Jalpaiguri; p. 315)

THE DISCOURSE OF VALUE III: THE IDYLLIC VILLAGE, BENGALI PASTORALISM, AND LITERARY KITSCH

Apart from the glories brought about by the village's antiquity and its participation in the life of the nation, there is also a present of the village that the essays in *Chhere asha gram* emphasize, but it is an eternal present. The village lives in an idyllic present into which erupts the beast of ethnic hatred. The writers of the essays are not the first to create this idyllic, pastoral picture of the Bengali village. Quintessentially a product of cities (mainly Calcutta), a picture of the ideal Bengali village had been developing since the 1880s, when a host of nationalist writers such as Bankimchandra Chatterjee and, later, Rabindranath Tagore drew on new perceptions of the countryside to create, for and on behalf on the urban middle classes, a powerfully nostalgic and pastoral image of the generic Bengali village. Thus, the older *basha/bari* distinction was rewritten into a much larger opposition between the city and the countryside. I do not have the space to develop the point here, but a few words may help set this literary convention in context.[13]

A cultural division between the western and the eastern parts of Bengal appears to be an old phenomenon. The name *East Bengal* as used to designate a geographic division may have been of modern colonial and administrative origin, but the languages and the ways of life of the people of the eastern side of Bengal were long an object of amused contempt for those of the western side, who called the easterners *bangals* (men from the East). We know, for example, that the great Bengali Vaisnava leader Chaitanya of the late fifteenth, early sixteenth century reportedly entertained his mother after his travels in the East by deliberately mimicking the manners and speech of the *bangal*.[14]

This tradition, in which the *bangal* features as the butt of jokes, does not surface in Calcutta until well into the 1850s, by which time the city is expanding under European rule and people from the eastern side are beginning to move there in large numbers.[15] Texts produced before that time—for example, Bhabanicharan Bandyopadhyay's *Kalikataka-malalaya* (1823)—can be found that center on a character who is a stranger to the ways of the city, but, in them, the stranger is not made to speak in the *bangal* accent.[16] By the 1860s, however, the *bangal* emerges as a standard figure of fun on the Calcutta stage, one the most famous characters being that of Rammanikya in Dinabandhu Mitra's temperance-inspired play *Sadhabar Ekadashi* (1866). Rammanikya immortalizes the pathetic attempts of the country bumpkin desperate to transform himself into the city sophisticate. His self-pity struck a chord with the sense of marginality that migrants from East Bengal felt in a Calcutta dominated by the dandy descendants of the residents of the western half of the province: "I have eaten so much rubbish, yet I cannot be like a Calcuttan. What have I not done that is not Calcuttan-like? I have gone whoring, made my woman wear fine *dhoti* [the normal sign of a widow], consumed biscuits from European houses, imbibed *bandil* [brandy]—yet in spite of all this I could not be *kalkatta*-like! What use is this sinning body? Let me throw myself into the river; let me be eaten by sharks and crocodiles."[17]

Both before and after Independence, this image of the man from East Bengal has supplied much of the urban humor of Calcutta. Sometimes, in fact, gifted artists from East Bengal have used this to their advantage. The pioneering Bengali stand-up comedian Bhanu Banerjee, who made a career in the 1940s and 1950s selling precisely the accent at which Calcuttans loved to laugh, is a case in point.[18] But some significant changes in the cultural location of East Bengal began to take place in the 1880s as an emergent Bengali literary nationalism started to work out—in the poetry and music of Bankimchandra Chatterjee, Rabindranath Tagore, and others—an image of Mother Bengal as a land of bounty. Accompanying all this was the idea of a Bengali "folk" situated in the countryside and evincing, as against the artificiality of the city of Calcutta, the qualities of the Bengali "heart" (another category essential to the romantic nationalism of the period).[19]

The village, as opposed to the city, became the true spiritual home of the (urban) Bengali. The riverine landscape of East Bengal was as critical to this development as were new ways of seeing that landscape, including the influence on the Bengali imaginative eye of Sanskrit literature, classical Indian music, and European writing, painting, and photography. Two major literary and intellectual figures—Tagore and Nirad Chaudhuri—should suffice as evidence. Tagore's *Chhinnapatrabali*, a collection of letters written during the 1880s and the 1890s when his duties as landlord forced him to travel extensively in East Bengal, can easily be read as one of the first literary efforts in modern Bengali prose to deploy the Western notion of perspective when describing the landscape:

> Some people's minds are like the *wet plate* of a *photograph;* unless the photo is printed on paper right away, it is wasted. My mind is of that type. Whenever I see a [natural] scene, I think I must write it down carefully in a letter.

> Our boat is anchored on the other side of Shilaidaha in front of a sandbank. It is a huge sandbank—a vast expanse, no end in sight. Only the river appears as a line from time to time. There are no villages, no humans, no trees, no grass. . . . Turning the head to the east one can see only the endless blue above and an infinite paleness down below. The sky is empty, and so is the earth, a poor, dry, and harsh emptiness below and a disembodied, vast emptiness above. Nowhere is to be seen such *desolation*.

I had sat outside for barely fifteen minutes yesterday when massive clouds collected in the western sky—very dense, disorderly clouds, lit up here and there by stealthy rays of light falling on them—just as we see in some paintings of storms.[20]

Nirad Chaudhuri's self-conscious discussion of the Bengali landscape and his experience of it in the 1920s shows the same changes to be still under way a few decades on. Chaudhuri's discussion is extremely aware of the recent origins of the practice of seeing the Bengal countryside as beautiful. "The curious thing was," writes Chaudhuri, "that the Bengalis taken collectively showed no awareness of their natural environment, not even of their great rivers." He adds: "Generally speaking, when modern Bengalis acquired a feeling for the beauties of nature they showed it by a vicarious enjoyment of those described in the source of their new feeling, namely, English literature. Thus English and Scottish landscapes in their imaginative evocation became the staple of the enjoyment." Chaudhuri's own experience of coming to grips with the landscape of Bengal shows the modernity of the landscape question in Bengali history. Indeed, one could argue that nationalist perceptions of the Bengal landscape owed much to the labor of cultural workers such as Chaudhuri himself, who writes:

When I grew up I began to put this question to myself: does the Bengali landscape have any beauty? . . . I could not be sure. . . . But one day I had an experience which I can regard as conversion in the religious sense. That was in 1927 during that very last stay at Kishorganj. I was always in the habit of taking long walks, and on that day I was strolling along the railway embankment northwards from Kishorganj. After I had gone about three miles I suddenly noticed a homestead with half-a-dozen huts to my left, which was silhouetted against the sunset. There was a long pool of water by the side of the railway line. . . . There was the usual pond before it. . . . The whole scene was like one of Constable's landscapes, and I can confirm the impression after seeing the Constable country. . . . I do not know if other Bengalis have felt like me, but for me it was like enlightenment bestowed in a blessed moment.[21]

It would be untrue to give the impression that this was all that there was to the way in which the city/country question was given shape in Calcutta's urbanism. The nostalgic, folksy image of the village never died. In the early decades of the twentieth century, however, after the emotionalism of the Swadeshi movement (1905–8) had subsided, realistic novels such as Saratchandra Chatterjee's *Pallisamaj* helped develop yet another stereotype of Bengali rural society. Bengali villages, so often described as abodes of peace, now became the obstacle to Bengali enlightenment. Factionalism, caste-based exploitation, and malarial diseases came to be seen as the predominant characteristic of life in rural Bengal, making villages the ideal scene for nationalist development work.[22] Yet the softer image, located in the lush water-washed landscape of East Bengal, remained and was celebrated, for instance, in Jibanananda Das's sonnet cycle from the 1930s *Rupashi Bangla* (Bengal the beautiful).[23]

A compromise between these two images of the Bengali village—the idyllic pastoral haunt of the nationalist imagination and the fallen social space calling for nationalist reform—was reached in Bibhutibushan Bandyopadhyay's famous novel *Pather panchali*. Published in 1927, it spoke to a dearly held urban image of the generic Bengali village—a place, it is true, marked by suffering, poverty, and, sometimes, a meanness of spirit, but yet the abode of some very tender sentiments of intimacy, innocence, and kinship. This was the Bengali village transformed by modern cultural values. The exact geographic location of the village of Nischindipur, in which the story of *Pather panchali* unfolds, was not relevant to the way in which Bengali readers appreciated the story. As Suniti Chatterjee, the noted linguist, said of the novel: "I have always lived in Calcutta, but I have affection for the village. I feel that Nischindipur is familiar to me. Likewise, the story of Apu and Durga [the protagonist and his sister] seems to be our own, even though we have grown up in the city."[24]

It is not surprising, then, that journeys to East Bengal, to the countryside, should be a major feature of the literature dealing with the beauty of the Bengali landscape. For, as I have said, the perception was urban. Tagore's eyes often frame the countryside through the window of the boat on which he traveled the countryside. He was capable of realistic and critical descriptions of rural life, but the eye that produced the following description saw the village from a distance: "Now, after a long time, being seated near the window of my *boat*, I have found some peace of mind. . . . I sit in a reclining position by the side of this open window. I feel the touch of a gentle breeze caressing my head. My body is weak and slothful having suffered a prolonged illness, and this nursing by nature, calm and soothing, feels very sweet at this time."[25]

Travel—by boat—is a major motif in Nirad Chaudhuri's appreciation of the Bengali landscape as well:

Consciously, I never credited Bengal with beautiful landscapes. Yet when I passed through one or other of most commonly seen aspects of the Bengali landscape, for instance, a great river (and I have journeyed in boat and steamer on all the big three), the rice fields either in their green or in their gold stretching out to the horizon and billowing under strong winds, the bamboo clumps or the great banian tree, there was not one occasion when I did not lose my sense of being a viewer only and became one with these scenes like Wordsworth's boy.

I shall never forget one such occasion. It was 14 April 1913, that I was going from Goalundo Ghat to Narayanganj in the river steamer *Candor*. . . . I had just read about Turner's paintings in a book. . . . The glow of his paintings, visualized by imagination, seemed to lie on the wide landscape all around me.[26]

Tagore, of course, was a landlord visiting the countryside on business, Chaudhuri a salaried clerk visiting his family in East Bengal during holidays. But, in either case, as in the case of so many other members of the Bengali *bhadralok*, it was a matter of accommodating the village and the country in the rhythm of urban life, in which the village and holidays were intimately associated.

Chhere asha gram repeats these urban-pastoral associations that informed the Bengali sense of a beautiful life, a life that, the authors of the essays said, was never theirs in the city. These associations appear, not as so many masterpieces of Bengali writing, but as hackneyed expressions derived from Tagore and other sources, as pieces of literary kitsch aimed at the shared nostalgia of the city's educated Hindu middle classes (the *bhadralok*). In other words, this memory places the idyllic village squarely in the middle of the country/city question as it had evolved in Calcutta's urban culture. Here, too, the beauty of the village is often tied to travel by boat and to the rhythms of holidays in the lives of urban workers or students, the holidays coinciding with religious festivals. I reproduce yet another long string of quotations to illustrate how pervasive these sentiments are:

> I remember the days of autumn. How long people would wait the whole year for this season to come. And what preparation! The people who lived afar were returning home. Every day, new boats would come and lay anchor on the banks of the Dhaleshwari. We boys would crowd the [riverside]. For a few days, Gangkhali was full of people. And everybody would renew their acquaintances. (Shabhar, Dhaka; p. 12)

> The steamers on the Narayanganj line would leave Goalundo . . . and stop at Kanchanpur. The wind on the Padma would carry to

our Station *ghat* [steps leading from the bank of a river to the water] the sound of the siren of departing steamers. And the sound would be heard in other villages across the Ilamora fields and the tanks of Aairmara. . . . All the people of this district knew that their relatives who lived in exile in Calcutta were coming by those steamers. (Notakhola, Dhaka; p. 47)

We are educated; we have tasted the intoxication of the city. We have lost our caste. That is why we feel international. Without tap water and machine-made bread nothing tastes good to our palate. . . . In our lives, the door that will allow us to return to the village has been shut forever. (Binyapher, Mymensingh; pp. 68–69)

We had to take the ferry across the Jamuna after alighting at the Sirajganj *ghat* and then take a boat to our village. I can clearly recall, even in darkness, the picture of the sun setting on the river. When the young sun, bright and bearing [the message of hope], appeared in the body of the sky, my head would automatically bow at its feet. I found life in the water of the river and youth in the sun. . . . The taste of the gravy of rice and curried Hilsa fish that I used to have at the Sirajganj Hotel those days still lingers in my mouth like the taste of nectar. (Sankrail, Mymensingh; pp. 89–90)

My [village,] Gomdandi, surrounded by the endless beauty of nature, had only green on all four sides. Whenever we could get over the seduction of the artificial environment of the city and find refuge in the green lap of the village, our mother, we would forget all the sadness and suffering of city life. . . . traveling on boats with white sails along the Karnaphuli in the month of Bhadra and Aswin, when the river overflowed both banks, the exiles' minds would thrill at the very sight of the paddies. (Gomdandi, Chittagong; p. 196)

The *puja* [holidays on account of religious festivals] are close. At this time of the year, every year, the mind yearns to go back to Shilaida[ha]. As soon as we got off at the Kustia station, our hearts would fill with an immeasurable sense of joy. (Shilaidaha, Kustia; p. 286)

I especially remember today the days of the Durga *puja* [worship]. Every year I would impatiently look forward to these days. A few days before the *puja* I would leave Calcutta for the village. The distance seemed unending. The moment I set foot in the village station after the long journey, I felt like a king. Who am I in Calcutta? I am only one among the innumerable ordinary men. In my village, at the very sight of me the stationmaster would ask with a smile, "So you have come back to *desh?*" (Phulbari, Dinajpur; p. 306)

It was within this country/city division that the village appeared both as an ideal and as an idyll, its idyllic qualities enhanced—in the experience of the writers and in their telling of their stories—by allusions to literature and festivals. As we have already seen, both types of allusion actually direct our attention to the city, where this literature was produced and the major Hindu festivals punctuate the annual and secular calendar of modern work. But both also imaginatively endow the village with its folk character, festivals being particularly important to such a construction.[27] The literary allusions are sometimes direct and sometimes buried in the very style of writing:

> Whenever I could break the harsh and gloomy bonds of the city and place myself within the affectionate and calming embrace of my mother country, I would remember the truth of the great message of the Kaviguru [Tagore]. . . . In a moment I would forget the insults, the suffering, and the weariness of the city. (Gabha, Barisal; pp. 111–12)

> Today I am a man of Calcutta. But I cannot forget her in the dust of whose . . . tender soil I was born. . . . The moment I get a holiday, I feel like running away to that village three hundred miles away. I wish I could walk along the tracks of that dream-tinged green village of Bikrampur and sing like I used to as a child: "Blessed is my life, Mother, that I have been born in this land."[28] (Bajrajogini, Dhaka; p. 4)

MEMORY AND ETHNICITY: THE PLACE OF THE MUSLIM

Where was the place of the Muslim—or, indeed, of people who were not Bengalis—in this idyll? Did the Bengali home that the village was supposed to be not have a place for the Bengali Muslims? The language of kinship is one of the means by which the other is absorbed into the idyllic and harmonious village. Muslims participated in the Hindu festivals and, thus, were narratively absorbed into the image of the eternal Bengali folk. The boatmen and other Muslims treated Hindus with civility and are, hence, placed within the pleasures of the imagined communal life of the village. Even the marketplace is seen as an extension of this harmony. As the following quotations show, the idyllic nature of this remembered village performed a particular function in the narrative structure of these memories of the Partition. If the village was always an abode of perfect ethnic harmony, the eruption of Muslim hostility toward the Hindus could only ever be a shocking and entirely unreasonable break with the past. The idyllic picture of the village helped enlarge the trauma of violence and dislocation:

> There was a woman who belonged to the Muslim community of a distant village. We called her Madhupishi [Auntie Madhu]. It was said that she had no family. She would often come to our house. We were apparently all she had—there is no counting the number of times she would say this. Never did the thought arise in our minds that Madhupishi was Muslim. She would often bring us presents from her house or fruit and herbs from the field. We would receive them with eagerness and joy. Not only this. A group of Bihari people, villagers from Bihar, . . . had become people of this village, sharing our soul. . . . Are they still there in my village? . . . In our childhood we noticed that the Muslims' joy at Durga *puja* was not any less than ours. As in the Hindu households, new clothes would be bought in their houses too. Muslim women would go from one neighborhood to another to see the images [of Durga]. (Shabhar, Dhaka; pp. 8, 13)

> The moment the college closed for the summer vacation, I restlessly anticipated my return home to the village. Barisal is full of waterways. When would the steamer arrive at the Gaurnadi station?—with what anticipation I would look forward to it. As soon as I reached the *ghat*, Shonamaddi, the [Muslim] boatman, would smile his ever-familiar smile and say, "Master, so you have arrived? Come, I have brought my boat. Of course, I knew that you would come today!" (Chandshi, Barisal; pp. 131–32)

> The Goddess Kali was a live [potent] goddess in this region. People used to come from many distant villages to worship [her] . . . seeking fulfillment of their desires. I have seen Muslim brothers make pledges [to the goddess] with folded hands. . . . I cannot recall seeing an instance of devotion to Kali that was so independent of caste or religion. (Shonarang, Dhaka; p. 58)

> "Babu, so you have come back to the village?" asks the Muslim peasant out of an ordinary sense of etiquette. . . . A strong, pungent smell assails my nostrils as I approach the house of Syed Munshi. He works both as a *kaviraj* [an ayurvedic doctor] and as a teacher. . . . He got calls whenever anything happened to small children in our village. There was no demand for "visits" [fees],

but often he would receive [gifts] of homegrown fruit and vegetables. Even today I consider them [the Muslims mentioned] the closest of my relatives. For so long we Hindus and Muslims have lived together like brothers—we have always felt a strong connection with everybody. . . . But today? (Dakatia, Khulna; p. 258)

In this idyllic home, it is the Muslim of the Muslim League who erupts as a figure of enigma, as a complete rupture from the past, a modernist dream of "junking the past" gone completely mad, a discordant image on a canvas of harmony. The following description of a Muslim man called Yaad Ali is typical:

They used to build the image of the goddess on our *chandimandap* [the courtyard of a well-to-do Hindu household used for communal worship]. Close to the time of the *pujas,* three potters would be at work late into the night, working by the light of lanterns. Until the time they were overwhelmed by sleep, a crowd of children . . . would sit there making many demands [on the potters]: "Brother Jogen, could you please paint my old doll? . . . My horse has a broken leg, Brother Jogen, could you please mend it?" "You children, don't talk when it is time for work!"—Yaad Ali would scold the children from the other side of the courtyard. ". . . Don't you listen to these rascals Mr. Pal; concentrate on painting; after all, this is all God's work," Yaad Ali would advise Jogen. But, even before we left the village, we noticed that Yaad had changed. He is a leader of the Ansars now. He would not even say the name of a Hindu god; he now explains Islam beautifully! (Kherupara, Dhaka; pp. 27–28)

The story of Yaad's transformation into an activist Muslim and the utter incomprehensibility of that phenomenon to the authors of the essays of *Chhere asha gram* give us a clue to the problem of this discourse of value within which the Hindu authors sought to place their Muslim brothers. As instances of public memory, these essays eschew the low language of prejudice and produce, instead, a language of cultural value. The home that the Hindu refugee has lost is meant to be more than just his home; it is the home of the Bengali nationality, the village in which in the 1880s nationalist writers had found the heart of Bengal. And this illustrates a fundamental problem in the history of the modern Bengali nationality—the fact that this nationalist construction of home was a Hindu home.

It is not that the Muslims did not share any of this language—after all, the national anthem of Bangladesh is a song of Tagore's that powerfully expresses the nostalgia that I have discussed. The point is, rather, that, for all the talk of harmony between Hindus and Muslims, not a single sentence can be found in *Chhere asha gram* suggesting the value (for both Hindus and Muslims) of Islamic ideas of the sacred. What *can* be found are passages that conceive of an East Bengal deprived of a vibrant Hindu community as dead (and this at a time when the Muslims of East Bengal would have been savoring their newfound independence):

> The villages, markets, settlements, of East Bengal are today speechless and without life, their consciousness wiped out by the horrors of the end of time [*kalpanta:* the measure of a day in the life of the supreme Hindu god, Brahma]. In that land of "thirteen festivals in twelve months" [a Hindu Bengali saying], no conch shell is sounded marking the advent of the darkness of evening, no ululation in the hesitant voice of the housewife is to be heard on Thursday evenings, the time for the worship of [the goddess] Lakshmi. The *ektara* [a musical instrument] is silent at the gatherings of the Vaisnavas, the string of the *gobijantra* [an instrument played by bauls] has perhaps acquired rust, while mice and cockroaches have probably built their worlds cutting into the leather of the drums of the devotees of Harisabha [place for Hindu devotional singing]. (Kherupara, Dhaka; p. 22)

In other words, without the sense of a Hindu home, East Bengal is reduced to an eerie emptiness!

This is where *Chhere asha gram* leaves us, with the central problem of the history of Hindu Bengali nationality. Hindu nationalism had created a sense of home that combined the sacred with the beautiful. And, even though this sense of home embodied notions of the sacred, it was not intolerant of the Muslim as such. The Muslim—that is, the non–Muslim League Muslim, the Muslim who did not demand Pakistan—had a place in it. But the home was still a Hindu home, its sense of the sacred constructed through an idiom that was recognizably Hindu. And no thought was given to what it might mean for a Hindu to be a guest in a Muslim home similarly constructed, one embodying Islamic notions of the sacred, as did the demand for Pakistan.

It is in this sense that what speaks of shared cultural values in the essays in *Chhere asha gram* also speaks, ultimately, of prejudice. In treating the Bengali Muslim's ethnic hatred as something inherently inexplicable and, hence, profoundly shocking, the essays refuse to acknowledge their own prejudice. I say this to underline the intimate relation that necessarily exists between values and prejudices. When unattended by critique, and in moments of crisis, not only do our values play a role in producing a sense of home, a sense of community among ourselves and with others, but they can also stop us from hearing what the other might be saying to us at that moment. My argument, then, is not one that recommends the "homelessness" of the modern; being at home is not something that we choose at will.[29] "Poetically, man dwells . . ."—true, but within the poetry lies the poison of inescapable prejudice, all the more unrecognizable because it comes disguised as value.

NINE The In-Human and the Ethical in Communal Violence

In concluding this book, I want to stay with the theme of the Partition and examine, briefly, how some of the recent writings of the memories of the violence of 1947 may help us think "the politics of difference." I do not approach this question as a specialist in the history of the Partition of India. My own relation to the history of the Partition is personal. My parents' lives and those of their families were affected by it.

I was born and grew up in a Calcutta struggling to accommodate the numberless refugees who migrated from East Pakistan through the 1950s and made that city their own. My mother's family was part of that story. I came to know about life in Dhaka through the two family albums of old photographs that my mother had held on to as the most precious of her possessions while the family moved about from one house to another in Calcutta in the riot-torn days of August 1946.

Growing up, all my cousins and I strongly identified with a sporting team called the East Bengal Club—the club with which most of the displaced people from East Bengal, now Bangladesh, associated themselves. We were called *ban-*

gals, while the older natives of Calcutta, who identified more with the western part of Bengal, were called *ghotis.*[1] The *ghotis* rooted for a rival and older soccer team, the Mohun Bagan Club.

We had not heard about academic critiques of essentialism in those days, so *bangals* and *ghotis* proceeded to elaborate and ritualize their differences with the enthusiasm of peoples whom anthropologists sometimes call *warring tribes.* We both spoke Bengali, but with different accents; we loved the Hilsa fish, while they loved prawns; our songs were set to different tunes; our traditions of courtesy were different; and every act of intermarriage was noticed and commented on. The incoming daughter-in-law often had to suffer jokes, if not rude and cruel remarks, at the expense of her natal family.

We mostly lived in different parts of the city. The northern part, the old colonial native town, was seen as predominantly *ghoti,* the "upstart" southern part, which was developed in the 1920s and later, as predominantly *bangal.* And, every time the two soccer clubs met, the spirit of rivalry between the *bangals* and the *ghotis* spilled over into areas far beyond the sporting ground. If the East Bengal Club won, the price of Hilsa went up, for every *bangal* household celebrated. Prawns suffered badly if the victory went to the other side. Sometimes, heads were broken on the playing field. Indeed, my own memory of the last soccer match that I attended, in the company of my friend Partha Chatterjee, is of a flying stone that accidentally hit me on the head after a minor riot broke out in the stands when our club lost.

Yet, over time, the city came to terms with these differences, and a composite urban culture grew up in which we learned to joke about and enjoy the things that made us seem different. And this enjoyment was never completely innocuous; it was also a part of our mutual rivalry. Our neighbors were a family of *ghotis,* and among them was a young man I knew as Bokada. My senior by quite a few years, he was a devoted supporter of the Mohun Bagan Club.

Those were our "radio days." I was—and still am—an extremely superstitious person whenever it came to East Bengal playing the *ghoti* club, Mohun Bagan. I had the idea that East Bengal would do badly if I did not stay glued to the radio set for the entire duration of the live commentary on the game. I would not eat or even sit down while the match was on as if my devotion and willingness to suffer for the club would somehow be magically transformed into a good-luck charm for them. Bokada knew about this secret. His tactic, therefore, was to stand on the road outside my parents' house and call out my name so that I had to leave the radio and answer him. I would be in an acute state of dilemma between my sense of politeness and my sense of loyalty to the club. We both recognized that this was part of the ongoing culture war between the *bangals* and the *ghotis,* and, while it bristled as a war tactic when the battle was on, I would laugh about Bokada's wiliness at other times and plan some suitable revenge.

This culture war actually fed the culture industries of post-Partition Calcutta. Radio and film played a key part in this process. Songs from East Bengal—through artists such as Nirmalendu Chaudhuri—became the staple of what the All India Radio popularized as the "folk" genre. On the screen and on the stage, two stand-up comedians, Bhanu Banerjee and Jahar Ray, came to embody the essentials of the *bangal* and the *ghoti,* respectively. Their simulated and orchestrated clashes were a major ingredient of the humor that Calcutta movies used in the 1950s and the early 1960s. Bhanu Banerjee and Jahar Ray became such a routine act that, eventually, a film called *Bhanu Goyenda Jahar Assistant* (*goyenda* translates as "detective") was made in the early 1960s depicting Banerjee as a *bangal* Holmes with Ray, a veritable *ghoti* Dr. Watson, in tow. Clearly, all the differences accentuated in the city by the refugee influx also helped create a culture industry. Commodification and consumption of difference became as much a way of living with difference as were humor and our occasional frictions.

Now, this was by no means the whole story of refugee resettlement in West Bengal and elsewhere. Of course, there was suffering—too much of it, in fact. Thanks to the recent writings of Menon, Bhasin, Butalia, Das, Pandey, and others, we now know that the Partition was neither a single event nor something confined merely to the time when the country was officially divided. People who were uprooted on both sides of the border faced enormous deprivation. I do not deny that. I mean my memories of the 1950s and the 1960s to illustrate and think through a distinction that I want to make between two ways of relating to difference: proximity and identity. These are abstract concepts, and let me first define them before fleshing them out with examples. I hope that this exercise will clarify why I make these distinctions.

By *identity,* I mean a mode of relating to difference in which difference is either congealed or concealed. That is to say, either it is frozen, fixed, or it is erased by some claim of being identical or the same. By *proximity,* I mean the opposite mode, one of relating to difference in which (historical and contingent) difference is neither reified nor erased but negotiated. The *ghotis* and *bangals* of my construction here (I repeat, in my *construction,* not always in reality), I would say, lived in proximity to, rather than in intimacy with, each other.

Why do I make this distinction? Because, it seems to me, the study of how people remember the Partition, the memories of the mayhem that accompanied it, cannot be separated from a question that is characteristic of the concerns of scholarship around the globe today. Of course, there have been specifically South Asian events inviting—and even inciting—the study of Partition violence. One may mention the organized anti-Sikh pogrom of 1984, the anti-Muslim and anti-Christian politics of the Bharatiya Janata Party (BJP), the endless taking of lives in Kashmir and Sri Lanka, the fiftieth birthday of the nation, and so on. But there is also a global context for these studies. Behind the contemporary interest in the Nazi Holocaust, the ethnic cleansing in the Balkans, the murderous events in Rwanda-Burundi, is a fundamental question of contemporary democratic thought.

The concept of diversity has become more salient in democracies today than that of development. All democratically minded people are wrestling with the question, How do we live with difference at a time when democracies increasingly accept and embrace the principle of infinite diversity? The earlier histories of the Partition were often straightforwardly historical. They sought to explain why the division of the country happened, its timing, the different political personalities, parties, and formations that contributed to it. The new histories—Menon and Bhasin's *Borders and Boundaries,* Butalia's *The Other Side of Silence,* Pandey's *Remembering Partition,* and Das's *Critical Events,* for example—focus more consciously on the experience of violence, suffering, and survival.[2] *Borders and Boundaries* and *The Other Side of Silence* also participate in our times by presenting powerful and cutting feminist critiques of the different, patriarchal ways in which nations and communities seek to possess "their" women.

At the heart of these histories and memories of violence is not so much the political-institutional history of the nation—although this still remains important—as the question of how humans create absolute others out of other humans. There is no act of human cruelty that is not accompanied by a certain lack of identification. In this sense, studies of the violence of the Partition are studies of the politics of difference. The ideologies that both the perpetrators and the victims of collective and social violence used to justify/understand the act of violence involved this process of "othering." As Butalia found out in the course of her research, memories of violence tended to locate it "somewhere outside, a distance away from the boundaries of the family and the community." "Violence is seen," she writes, "as relating only to the other." A fundamental problem, in other words, in the narration of social—and not individual, pathological, or casual—violence is the difficulty of recognizing this violence as also belonging to the self that speaks. "Some-how," says Butalia, "when we speak of the violence of Partition, we do not touch the violence within ourselves."[3]

It is clear that the inhumanity of collective violence is, after all, hu-man. The inhuman is in humans and, in that sense, is better written as *in-human.* Yet both fictional and autobiographical depictions of vio-lence that was nothing but social consign it to a time and space marked, paradoxically, by an assumed death of the social. "You see," said Krishna Thapar talking to Menon and Bhasin, "we did not do less to the Mus-lims—we had also become such brutes. . . . We lost all humanity." Or you have the trope of what I call *thingification.* (Commodification would be a special case of thingification.) Women were sold, said the for-mer activist Kamlaben Patel, "in the same way that baskets of grapes or oranges are sold or gifted."[4] In conversation with Butalia, Patel said: "I found it difficult to believe human beings could be like this. It was as if the demons had come down on earth." Butalia herself resorts to the nonhuman image of the thing to capture the moment when the other-ing of others becomes absolute: "The transformation of the 'other' from a human being to the enemy, a *thing* to be destroyed before it destroyed you, became the all-important imperative."[5] Kavita Daiya has uncov-ered a similar series of rhetorical moves in representations of Partition vi-olence in fiction and film. Stories such as "The Woman in the Red Rain-coat" or "Colder than Ice" by Manto, for example, portray the desire for "ethnic sexual violence" by reducing women to mere bodily things, sometimes even dead bodies.[6]

These narratives of Partition violence, then—to use words once writ-ten by Sartre—"lay claim to and deny the human condition at the same time," such is the contradictory explosiveness of their rhetoric.[7] It is ob-vious that, for all the rendering of the human into a mere thing that col-lective violence may appear to perform, the recognition by one human of another as human is its fundamental precondition. It is humans who torture, rape, oppress, exploit, other humans. We cannot do these things to objects. We cannot call objects *Muslim* or *Hindu* except in reference to their relation to humans. Humans can torture other live beings, but they do not do so in a collective spirit of historical revenge. That is why it must be said that, even in denying the humanity of the victim of vio-lence, the perpetrator of violence and torture does, to begin with, rec-ognize the victim as human. In this unintentional practice of mutual hu-man recognition lies the ground for the conception of proximity. The denial of the victim's humanity, thus, proceeds necessarily from this ini-tial recognition of it. It is the very perverse nature of this recognition of one human by another that the language of memories seeks to capture through a paradoxical set of images and metaphors that speak of the death of the human.

This paradox cannot be resolved. We cannot produce narratives that relive and celebrate the moment of inhumanity even though we can all imagine the boastful stories of cruelty that would have circulated among men who killed in the days of the riots. But they are like the well-known yet suppressed stories of barbarism of yesterday that underlie today's civility in every society. That barbarism is a practice of a certain kind of social, one that can be written about only as though it signified the death of the social. Faced with such banality of evil, the question arises, Why remember? Is not remembering potentially dangerous? Is not murderous violence better dealt with simply by forgetting it? Butalia tackles this question head-on. She writes: "Over the years, despite many uncertainties, I have become increasingly convinced that while it may be dangerous to remember, it is also essential to do so—not so that we can come to terms with it but because unlocking memory and remembering is an essential part of beginning the process of resolving, perhaps even of forgetting."[8]

So the call to memory is a plea for a talking cure. And, as in the case of all talking cures, there is no guarantee that the cure will be permanent. It is an ethical call. It is a call that issues from one's immersion in the present, amid violence, as one asks the question, How do I comport myself toward the politics of difference? The new histories of the Partition and its attendant violence depart from older social-science histories in abjuring aspirations toward social engineering. When we recognize the banality of evil, we do not look for utopian blueprints of social orders from which the evil of violence will be eternally banished. The call to remember that Butalia, Menon and Bhasin, Pandey, and others issue is not in search of permanent, a priori solutions to the ways in which modernity, governmentality, and their institutional arrangements can exacerbate the in-human. What animates contemporary investigations of the memories of the violence of 1947 and beyond is the question of how to live with difference today.

It was with this larger question in mind that I made the distinction between *proximity* and *identity*. I see the distinction illustrated by the memories incited to speech by the new historians. Depending on the circumstances surrounding them, both the practices of proximity and those of identity can kill us or save us.

Sometimes, I see both principles embodied in the same narrative. Consider the story of a *tahsildar* [holder of an administrative office] in the western Punjab as told to Menon and Bhasin by Dayawati Kalra of Gandhi Vanita Ashram in Jalandhar. This man "would take Hindu young men from the camp and kill them." Surely, this act was to do with extirpating that which was not identical to the self. Yet, in an opposite gesture of making the different the same, the same man treated an abducted non-Muslim woman "like a daughter for over a year. Only when no one came for her did he suggest marriage to his son. No one else would have done so much. He was honourable." A more complicated case is that of a woman—"K"—whose brother spoke to Menon and Bhasin when they met him in Jammu in 1992. This non-Muslim woman had been forced into a Muslim family—an example, we could say, of the practice of identity tending to kill. We are told that she "lived on in Pakistan, had two sons and four daughters and commanded great respect in her family and community." Yet "she had complete freedom, . . . didn't believe in Islam, was not obliged to read the Qoran or say her namaaz. But her name was changed to Sarwar Jahan."[9] In this instance, practices born of identity clearly gave way—within historical limits—to those of proximity in the heart of the new family that was once foisted on her.

The new studies of the memories of Partition violence are salutary in reminding us that there is no a priori way of resolving, ahead of any concrete investigation, whether the practices of proximity are necessarily better than those of identity, or vice versa. Uncovering the patriarchal violence and undemocracy of the Indian and Pakistani governments' program to recover "abducted women" and restore them to their families, Menon and Bhasin effectively use the universalist and allegedly unmarked identity of the citizen to produce a cogent feminist critique of the program. They write: "The process of recovery, of putting abducted women back into place, was not conceived by the state as a relationship of *women as missing citizens* of the new state (if so, it would have endowed them with civil rights); rather, it chose to treat them as *missing members of religious and cultural communities* on whose behalf choices had to be made."[10]

As this particular example illustrates, the ethical space within which I am seeking to locate the practices of identity and proximity is never completely autonomous of the larger political field of governments, political parties, movements, and other institutions. Some practices of proximity, for instance, fell into disrepute once the larger movements for nationalisms, democracy, and social equality took hold of people's imagination. Menon and Bhasin quote a Hindu woman who saw the past as a time of peace in which practices of proximity and nonidentity did not necessarily give offense. She said, speaking of the past of Hindu-Muslim relations in the Punjab: "Roti-beti ka rishta nahin rakhte the, baki saab theek tha" (Menon and Bhasin give a somewhat Christian-sounding translation of this sentence: "We neither broke bread with them nor intermarried, the rest was fine").[11] Yet Butalia cites the case of a Bir Bahadur Singh for whom such practices of proximity, in retrospect, looked like exclusionary politics of identity: "They [Muslims] would eat in our houses but we would not eat in theirs and this is a bad thing, which I now realize. If they would come to our houses we would have two utensils in one corner of the house, and we would tell them, pick these up and eat in them; they would then wash them and keep them aside and this was such a terrible thing. This was the reason Pakistan was created. . . . All our dealings with them were so low that I am even ashamed to say it."[12]

There is no gainsaying the fact that the larger political context of 1947 influenced one's reading of these practices. Think of Beth Roy's *Some Trouble with Cows* documenting a rural riot between Hindu and Muslim peasants in East Pakistan soon after Independence. Surely, it was the larger political fact of Pakistan having been established that encouraged the Muslim peasants involved in this conflict to say to their Hindu neighbors, "We won't allow any Hindus to stay here," and the Hindus to say, "We won't allow any Muslims to stay this side of the river. We'll push them to the other side."[13] There is, in that sense, no "small voice of history" autonomous of the larger political sphere.[14] But the practices of proximity and identity still wrestled in many narratives as possible alternative ethical ways of relating to difference. They do not admit of resolutions that are free of all contexts.

But, in bringing this essay to a close, let me repeat here a story from the life of the noted Bengali filmmaker Mrinal Sen. It is a story that I have recounted elsewhere, but it is relevant to the issues under discussion.

Sen grew up in the 1920s and 1930s in a nationalist Congressite family in Faridpur. His family did not shun the company of Muslims. Once, says Sen, his oldest brother, then a high school student, showed their father a poem written by a Muslim boy from his class. Moved by the writing, Sen's father encouraged his son to invite this boy home. The young Muslim poet came, was befriended by the family, and, in Sen's words, became one of them: "My eldest brother brought his friend home. The boy turned up with his feet covered with dust, a pure peasant boy. The nickname of this poet was Sadhu. He would move in and out of our household as though he were a boy of this family. It was after I had grown up a little more that I came to know that he was not our brother."[15]

This poet, Sen reveals, was none other than the famous and gifted Muslim Bengali poet Jasimuddin. But Sen's narrative lets us see how a crisis set in, threatening to undermine this bond of putative kinship as the demand for Pakistan gathered strength. Jasimuddin was not unaf-

fected by the sentiments growing in the minds of many Bengali Muslims. Nor, from an opposing point of view, was Sen's father. Sen writes:

> There were no communal troubles in Faridpur. But Hindu-Muslim
> conflict was on the rise in other places and had an impact on Farid-
> pur as well. The grown-ups had to be a little careful therefore. . . .
> I noticed that a certain Hinduness asserted itself in my father
> whenever there was a communal conflict somewhere else. There
> would be furious arguments and counterarguments. And Jasimud-
> din would argue taking the side of Muslims. One day Jasimuddin
> said to my mother, "Mother, if it is true that I am one of your sons,
> why do you feed me seating me outside? Why is it that you never
> let me sit with your sons to eat from the same plate?"[16]

It is Sen's narrative resolution of the emotional impasse that this moment creates that allows us to see the contestation between the practices
of proximity and those of identity. He continues: "My mother found
herself in difficulty. What Jasim said was not untrue after all. But my
mother was helpless. She explained to him that she had no objection to
having him sit inside while feeding him but that the servants of the
household would not accept this arrangement. Her eyes glistening with
tears, she said, 'Sadhu, you may not know this, but it is I who washes up
after you.'"[17]

This is a poignant moment in stories of Hindu Bengali generosity.
The Hindu Bengali mother, who acts as a critical nodal point in the affective structure of kinship, speaks here for Hindu liberalism (in a loose,
not a doctrinal, sense) in acknowledging the call for justice in the griev-
ance of the Muslim person whom she has recognized as her son. At the
same time, she pleads helplessness, blaming—like men everywhere have
done at many critical moments in the history of modernity—tradition
and unreason, now allegedly embodied in the subaltern characters of the
household, the ignorant servants. But she does not stop there. Tearfully,
she makes a claim on the Muslim's sentiment: the mother has both accepted and transgressed difference for the sake of her feelings for her
Muslim son. Why would not the Muslim reciprocate?

Yet, however full of pathos this gesture may be, there is a deafness to
the other that structures her question from within. Jasimuddin, the
Muslim in Sen's story, was declining the role of good guest in a household that defined itself as Hindu. He was asking for a change in the rules
that defined hospitality and that decided the question of who was in the
position of offering it. Was he within his rights to do so? It is this larger
political question that goes unacknowledged and undiscussed in the
Hindu response in this story. Like numerous Hindu Bengali stories of

this kind, Sen's stands witness to a historic Hindu Bengali deafness to the call of the other. This deafness was as constitutive of ethnic distance as may be the more explicit elements of violence. It was a mark, indeed, of one's participation in the politics of ethnicity. To be deaf to the call for justice in Muslims' historical demand for a home embodying their own imagination of dwelling was to express prejudice, however silent that expression may have been.

In saying this, I do not mean to blame the Hindus, in particular those who were displaced, for their cup of suffering was more than full. I myself grew up around such suffering, as did many of my contemporaries. I mean, rather, to emphasize the importance of being sensitive to the larger field of the political within which the ethical must be situated. As I have said, there is no way of choosing between identity and proximity in an a priori manner. But let me end with a personal anecdote about the practice of proximity in a post-Partition context. It suggests, I think, that the relation between identity and proximity is not one of an either/ or quality.

I took my parents to Bangladesh in 1991 to visit my ancestral homes on both sides. My parents had not been back since the Partition. We went to the village in Bikrampur where my father spent his childhood and later his holidays when he studied and worked in Calcutta. We discovered that the Muslim family that used to work for my father's family was in occupation of the house. They had lived there since Independence. Their first worry was that we might have come back to reclaim property. They were a little tense in the beginning. The old man in the family was my father's age and remembered our family. He remembered some of the weddings that took place in that house. The first thing he said, to the consternation of his family, was: "All this is yours. You can take it back if you want." That was the field of the political coming into our conversations. Once we assured them, however, that we had come simply to see the house, that I lived outside India and had no practical interest in acquiring property in Bangladesh, they relaxed. And then a space opened up for what I have called *the practice of proximity*, that is, the practice of relating to historical and contingent difference by acknowledging and negotiating it.

They asked us to sit down in the garden outside the house. My mother was with the women of the household. A number of curious children had thronged around us. The old man's son, a politically active member of the local village council, was keeping a courteous but cautious eye on the proceedings. And the question arose about the seating arrangement. They had two comfortable chairs out and one not-so-comfortable stool. Whoever sat on the stool would also be at a lower level than those on the chairs. The old man offered me and my father the two chairs and made a gesture of taking the stool for himself, saying, "You are the masters, you should sit on the chairs." My father immediately countered saying, "No, no, those days are gone; we are not masters and servants. You should sit on the chair." The situation came to a successful resolution through my saying, "But you are both old and senior to me; it is I who should sit on the stool." Everybody found that acceptable. We had each acknowledged different kinds of difference, and even inequalities and equalities, without letting them give offense. We had, in other words, successfully negotiated some very historical and contingent differences. My parents and I returned that evening with very pleasant memories of the generous hospitality offered to us by the Muslim family.

I know that this resolution was contingent and temporary. It would not have happened if we were there in the larger political field and made a claim on the property. The larger field of the political exists, and we, as individuals, are rarely in a position to choose it. We find ourselves in it, we feel called to it, and we try to mold it to the extent that we can. But the political does not exhaust or foreclose the space of the ethical. Purely political and sociological histories often lose themselves in the impulse of causal analysis and, thus, in the designs of utopian social engineering. The new historians of the Partition remind us of the profound banality of evil. Their focus is on the normal and the everyday. The category of the everyday has now received a positive and theoretical valorization through our readings of Henri Lefebvre and Walter Benjamin and the like. The new histories of the Partition point to the irruptions into the moment of the everyday of the practices of both proximity and identity in the politics of difference. The explorations of history and memory show that only a capacity for a humanist critique can create the ethical moment in our narratives and offer, not a guarantee against the prejudice that kills, but an antidote with which to fight it. History must, like literature and philosophy, imbibe this spirit of critique.

NOTES

INTRODUCTION

1. See the thoughtful discussions in Dilip Parameshwar Gaonkar, "On Alternative Modernities," *Public Culture* 11, no. 1 (1999): 1–18; Arjun Appadurai, *Modernity at Large: Cultural Dimensions of Globalization* (Minneapolis: University of Minnesota Press, 1996), in particular, chaps. 1 and 5; and Lisa Rofel, "Rethinking Modernity: Space and Factory Discipline in China," in *Culture, Power, Place: Explanations in Critical Anthropology*, ed. Akhil Gupta and James Ferguson (Durham, N.C.: Duke University Press, 1997).

2. My position is, thus, somewhat different from that adopted in Bruno Latour's *We Have Never Been Modern* (trans. Catherine Porter [New York: Harvester, 1993]).

3. Aijaz Ahmad's *In Theory: Classes, Nations, Literatures* (London: Verso, 1992) is a good example of such polarized debate between Marxism and postmodernism.

4. Dipesh Chakrabarty, *Provincializing Europe: Postcolonial Thought and Historical Difference* (Princeton, N.J.: Princeton University Press, 2000).

5. See Hannah Arendt, *The Human Condition*, 2d ed. (Chicago: University of Chicago Press, 1998).

CHAPTER ONE

1. Arif Dirlik, "The Aura of Postcolonialism: Third World Criticism in the Age of Global Capitalism," in *Contemporary Postcolonial Theory: A Reader*, ed. P. Mongia (London: Arnold, 1996), 302.

2. See Walter Benjamin, "A Small History of Photography," in *One-Way Street and Other Writings*, trans. Edmund Jephcott and Kingsley Shorter (London: New Left Books, 1979).

3. See my discussion of the relation between nationalism and Marxism in Indian historiography in "Marxism and Modern India," in *After the End of History*, ed. A. Ryan (London: Collins & Brown, 1992), 79–84. Sanjey Seth's *Marxism, Theory, and Nationalist Politics: The Case of Colonial India* (Delhi: Sage, 1995) provides a

good analysis of the historical connections between Marxist thought and nationalist ideologies in British India.

4. See Bipan Chandra, *The Rise and Growth of Economic Nationalism in India: Economic Policies of Indian National Leadership, 1880–1905* (Delhi: People's, 1969); Anil Seal, *The Emergence of Indian Nationalism: Competition and Collaboration in the Later Nineteenth Century* (Cambridge: Cambridge University Press, 1968); A. R. Desai, *Social Background of Indian Nationalism* (Bombay: Asia, 1966); D. A. Low, ed., *Soundings in Modern South Asian History* (Canberra: Australian National University Press, 1968); B. S. Cohn, *An Anthropologist among the Historians and Other Essays* (Delhi: Oxford University Press, 1988); and Morris David Morris and D. Kumar, eds., *Indian Economy in the Nineteenth Century: A Symposium* (Delhi: Indian Economic and Social History Association, 1969).

5. The subtitle of Seal's *Emergence of Indian Nationalism* refers to the two themes of competition and collaboration.

6. See John Gallagher, Gordon Johnson, and Anil Seal, eds., *Locality, Province, and Nation: Essays on Indian Politics, 1870–1940* (Cambridge: Cambridge University Press, 1973).

7. In contradistinction to the so-called horizontal affiliations of class.

8. Anil Seal, "Imperialism and Nationalism in India," in ibid., 2.

9. See Bipan Chandra, *Nationalism and Colonialism in Modern India* (New Delhi: Orient Longman, 1979).

10. As one respected Indian historian wrote responding to the work of the Cambridge scholars: "Once, not so very long ago, to countless Indians nationalism was a fire in the blood" (Tapan Raychaudhuri, "Indian Nationalism as Animal Politics," *Historical Journal* 22, no. 3 [1979]: 747–63).

11. See Gyanendra Pandey, *The Ascendancy of the Congress in Uttar Pradesh, 1926–1934: A Study in Imperfect Mobilization* (Delhi: Oxford University Press, 1978); Majid Siddiqi, *Agrarian Unrest in North India: The United Provinces, 1918–1922* (Delhi: Vikas, 1978); Kapil Kumar, *Peasants in Revolt: Tenants, Landlords, Congress, and the Raj in Oudh, 1886–1922* (New Delhi: Manohar, 1984); David Arnold, *The Congress in Tamilnadu: National Politics in South Asia, 1919–1937* (New Delhi: Manohar, 1977); Histesranjan Sanyal, *Swarajer Pathe* (Calcutta: Papyrus, 1994); and David Hardiman, *Peasant Nationalists of Gujarat: Kheda District* (Delhi: Oxford University Press, 1981). See also the essays in D. A. Low, ed., *Congress and the Raj* (London: Heinemann, 1977).

12. See Ranajit Guha, introduction to *A Subaltern Studies Reader,* ed. Ranajit Guha (Minneapolis: University of Minnesota Press, 1998).

13. Ranajit Guha, "On Some Aspects of the Historiography of Colonial India," in *Subaltern Studies I: Writings on South Asian History and Society,* ed. Ranajit Guha (Delhi: Oxford University Press, 1982), 3.

14. See Antonio Gramsci, "Notes on Italian History," in *Selections from the Prison Notebooks,* ed. and trans. Quintin Hoare and Geoffrey Nowell Smith (New York: International, 1973).

15. Ranajit Guha, preface to *Subaltern Studies III: Writings on Indian History and Society,* ed. Ranajit Guha (Delhi: Oxford University Press, 1984), vii.

16. Ranajit Guha, "On Some Aspects of the Historiography of Colonial India," in *Selected Subaltern Studies,* ed. Ranajit Guha and Gayatri Chakravorty Spivak (New York: Oxford University Press, 1988), 3–4.

17. Ibid., 4–5.

18. E. J. Hobsbawm, *Primitive Rebels: Studies in Archaic Forms of Social Movement in the Nineteenth and Twentieth Centuries* (Manchester: Manchester University Press, 1978), 2.

19. See Ranajit Guha, *Elementary Aspects of Peasant Insurgency in Colonial India* (Delhi: Oxford University Press, 1983), chaps. 1 and 2.

20. Seal, *Emergence of Indian Nationalism,* 1.

21. Guha examines and critiques such Marxist positions in "The Prose of Counter-Insurgency," in *Selected Subaltern Studies,* ed. Ranajit Guha and Gayatri Chakravorty Spivak (New York: Oxford University Press, 1988), 45–86.

22. Guha, *Elementary Aspects,* 75.

23. Ibid., 6.

24. Hobsbawm, *Primitive Rebels,* 3.

25. Guha, *Elementary Aspects,* 6.

26. Guha, "On Some Aspects," 4.

27. Ibid., 5–6.

28. Ranajit Guha, "Colonialism in South Asia: A Dominance without Hegemony and Its Historiography," in *Dominance without Hegemony: History and Power in Colonial India* (Cambridge, Mass.: Harvard University Press, 1997), 97–98.

29. Guha, "On Some Aspects," 5–6.

30. This aspect of the project later came to be developed by Partha Chatterjee, Gyanendra Pandey, and Shahid Amin (see the discussion below).

31. Eugen Weber, *Peasants into Frenchmen: The Modernization of Rural France, 1870–1914* (Stanford, Calif.: Stanford University Press, 1976), xvi.

32. See E. P. Thompson on *experience:* "A category which, however imperfect it may be, is indispensable to the historian, since it comprises mental and emotional response, whether of an individual or of a social group, to many inter-related events" ("The Poverty of Theory; or, An Orrery of Errors," in *The Poverty of Theory and Other Essays* [London: Merlin, 1979], 199). See also Keith Thomas, "History and Anthropology," *Past and Present,* no. 24 (April 1963): 3–18.

33. See Guha, *Elementary Aspects,* chaps. 1 and 2.

34. Guha's own reading strategies are spelled out in "The Prose of Counter-Insurgency" and are implicit throughout *Elementary Aspects.*

35. To be fair, not only does Thompson ("The Poverty of Theory," 210, 222) write about "voices clamour[ing] from the past"—"not the historian's voice, please observe; *their* [i.e., the historical characters'] *own voices*"—but he also has much to say about how historians interrogate their sources in order to listen to the lost voices of history.

36. This is best exemplified in Guha's "The Prose of Counter-Insurgency." See also Gayatri Chakravorty Spivak, introduction to Guha and Chakravorty Spivak, eds., *Selected Subaltern Studies.*

37. On this retirement, see Guha's introduction to *Subaltern Studies VI* (Delhi: Oxford University Press, 1988).

38. Edward Said, foreword to Guha and Chakravorty Spivak, eds., *Selected Subaltern Studies,* v.

39. Gayatri Chakravorty Spivak, "Subaltern Studies: Deconstructing Historiography," in Guha and Chakravorty Spivak eds., *Selected Subaltern Studies,* 3–32.

40. Rosalind O'Hanlon, "Recovering the Subject: Subaltern Studies and Histories of Resistance in Colonial South Asia," *Modern Asian Studies* 22, no. 1 (1988): 189–224.

41. Gayatri Chakravorty Spivak, "Can the Subaltern Speak?" in *Colonial Discourse and Postcolonial Theory: A Reader,* ed. P. Williams and L. Chrisman (New York: Columbia University Press, 1994), 66–111.

42. See Ranajit Guha, "Chandra's Death," in Guha, ed., *A Subaltern Studies Reader,* 34–62; Partha Chatterjee, "The Nationalist Resolution of the Woman Question," reprinted as "The Nation and Its Women" in his *The Nation and Its Fragments: Colonial and Post-Colonial Histories* (Princeton, N.J.: Princeton University Press, 1993); and Susie Tharu and Tejaswini Niranjana, "Problems for a Contemporary Theory of Gender," in *Subaltern Studies IX,* ed. Shahid Amin and Dipesh Chakrabarty (Delhi: Oxford University Press, 1996), 232–60.

43. Partha Chatterjee, *Nationalist Thought and the Colonial World* (London: Zed, 1986).

44. Gyanendra Paney, *Remembering Partition: Violence, Nationalism, and History in India* (Cambridge: Cambridge University Press, 2001).

45. Gyanendra Pandey, *The Construction of Communalism in Colonial North India* (Delhi: Oxford University Press, 1990), and "In Defense of the Fragment: Writing about Hindu-Muslim Riots in India Today" in Guha, ed., *A Subaltern Studies Reader,* 1–33; Chatterjee, *The Nation and Its Fragments;* Shahid Amin, *Event, Memory, Metaphor* (Berkeley and Los Angeles: University of California Press, 1995).

46. Gyan Prakash has led the debate on nonfoundational histories with his well-known essay "Writing Post-Orientalist Histories of the Third World: Perspectives from Indian Historiography" (*Comparative Studies in Society and History* 32 [April 1990]: 383–408). Ranajit Guha's "An Indian Historiography of India: Hegemonic Implications of a Nineteenth-Century Agenda" (in his *Dominance without Hegemony*), Chatterjee's "The Nation and Its Pasts" (in his *The Nation and Its Fragments*), Gyanendra Pandey's "*Subaltern Studies:* From a Critique of Nationalism to a Critique of History" (Johns Hopkins University, 1997, typescript), and Shahid Amin's "Alternative Histories: A View from India" (University of Delhi, 1997, typescript) are contributions to the debates on historiography and the status of historical knowledge to which *Subaltern Studies* has given rise. In this connection, see also Shail Mayaram's treatment of memory and history in her "Speech, Silence, and the Making of Partition Violence in Mewat," in Amin and Chakrabarty, eds., *Subaltern Studies IX,* 126–64; and Ajay Skaria, *Hybrid Histories* (Delhi: Oxford University Press, 1999).

47. Exemplified by the analysis of the discourses of science and modernity in colonial India in Gyan Prakash's *Another Reason: Science and the Imagination of Modern India* (Princeton, N.J.: Princeton University Press, 1999). See also, e.g., Gyan Prakash, "Science between the Lines," in Amin and Chakrabarty, eds., *Subaltern Studies IX,* 59–82.

48. David Arnold, *Colonizing the Body: State Medicine and Epidemic Diseases in Nineteenth-Century India* (Berkeley and Los Angeles: University of California Press, 1993); David Hardiman, *The Coming of the Devi: Adivasi Assertion in Western India* (Delhi: Oxford University Press, 1987), and *Feeding the Baniya: Peasants and Usurers in Western India* (Delhi: Oxford University Press, 1996); Gautam Bhadra, *Iman o nishan: Unish shotoke bangaly krishak chaitanyer ek adhyay, c. 1800–1850* (Calcutta: Subarnarekha for the Centre for Studies in Social Sciences, 1994).

49. For a more detailed exposition of this point, see my *Provincializing Europe: Postcolonial Thought and Historical Difference* (Princeton, N.J.: Princeton University Press, 2000).

50. I have developed some of these thoughts further in an essay on contemporary Aboriginal history in Australia—"Reconciliation and Its Historiography: Some Preliminary Thoughts," *UTS Review* 7, no. 1 (May 2001): 6–16.

CHAPTER TWO

1. Sumit Sarkar, "The Fascism of the Sangh Parivar," *Economic and Political Weekly,* 20 January 1993, 164–65.

2. Ibid., 167.

3. See, e.g., Tom Brass, "A-Way with Their Wor(l)ds: Rural Labourers through the Postmodern Prism," *Economic and Political Weekly,* 5 June 1993, 1162–68; and K. Balagopal, "Why Did December 6, 1992, Happen?" *Economic and Political Weekly,* 24 April 1993, 790–93.

4. Christopher Norris, *The Truth of Postmodernism* (Oxford: Oxford University Press, 1993).

5. Sumit Sarkar, *The Swadeshi Movement in Bengal, 1903–1908* (Delhi: People's, 1977).

6. Ibid., 316.

7. Ibid., 24.

8. Alexander Duff quoted in M. A. Laird, *Missionaries and Education in Bengal, 1793–1837* (Oxford: Clarendon, 1972), 207.

9. Ibid., 86–87, 207–8.

10. It is a well-worn point of European history that the idea of an irrevocable opposition between science/rationalism and religion goes against all available evidence. For a recent collection of careful discussions, see David C. Lindberg and Ronald I. Numbers, eds., *God and Nature: Historical Essays of the Encounter between Christianity and Science* (Berkeley and Los Angeles: University of California Press, 1986).

11. C. B. A. Behrens, *Society, Government, and the Enlightenment: The Experiences of Eighteenth-Century France and Prussia* (London: Thames & Hudson, 1985), 26.

12. Preserved Smith, *The Enlightenment, 1687–1776* (New York, 1966), 117.

13. See the interesting discussion in A. K. Ramanujan, "Is There an Indian Way of Thinking? An Informal Essay," in *India through Hindu Categories,* ed. McKim Marriott (New Delhi: Sage, 1990), 45–58. Ramanujan discusses the case of his own scientist father, who was both an astronomer and "an expert astrologer": "I had just been converted by Russell to the 'scientific attitude.' . . . I looked for consistency in [my father], a consistency he did not seem to care about or even think about" (42–43).

14. See Sarkar, "The Fascism of the Sangh Parivar."

15. Rajendralal Mitra quoted in Andrew Sartori, "Raja Rajendralal Mitra and the Fractured Foundations of National Identity" (master's thesis, University of Melbourne, 1993), 60. The thoughts expressed here owe much to Sartori's analysis of this passage.

16. G. W. F. Hegel, *Phenomenology of Spirit,* trans. A. V. Miller (Oxford: Clarendon, 1977), 330.

17. Sarkar, *The Swadeshi Movement,* 34–35.

18. See the discussion in my *Provincializing Europe: Postcolonial Thought and Historical Difference* (Princeton, N.J.: Princeton University Press, 2000), chap. 2.

19. Barun De, "The Colonial Context of the Bengal Renaissance," in *Indian Society and the Beginnings of Modernisation, 1830–1850,* ed. C. H. Phillips and Mary

Doreen Wainwright (London: University of London, School of Oriental and African Studies, 1976), 123–24.

20. Ibid., 121–25.

21. Sumit Sarkar, *Modern India* (Delhi: Macmillan, 1983), 1.

22. Susie Tharu and K. Lalitha, eds., *Women Writing in India: 600 B.C. to the Early 20th Century* (Delhi: Oxford University Press, 1991), 184.

23. Gyan Prakash's *Another Reason: Science and the Imagination of Modern India* (Princeton, N.J.: Princeton University Press, 1999) goes a long way toward addressing this problem.

24. Salman Rushdie, *Midnight's Children* (London: Cape, 1984), 34.

25. Ibid., 42.

26. On this aspect of English history, see Peter Stallybrass and Allon White, *The Politics and Poetics of Transgression* (London: Methuen, 1986).

27. Eugen Weber, *Peasants into Frenchmen: The Modernization of Rural France, 1870–1914* (Stanford, Calif.: Stanford University Press, 1976).

28. Jacques Derrida, "Force of Law: The 'Mystical Foundation of Authority,'" in *Deconstruction and the Possibility of Justice,* ed. Drucilla Cornell, Michel Rosenfeld, and David Gray Carlson (New York: Routledge, 1992), 21, 31.

29. Weber, *Peasants into Frenchmen,* 478.

30. The police in India are routinely accused by civil-liberties groups of violating human rights.

31. Roland Barthes, *Image-Music-Text,* trans. Stephen Heath (London: Fontana, 1977), 95.

32. See Ranajit Guha, *Elementary Aspects of Peasant Insurgency in Colonial India* (Delhi: Oxford University Press, 1983).

33. Antonio Gramsci, *Selections from the Prison Notebooks,* ed. and trans. Quintin Hoare and Geoffrey Nowell Smith (New York: International, 1972), 52, 54–55.

34. For more extensive discussion of the concept of the fragment, see Gyanendra Pandey, "In Defense of the Fragment: Writing about Hindu-Muslim Riots in India Today," in *A Subaltern Studies Reader,* ed. Ranajit Guha (Minneapolis: University of Minnesota Press, 1998), 1–33; and Partha Chatterjee, *The Nation and Its Fragments: Colonial and Post-Colonial Histories* (Princeton, N.J.: Princeton University Press, 1993).

35. Heidegger speaks about ridding "ourselves of the habit of always hearing only what we already understand" (see Martin Heidegger, "The Nature of Language," in *On the Way of Language,* trans. Peter D. Hertz [1971; reprint, New York: Harper & Row, 1982], 58). Should Heidegger's name raise politically correct hackles because of his Nazi past, let us remember that the Nazis sometimes mounted the same objection to his thought as those raised by the old Left against poststructuralism: "In his last rector's speech [said a Nazi evaluation of Heidegger] philosophy tends in practice to . . . dissolve into an aporetic of endless questioning. . . . In any case, one ought not to be silent about certain themes of the philosophy of 'care' [*Sorge*] which, like our anguish, could lead to truly paralyzing effects" (Victor Farias, *Heidegger and Nazism,* trans. Paul Burrelli [Philadelphia: Temple University Press, 1989], 165).

36. My debt to Levinas and Derrida and their numerous commentators will be obvious at this point.

37. Lydia Liu, "Translingual Practice: The Discourse of Individualism between China and the West," *Positions: East Asia Cultures Critique* 1, no. 1 (spring 1993): 191.

CHAPTER THREE

1. Ashis Nandy, "Science, Authoritarianism, and Culture," in *Traditions, Tyranny, and Utopia: Essays in the Politics of Awareness* (Delhi: Oxford University Press, 1987), 121, 124. Nandy complicates the issue in a later essay (see his "From Outside the Imperium," in ibid., 153).

2. Nandy, "Science, Authoritarianism, and Culture," 125.

3. Ashis Nandy, "Reconstructing Childhood," in *Traditions, Tyranny, and Utopia: Essays in the Politics of Awareness* (Delhi: Oxford University Press, 1987), 73–74.

4. Nandy, "From Outside the Imperium," 147–48.

5. My reference here is obviously to Foucault's well-known discussion (in "What Is Enlightenment?" in *The Foucault Reader,* ed. Paul Rabinow [New York: Pantheon, 1984]) of Baudelaire's essay "The Painting of Modern Life."

6. Ashis Nandy, "Sati in Kali Yuga," in *The Savage Freud and Other Essays on Possible and Retrievable Selves* (Princeton, N.J.: Princeton University Press, 1995), 47, 41 n. 15. Kumkum Sangari quoted in Rajeswari Sundar Rajan, *Real and Imagined Women: Gender, Culture, and Postcolonialism* (London: Routledge, 1993), 7.

7. Nandy, "Sati in Kali Yuga," 40–41.

8. Ibid., 38–39.

9. Ibid., 49.

10. Jacques Derrida, *Specters of Marx: The State of the Debt, the Work of Mourning, and the New International,* trans. Peggy Kamuf (New York: Routledge, 1994).

CHAPTER FOUR

1. Gandhi quoted in Susan Bean, "Gandhi and *Khadi,* the Fabric of Indian Independence," in *Cloth and Human Experience,* ed. Annette B. Weiner and Jane Schneider (Washington, D.C.: Smithsonian Institute Press, 1991), 367.

2. Ibid.

3. See Emma Tarlo, *Clothing Matters: Dress and Identity in India* (Chicago: University of Chicago Press, 1996), chaps. 3 and 4.

4. Gopalchandra Ray, *Saratchandra,* 3 vols. (Calcutta: Mitra O Ghosh, 1966), 2:143. The italicized portions appear in English in the original.

5. *Sunday* (Calcutta), 27 November–3 December 1994, front cover.

6. Bean, "Gandhi and *Khadi,*" 366 (Nehru), 366.

7. On this question, see Uday Mehta, *Liberalism and Empire* (Chicago: University of Chicago Press, 1999).

8. There is some discussion of the issue in my *Rethinking Working-Class History: Bengal, 1890–1940* (Princeton, N.J.: Princeton University Press, 1989), chap. 4.

9. See the discussion in John Rosselli, "The Self-Image of Effeteness: Physical Education and Nationalism in Nineteenth-Century Bengal," *Past and Present,* no. 86 (February 1980): 121–48.

10. The tradition goes back to one of the earliest Bengali tracts of history, *Banglar itihas* (1848), written by the nineteenth-century social reformer Vidyasagar. The text was a direct translation of John Clark Marshman's *Outlines of the History of Bengal for the Use of Youths in India,* published in the 1830s.

11. J. C. Ghosh, *Bengali Literature* (1948; reprint; New York: AMS, 1978), 145.

12. See the discussion in Asitkumar Bandyopadhyay, preface to *Vidyasaagar rachanabali* (4 vols.), ed. Debkumar Bosu (Calcutta: Mandal, 1966), 1:36–37.

13. Tapan Raychaudhuri, *Europe Reconsidered: Perceptions of the West in Nineteenth Century Bengal* (Delhi: Oxford University Press, 1988), 306.

14. M. K. Gandhi, *An Autobiography; or, The Story of My Experiments with Truth* (1927), trans. Mahadev Desai (1966; reprint, Boston: Beacon, 1957), 13–14.

15. See Lloyd Rudolph and Susanne Rudolph, *The Modernity of Tradition* (Berkeley and Los Angeles: University of California Press, 1968).

16. See chap. 5 below.

17. My understanding of this point is indebted to Madhu Kishwar, "Gandhi on Women," *Economic and Political Weekly*, 5, 12 October 1985, 1691–1702, 1753–58.

18. Gandhi quoted in ibid., 1693.

19. G. D. Tendulkar quoted in ibid., 1755.

20. Erik Erikson, *Gandhi's Truth* (New York: Norton, 1969).

21. In her effective feminist critique of Gandhi's views on women, Kishwar, e.g., repeats a commonly made observation: "There are obsessive and repeated references to 'lust' in his autobiography" ("Gandhi on Women," 1754–55).

22. Gandhi, *Autobiography*, 157.

23. See William C. Spengemann, *The Forms of Autobiography: Episodes in the History of a Literary Genre* (New Haven, Conn.: Yale University Press, 1980), 5.

24. Gandhi, *Autobiography*, xiv.

25. Nirmal Kumar Bose, *My Days with Gandhi* (Bombay: Orient Longman, 1974), 20, 67–68.

26. See the discussion in my *Provincializing Europe: Postcolonial Thought and Historical Difference* (Princeton, N.J.: Princeton University Press, 2000), chap. 1.

27. Slavoj Žižek, *The Sublime Object of Ideology* (London: Verso, 1989), 30, 36–37.

28. For a beginning on these questions, see Sudipta Kaviraj, "Filth and the Public Sphere: Concepts and Practices about Space in Calcutta," *Public Culture* 10, no. 1 (fall 1997): 83–114.

CHAPTER FIVE

1. V. S. Naipaul, *India: A Million Mutinies Now* (New York: Viking, 1990), 1–2.

2. See Paul Rabinow, *French Modern: Norms and Forms of the Social Environment* (Cambridge, Mass.: MIT Press, 1989), 30–34; and Peter Stallybrass and Allon White, *The Politics and Poetics of Transgression* (London: Methuen, 1986).

3. Wellesley quoted in S. W. Goode, *Municipal Calcutta: Its Institutions in Their Growth and Origin* (Edinburgh, 1916), 237.

4. Sherring quoted in Nita Kumar, *The Artisans of Banaras: Popular Culture and Identity* (Princeton, N.J.: Princeton University Press, 1988), 78.

5. A. U., *Overland, Inland, and Upland: A Lady's Notes of Personal Observations and Adventure* (London: Seeley, Jackson & Halliday, 1874), 55–56.

6. Ibid., 47–50, 51–53.

7. Naipaul quoted in Michael Thompson, *Rubbish Theory: The Creation and Destruction of Value* (Oxford: Oxford University Press, 1979), 3. For Naipaul's later thoughts on his early writings on India, see his *India*, esp. 6–9.

8. Gandhi quoted in Bhikhu Parekh, *Gandhi's Political Philosophy: A Critical Examination* (Notre Dame, Ind.: University of Notre Dame Press, 1989), 49–50.

9. Nirad C. Chaudhuri, *The Autobiography of an Unknown Indian* (Calcutta: Jaico, 1968), 269, 376.

10. Kumar, *The Artisans of Banaras*, 78–79.

11. Thompson, *Rubbish Theory*, 4.

12. Mary Douglas, *Purity and Danger* (1966; reprint, London: Routledge & Kegan Paul, 1984).

13. I have elaborated on this theme in *Provincializing Europe,* chap. 8.

14. Gloria Goodwin Raheja, *The Poison in the Gift: Ritual, Prestation, and the Dominant Caste in a North Indian Village* (Chicago: University of Chicago Press, 1988), 43, 47.

15. The implications of this have been discussed in some detail in Ranajit Guha, *Elementary Aspects of Peasant Insurgency in Colonial India* (Delhi: Oxford University Press, 1983), 281–82.

16. This is based on my conversations over the years with Hilary Standing, whose doctoral research was conducted among the Mundas. Of course, Standing bears no responsibility for my statement.

17. See Gyanendra Pandey, *The Construction of Communalism in Colonial North India* (Delhi: Oxford University Press, 1990), 108–200; as well as Sudhir Kakar, "Some Unconscious Aspects of Ethnic Violence in India," in *Mirrors of Violence: Communities, Riots, and Survivors in South Asia,* ed. Veena Das (Delhi: Oxford University Press, 1990); and Amrit Srinivasan, "The Survivor in the Study of Violence," in ibid.

18. On this, see Veena Talwar Oldenberg, *The Making of Colonial Lucknow* (Princeton, N.J.: Princeton University Press, 1984), 14; Sandria Freitag, *Collective Action and Community: Public Arenas in the Emergence of Communalism in North India* (Berkeley and Los Angeles: University of California Press, 1989), 118; and Jim Masselos, "Power in the Bombay 'Mohalla,' 1904–1915: An Initial Exploration into the World of the Indian Urban Muslim," *South Asia* 6 (1976): 75–95.

19. See Kumar, *The Artisans of Banaras,* 71–72.

20. Henry Whitehead, *The Village Gods of South India* (Calcutta: Association Press, 1921), 35, 38–39; on the worship of Pedamma, see generally 48–54.

21. I. J. Catanach, "Plague and the Indian Village, 1896–1914," in *Rural India: Land, Power, and Society under British Rule,* ed. Peter Robb (Delhi: Segment, 1986), 228.

22. Ralph W. Nicholas, "The Goddess Sitala and Epidemic Smallpox in Bengal," *Journal of Asian Studies* 41, no. 1 (November 1981): 37.

23. Diane M. Coccari, "Protection and Identity: Banaras's Bir Babas as Neighbourhood Guardian Deities," in *Culture and Power in Banaras: Community, Performance, and the Environment,* ed. Sandria B. Freitag (Berkeley and Los Angeles: University of California Press, 1989), 141. See also Diane M. Coccari, "The Bir Babas of Banaras and the Deified Dead," in *Criminal Gods and Demon Devotees: Essays on the Guardians of Popular Hinduism,* ed. Alf Hiltebeitel (Albany: State University of New York Press, 1989), 251–70.

24. For a recent discussion, see Anand A. Yang, *The Limited Raj: Agrarian Relations in Colonial India, Saran District, 1793–1920* (Berkeley and Los Angeles: University of California Press, 1989), 13–30.

25. See Rajat Kanta Ray, "The Bazaar: Changing Structural Characteristics of the Indigenous Section of the Indian Economy before and after the Great Depression," *Indian Economic and Social History Review* 25, no. 3 (July–September 1988): 263–318; Oldenberg, *Colonial Lucknow,* 13–14; and Stephen P. Blake, "Cityscape of an Imperial Capital: Shahjahanabad in 1739," in *Delhi through the Ages: Essays in Urban History, Culture, and Society,* ed. R. E. Frykenberg (Delhi: Oxford University Press, 1986), 158–60. See also Anand Yang, *Bazaar India:*

Markets, Society, and the Colonial State (Berkeley and Los Angeles: University of California Press, 1998).

26. Jennifer Alexander, *Trade, Traders, and Trading in Rural Java* (Singapore: Oxford University Press, 1987), 165–67. I am grateful to Charles Coppel for directing me to this interesting ethnography.

27. Akos Ostor, *Culture and Power: Legend, Ritual, Bazaar, and Rebellion in a Bengali Society* (Delhi: Sage, 1984), 106.

28. S. P. Punalekar, *Weekly Markets in the Tribal Talukas of Surat Valsad Region* (1957; reprint, Surat: Centre for Social Studies, 1978), pt. 1, pp. 37, 93–94.

29. Ostor, *Culture and Power,* 135.

30. Alexander, *Rural Java,* 181.

31. This statement, of course, in no way denies the validity of Meaghan Morris's perceptive and stimulating analysis of how modern shopping centers can become focal points for social life even in "postindustrial" cultures. But this could happen in spite of their designs. See Meaghan Morris, "Things to Do with Shopping Centres," in *Grafts: Feminist Cultural Criticism,* ed. Susan Sheridan (London: Verso, 1988).

32. Anthony D. King, *Colonial Urban Development* (London: Routledge & Kegan Paul, 1976), 52–53.

33. Punalekar, *Weekly Markets,* pt. 1, pp. 89, 105.

34. King, *Colonial Urban Development,* 56.

35. Ostor, *Culture and Power,* 95–96.

36. On the mythology of Ganesh, see Paul B. Courtright, *Ganesa: Lord of Obstacles, Lord of Beginnings* (New York: Oxford University Press, 1985).

37. Ostor, *Culture and Power,* 100–101.

38. Freitag, *Collective Action,* 139–41.

39. See Kumar, *The Artisans of Banaras,* 79.

40. Guha, *Elementary Aspects,* 258–59.

41. Punalekar, *Weekly Markets,* pt. 1, pp. 48–49.

42. Kumar, *The Artisans of Banaras,* 89.

43. Raj Chandavarkar, "Workers' Politics and the Mill Districts in Bombay between the Wars," *Modern Asian Studies* 15, no. 3 (1981): 606–7.

44. Ghalib quoted in Faisal Fatehali Devji, "Gender and the Politics of Space: The Movement for Women's Reform in Muslim India, 1857–1900," *South Asia* 14, no. 1 (June 1991): 148.

45. John Foreman quoted in Carlos Quirino, *The First Filipino: A Biography of Jose Rizal* (Manila: Philippine Education Co., 1979), 25. I am grateful to Joseph Sales for referring me to this book. See also the very illuminating discussion in Timothy Mitchell, *Colonising Egypt* (Cambridge: Cambridge University Press, 1989).

46. See John Campbell Oman, *Cults, Customs, and Superstitions of India* (London: T. F. Unwin, 1908), pt. 2, pp. 218–28.

47. See, e.g., David Arnold, "Cholera and Colonialism in British India," *Past and Present,* no. 113 (November 1986): 127; and Oldenberg, *Colonial Lucknow,* 99–144.

48. Michel Foucault, *The Birth of the Clinic: An Archeology of Medical Perception* (New York: Vintage, 1975), 25.

49. Chaudhuri, *Autobiography,* dedication.

50. See Arnold, "Cholera and Colonialism."

51. All this, of course, is true only of the ideals. The Indian reality continues to be marked by the ironic combination of longer life for most, made possible by the management of epidemics and natural disasters, and persistent malnutrition for the major-

ity. One could be forgiven for thinking that Indian public-health programs were aimed at ensuring that the elite enjoyed good health *and* long life by removing the conditions for epidemics, which do not respect class divisions, from the lives of the poor.

52. Kumar, *The Artisans of Banaras,* 243.

53. Ibid.

54. Ray Ileto, "Cholera and the Origins of the American Sanitary Order in the Philippines," in *Imperial Medicine and Indigenous Societies,* ed. David Arnold (Delhi: Oxford University Press, 1989), 125.

CHAPTER SIX

1. Rushdie cited in Talal Asad, "Ethnography, Literature, and Politics: Some Readings and Uses of Salman Rushdie's *The Satanic Verses,*" *Cultural Anthropology* 5, no. 3 (August 1990): 243.

2. Klaus K. Klostermaier, *A Survey of Hinduism* (Albany: State University of New York Press, 1989), 412.

3. G. W. F. Hegel, *The Philosophy of History,* trans. J. Sibree (New York: Dover, 1956), 161, 163.

4. V. S. Naipaul, *India: A Million Mutinies Now* (London: Heinemann, 1990), 420.

5. Romila Thapar, "Imagined Religious Communities? Ancient History and the Modern Search for a Hindu Identity," *Modern Asian Studies* 23, no. 2 (1989): 219.

6. Some of the unfortunate consequences of such standardization in postcolonial India have been recently traced by Madhu Kishwar in her "Codified Hindu Law: Myth and Reality," *Economic and Political Weekly,* 13 August 1994, 2145–67.

7. Our eyes have been opened to these aspects of modernity by the pathbreaking work of Michel Foucault, among others. My particular observations on India owe much to the pioneering research of Bernard Cohn and to the illuminating work of Richard Smith, Arjun Appadurai, Carol Breckenridge, Nicholas Dirks, Rashmi Pant, N. G. Barrier, Gyan Prakash, and others.

8. Ian Hacking, *The Taming of Chance* (Cambridge: Cambridge University Press, 1991), 24.

9. See Michel Foucault, "Governmentality," in *The Foucault Effect: Studies in Governmentality,* ed. G. Burchell, C. Gordon, and P. Miller (London: Harvester Wheatsheaf, 1991), 87–104.

10. T. H. Hollingsworth, *Historical Demography* (London: Hodder & Stoughton, 1969), 78.

11. See Kenneth W. Jones, "Religious Identity and the Indian Census," in *Census in British India: New Perspectives,* ed. N. G. Barrier (Delhi: Manohar, 1984), 74.

12. For a fine analysis and history of the word *communalism,* see Gyanendra Pandey, *The Construction of Communalism in Colonial North India* (Delhi: Oxford University Press, 1990), chap. 7.

13. M. Galanter, *Competing Equalities: Law and the Backward Classes in India* (Delhi: Oxford University Press, 1984), 130.

14. Ian Hacking, "Making Up People," in *Reconstructing Individualism: Autonomy, Individuality, and the Self in Western Thought,* ed. T. Heller, M. Sosna, and D. E. Wellbery (Stanford, Calif: Stanford University Press, 1986), 227–28.

15. See Sudipta Kaviraj, "On the Construction of Colonial Power: Structure, Discourse, Hegemony" (paper presented at the conference "Imperial Hegemony," Berlin, 1–3 June 1989).

16. Hacking, "Making Up People," 227.

17. Kaviraj, "On the Construction of Colonial Power," 5.

18. See E. F. Irschick, *Politics and Social Conflict in South India: The Non-Brahmin Movement and Tamil Separatism, 1916–1929* (Berkeley: University of California Press, 1969), app. 1.

19. Jones, "Religious Identity," 91.

20. Lucien Febvre, "*Civilisation:* Evolution of a Word and a Group of Ideas," in *A New Kind of History: From the Writings of Febvre,* ed. P. Burke (London: Routledge & Kegan Paul, 1973), 219–57.

21. R. Bandyopadhyay, *Neetibodh,* 8th ed. (Calcutta, 1858), 12–13.

22. The barrister Geoffrey Robertson hosted a series of Australian Broadcasting Corp. television programs cast as mock trials and entitled *Hypotheticals,* in which topical issues were debated by interested parties and "expert witnesses."

23. Talal Asad, "Multiculturalism and British Identity in the Wake of the Rushdie Affair," in *Genealogies of Religion: Discipline and Reasons of Power in Christianity and Islam* (Baltimore: Johns Hopkins University Press, 1993), 239–68.

24. Ashin Das Gupta, personal communication, 12 December 1988. (The late Professor Das Gupta was the director of the National Library in Calcutta.)

25. See J. Rawls, *A Theory of Justice* (1971; reprint, London: Oxford University Press, 1976), 137–38. As is well-known, Rawls has both modified and presented reinterpretations of his original theory in subsequent publications. A good overview of the debate around Rawls is available in Chandran Kukathas and Philip Petit, *Rawls: "A Theory of Justice" and Its Critics* (Cambridge: Cambridge University Press, 1990).

26. Chantal Mouffe, "Rawls: Political Philosophy without Politics," in *Universalism vs. Communitarianism: Contemporary Debates in Ethics,* ed. David Rasmussen (Cambridge, Mass.: MIT Press, 1990), 223.

27. Ibid., 222.

CHAPTER SEVEN

1. I have attempted a critique of citizenship narratives in *Provincializing Europe: Postcolonial Thought and Historical Difference* (Princeton, N.J.: Princeton University Press, 2000), chap. 1. Alasdair Macintyre, *After Virtue: A Study in Moral Theory,* 2d ed. (London: Duckworth, 1985), 71.

2. Sivanath Sastri, "Rammohun Roy: The Story of His Life," in *The Father of Modern India: Commemoration Volume of the Rammohun Roy Centenary Celebrations, 1933,* ed. Satis Chandra Chakravarti (Calcutta: Rammohun Roy Centenary Committee, 1935), pt. 2, p. 20.

3. Subal Chandra Mitra, *Iswar Chandra Vidyasagar: A Story of His Life and Work* (Calcutta: Sarat Chandra Mitra, 1902), 261.

4. See, e.g., Asok Sen, *Iswarchandra Vidyasagar and His Elusive Milestones* (Calcutta: Riddhu-India, 1976); and Lata Mani, "Contentious Traditions: The Debate on *Sati* in Colonial India," in *Recasting Women: Essays in Indian Colonial History,* ed. Kumkum Sangari and Sudesh Vaid (New Brunswick, N.J.: Rutgers University Press, 1990), 88–126.

5. Saradasundari Devi, *Atmakatha* (1913), reprinted in *Atmakatha* (5 vols.), ed. Nareschandra Jana, Manu Jana, and Kamal Kumar Sanyal (Calcutta: Ananya, 1980–87), 1:7–40; Nistarini Devi, *Shekele katha* (ca. 1913), reprinted in ibid., 2:3–49; Kalyani Datta, "Baidhyabya kahini" (Tales of widowhood), *Ekshan,* no. 20 (autumn 1991): 41–54.

6. Datta, "Baidhyabya kahini," 43.

7. Ibid., 42–43, 46.

8. Ibid., 50–51.

9. N. Devi, *Shekele katha,* 2:33.

10. On expressivisim, see the discussion in Charles Taylor, *Hegel* (Cambridge: Cambridge University Press, 1975), chap. 1.

One important form that cruelty to widows took within Bengali families—the withdrawal of affection—must be distinguished from the withdrawal of affection that results from the death of love within a modern, romantic relationship, a withdrawal that, while still a source of pain, can be justified on the grounds that to show love when one no longer feels love is hypocritical. The modern lives in fear of appearing inauthentic.

11. Datta, "Baidhyabya kahini," 48.

12. S. Devi, *Atmakatha,* 1:14.

13. Ibid.

14. Ibid., 26.

15. Datta, "Baidhyabya kahini," 49–50.

16. Ibid., 53.

17. Ibid., 41.

18. B. B. Majumdar, *Heroines of Tagore: A Study in the Transformation of Indian Society* (Calcutta: K. L. Mukhopadhyay, 1968), 123.

19. Rabindranath Tagore [Thakur], *Galpaguchha* (Calcutta: Visvabharati Granthalaya, 1973), 1001.

20. I am obviously following here the analysis presented in J. F. Lyotard's *The Differend: Phrases in Dispute,* trans. Georges Van Den Abbeele (Minneapolis: University of Minnesota Press, 1988).

21. For the suggestion of an answer in the affirmative, see Nancy Fraser, "What's Critical about Critical Theory? The Case of Habermas and Gender," in *Feminism as Critique,* ed. Seyla Benhabib and Drucilla Cornell (Cambridge: Cambridge University Press, 1987), 31–55.

22. Emmanuel Levinas, *Ethics and Infinity: Conversations with Philippe Nemo,* trans. Richard A. Cohen (Pittsburgh: Duquesne University Press, 1985), 77, 81.

23. Ibid., 86, 89.

24. Tagore, *Galpaguchha,* 1004.

CHAPTER EIGHT

1. See Urvashi Butalia, "Community, State, and Gender: On Women's Agency during Partition," *Economic and Political Weekly,* 24 April 1993, WS12–WS24; Ritu Menon and Kamla Bhasin, "Recovery, Rupture, Resistance—Indian State and Abduction of Women during Partition," *Economic and Political Weekly,* 24 April 1993, WS2–WS11; Veena Das, *Critical Events: An Anthropological Perspective on Contemporary India* (Delhi: Oxford University Press, 1995); Gyanendra Pandey, "The Prose of Otherness," in *Subaltern Studies VIII: Essays in Honour of Ranajit Guha,* ed. David Arnold and David Hardiman (Delhi: Oxford University Press, 1994), 188–221; and Anne Hardgrove, "South Asian Women's Communal Identities," *Economic and Political Weekly,* 30 September 1995, 2427–30.

2. My thoughts here are influenced by Friedrich Nietzsche, "On the Uses and Disadvantages of History for Life," in *Untimely Meditations,* trans. R. J. Hollingdale (Cambridge: Cambridge University Press, 1989), 57–124.

3. Dakshinaranjan Basu, comp. and ed., *Chhere asha gram* (The abandoned village) (Calcutta: Jugantar, 1975).

4. See Ahmad Kamal, "The Decline of the Muslim League in East Pakistan,

1947–1954" (Ph.D. diss., Australian National University, 1989), chap. 1; and Beth Roy, *Some Trouble with Cows: Making Sense of Social Conflict* (Berkeley and Los Angeles: University of California Press, 1994).

5. See Prafulla K. Chakrabarti, *The Marginal Men* (Calcutta: Lumière, 1990).

6. The authors' village and district—in that order—are given in parentheses at the end of each quotation, as is the page number in *Chhere asha gram* for the quotation.

7. Sir Monier Monier-Williams, *A Sanskrit-English Dictionary* (1899; reprint, Delhi: Motilal Banarsidass, 1986).

8. See the discussion in Ronald B. Inden and Ralph W. Nicholas, *Kinship in Bengali Culture* (Chicago: University of Chicago Press, 1977), 7.

9. See my *Provincializing Europe: Postcolonial Thought and Historical Difference* (Princeton, N.J.: Princeton University Press, 2000), chap. 8.

10. These italicized lines bear a literary allusion. They quote a well-known line from a nationalist poem on Bengal written by Satyendranath Datta.

11. See Dineshchandra Sen, *Brihat Banga* (Calcutta: Kalikata Bisvabidyalaya, 1935); and Satyajit Chaudhuri, Debaprasad Bhattacharya, and Nikhilesvara Sen Gupta, eds., *Haraprasad Shastri smarakgrantha* (Calcutta: Sanyal Prakasan, 1978).

12. See Jadunath Sarkar, introduction to *Bangalir Itihash: Adi Parba,* by Niharranjan Ray (Calcutta: Paschimbanga Niraksharata Durikaran Samiti, 1980).

13. I have discussed this question in more detail in *Provincializing Europe,* chap. 6. See also my "Afterword: Revisiting the Modernity/Tradition Binary," in *Mirror of Modernity: Invented Traditions of Modern Japan,* ed. Stephen Vlastos (Berkeley and Los Angeles: University of California Press, 1998).

14. See Girijasankar Raychaudhuri, *Bangla charit granthe Sri Chaitanya* (Calcutta: Kalikata Bisvabidyalaya, 1949), 89.

15. See S. N. Mukherjee, *Calcutta: Myths and History* (Calcutta: Subarnarekha, 1977).

16. This text is discussed in my *Provincializing Europe,* chap. 8.

17. Dinabandhu Mitra, "Sadhabar Ekadashi," in *Dinabandhu rachanabali* (The collected works of Dinabandhu), ed. Kshetra Gupta (Calcutta: Sahitya Samshad, 1967), 136.

18. Bhanu Banerjee made his first comic recording using the *bangal* accent in 1941 (Pinaki Banerjee, personal communication, 10 October 1995 [Pinaki Banerjee is Bhanu Banerjee's son]).

19. See Rabindranath Tagore's *Loka Sahitya* (Folk literature), now reprinted in *Rabindrarachanabali,* 15 vols. (Calcutta: Government of West Bengal, 1961), 13: 663–734.

20. Rabindranath Tagore, "Chhinnapatrabali," in *Rabindrarachanabali,* 11:90, 8, 30. The italicized words in these quotations appear in English in the original.

21. Nirad C. Chaudhuri, *Thy Hand, Great Anarch! India, 1921–1952* (London: Chatto & Windus, 1987), 205, 207–8, 209–10. See also the discussion in Satyendranath Ray, "Prachin bangla sahitye prakriti o puran," *Visva-Bharati Patrika,* July–September 1964, 25–56.

22. Saratchandra Chattopadhyay, *Pallisamaj,* in *Saratsahitya samagra* (Calcutta: Ananda, 1987), 1:137–84.

23. See the discussion in Clinton B. Seely, *A Poet Apart: A Literary Biography of the Bengali Poet Jibanananda Das* (Newark: University of Delaware Press, 1990), 89–90.

The sonnets were published only posthumously, in the 1950s. Their popularity soared during the 1971 Bangladeshi war of liberation.

24. Chatterjee quoted in Taraknath Ghosh, *Jibaner panchalikar bibhutibhushan* (Kalikata: Sankha Prakasana, 1983), 38. It goes to the credit of the filmmaker Satyajit Ray that he could convey a sense of the generic Bengali village, essentially a literary and linguistic construction, through what is essentially a visual medium.

25. Tagore, "Chhinapatrabali," 82. The italicized word appears in English in the original. See also the discussion in *Provincializing Europe,* chap. 6.

26. Chaudhuri, *Thy Hand, Great Anarch!* 208–9.

27. The literature on this point is vast, but little work has been done so far on the various constructions of rurality that have been critical to the development of a *bhadralok* literary orientation to the world in the urban milieu of Calcutta. The works of Dineshchandra Sen, Dinendranath Ray, Abanindranath Tagore, and Yogeshchandra Ray Bidyanidhi—to name a few—would repay examination on this point.

28. The writer is quoting a line from a nationalist song composed by Tagore.

29. See the discussion in William Conolly, *Political Theory and Modernity* (Oxford: Blackwell, 1988).

CHAPTER NINE

1. For a discussion of the word *bangal,* see chap. 8.

2. Ritu Menon and Kamla Bhasin, *Borders and Boundaries: Women in India's Partition* (New Delhi: Kali for Women; New Brunswick, N.J.: Rutgers University Press, 1998); Urvashi Butalia, *The Other Side of Silence: Voices from the Partition of India* (1998; reprint, Durham, N.C.: Duke University Press, 2000); Gyanendra Pandey, *Remembering Partition: Violence, Nationalism, and History in India* (Cambridge: Cambridge University Press, 2001); Veena Das, *Critical Events: An Anthropological Perspective on Contemporary India* (Delhi: Oxford University Press, 1995).

3. Butalia, *The Other Side of Silence,* 170, 170, 169. Gyanendra Pandey ("The Prose of Otherness," in *Subaltern Studies VIII: Essays in Honour of Ranajit Guha,* ed. David Arnold and David Hardiman [Delhi: Oxford University Press, 1994], 188–221) makes a similar point.

4. Menon and Bhasin, *Borders and Boundaries,* 174, 76.

5. Bhutalia, *The Other Side of Silence,* 105, 58.

6. See Kavita Daiya, "Rethinking Violence, Nationalism, and Minority Citizenship: Public Sphere Cultures in Postcolonial South Asia" (Ph.D. diss., University of Chicago, 2000), chap. 2.

7. Jean-Paul Sartre, foreword to Franz Fanon, *The Wretched of the Earth* (New York: Grove, 1965), 20.

8. Butalia, *The Other Side of Silence,* 283.

9. Menon and Bhasin, *Borders and Boundaries,* 93, 95.

10. Ibid., 161.

11. Ibid., 12.

12. Butalia, *The Other Side of Silence,* 31.

13. Beth Roy, *Some Trouble with Cows: Making Sense of Social Conflict* (Berkeley and Los Angeles: University of California Press, 1994), 22.

14. See Ranajit Guha, "The Small Voice of History," in *Subaltern Studies IX,* ed. Shahid Amin and Dipesh Chakrabarty (Delhi: Oxford University Press, 1996).

15. Mrinal Sen, "Chhabi karar ager dinguli," in *Mrinal Sen,* ed. Pralay Sur (Calcutta: Banisilpa, 1987), 11. I am grateful to Kunal Sen for the loan of this book.

16. Ibid., 11.

17. Ibid., 12.

INDEX

abducted women, 144
Achenwall, Gottfried, 84
affirmative action, 86, 87
Ahmad, Aijaz, 149n. 3
Aiyer, G. Subramania, 102
Alexander, Jennifer, 72, 73
Althusser, Louis, 16
Ambedkar, Bhimrao Ramji, 39
Amin, Shahid, 17, 151n. 30, 152n. 46
Anglophilia, 42
anti-Brahmanism, 89, 92
Appadurai, Arjun, 149n. 1
Area of Darkness, An (Naipaul), 67
Arendt, Hannah, xxiv
Arnold, David, 6, 18, 76
Asad, Talal, 92
Assam, 91
Aurobindo, 23
auspiciousness, 70, 109
autobiography, confessional, 60–61

backwardness, xx, 9, 78
"Baidhyabya kahini" (Datta), 105
Banaras, 66, 68, 71, 78
Bandyopadhyay, Bhabanicharan, 127
Bandyopadhyay, Bibhutibushan, 130
Banerjee, Bhanu, 128, 140, 162n. 18
Bangiya Sahitya Parishad, 124
Bangladesh: Bengali Muslim sense of eth-
    nicity and Pakistani nationalism, 94;
    language and liberation war of, 86; na-

tional anthem of, 135–36; returning
to visit, 147–48. *See also* East Bengal
Banglar itihas (Vidyasagar), 155n. 10
Barthes, Roland, 33
Basu, Dakshinaranjan, 115
bazaars, 71–75; as dirty and disorderly,
    67, 76; entertainers in, 74–75; famil-
    iarity and trust in, 72–73; kinds of, 71;
    multiple functions of, 73; regulating,
    77; as representing the outside, 71–72;
    riots starting in, 74; rituals of enclosure
    in, 74; rumors in, 74, 76; speech as
    privileged in, 73, 74
Bean, Susan, 53
Behrens, C. B. A., 153n. 11
Bengal: cultural division between eastern
    and western, 127; *khadi* worn by na-
    tionalists in, 52–53; as motherland,
    121; Partition in, 115–48; Swadeshi
    movement, 22–23, 24, 26–27, 125,
    129. *See also* Bengali villages; Calcutta;
    East Bengal
Bengali villages, 121–33; antiquity of,
    123–26; Hindu festivals in, 133; idyl-
    lic image of, 126–33; as mother fig-
    ures, 122; Muslims in, 133–37; as sa-
    cred, 121–23; as spiritual home of
    urban Bengalis, 128
Benjamin, Walter, 4, 148
Bentham, Jeremy, 84–85
Bhabha, Homi, 18

165

Oldenberg, Veena Talwar, 76
open space (outside): caste system and, 75;
as exciting, 76; Indian use of, 65–79;
as needing to be tamed, 76; protection
required in, 73–74; rubbish thrown
outside, 67–68, 76, 79; streets, 71,
73, 75, 77. *See also* bazaars
Orientalism, 81
Ostor, Akos, 72, 73
othering, 141
Other Side of Silence, The (Butalia), 141
outside. *See* open space (outside)

Pallisamaj (Chatterjee), 129–30
Pandey, Gyanendra: call to remember of,
143; *The Construction of Communalism in Colonial North India,* 17; "In
Defense of the Fragment," 17; on
nonfoundationalist history, 152n. 46;
on Partition, 140, 141; and postnationalist critique, 17, 151n. 30; on reactionary side of nationalism, 6; *Remembering Partition,* 141
Pantalu, Viresalingam, 102
Partition in Bengal, 115–48; as inexplicable, 117–19; the language of homelessness, 120–22; violence in, 116,
141–45; women in, 116, 141, 142,
144
Patel, Kamlaben, 142
Pather panchali (Bandyopadhyay), 130
peasants: citizenship granted to, 19; docu-
mentary evidence not left by, 15;
modernity employed in struggles of,
30; religion and political action by, 22;
revolts by, 9–11, 34; rumors in mobilization of, 74; in transition to capitalism, 10–12, 19; violence in making individuals of, 32
Peasants into Frenchmen (Weber), 15
Pedamma, 70, 71
pluralism, 90, 91, 94, 95, 96
political, the: the ethical as situated in,
147–48; *khadi* and the political man,
51–64; politics of difference, 141–48;
prepolitical consciousness, 9, 11–12,
14, 15; religion and politics, 22–24,
26–27; subalterns as political actors,
8–11, 19, 22
political philosophy: practical utility of
Left-liberal, 33; translating categories
of, xxii–xxiii

postcolonial studies: Dirlik's critique of, 3;
postcolonial critique as postnationalist,
17; *Subaltern Studies* and, 14, 18, 19
postmodernism, 17–18, 21
Prakash, Gyan, 17, 152n. 46
prejudices, values and, 136–37
premodern, the, xix, 14
prepolitical consciousness, 9, 11–12, 14, 15
privacy, 61–62, 77
private sphere, 95, 96
progress, xix, 90
"Prose of Counter-Insurgency, The"
(Guha), 151n. 21
Provincializing Europe (Chakrabarty),
xxiii–xiv
proximity, versus identity, 140, 142, 143–
48
public health: capitalism requiring, 77;
epidemic control, 76; Gandhi's concern with, 59, 62; in India, 77, 158n.
51; as modern concern, 66
public sphere: Hinduism and caste affected by, 83; religion and morality ex-
cluded from, 95, 96
Punalekar, S. P., 73, 74–75
Punjab, 91

racism: communalism as, 86; ethnic mobi-
lization and, 93; fixed ethnic categories
required by, 96; Indians denying, 82
Raheja, Gloria Goodwin, 70
Ramanujan, A. K., 20, 153n. 13
Ramayana, 57
Ranade, M. G., 102
rationalism: colonizing violence and, 32;
critiques of, 21–22, 37; hyperrational-
ism and the colonial modern, 22–29;
and religion, 25, 153n. 10; subaltern
histories and post-Enlightenment, 20–
37. *See also* reason
Rawls, John, 95, 96, 160n. 25
Ray, Anilbaran, 53
Ray, Dinendranath, 163n. 27
Ray, Jahar, 140
Ray, Satyajit, 163n. 24
Raychaudhuri, Tapan, 57–58, 150n. 10
reason: emotion opposed to, 24, 26; un-
reasonable origins of, 29–32. *See also*
rationalism
"Reconciliation and Its Historiography:
Some Preliminary Thoughts"
(Chakrabarty), 153n. 50